Workshop Formulas, Tips & Data

By Kenneth M. Swezey

Updated by Robert Scharff

Sterling Publishing Co., Inc.   New York

Library of Congress Cataloging-in-Publication Data

Swezey, Kenneth M., d. 1972.
    Workshop formulas, tips & data / Kenneth M. Swezey ; updated by
Robert Scharff.
    p.   cm.
    Rev. ed. of: Formulas, methods, tips and data for home and
workshop, 1989.
    Includes index.
    ISBN 0-8069-6791-9
    1. Handicraft—Handbooks, manuals, etc. 2. Workshop recipes.
I. Scharff, Robert. II. Swezey, Kenneth M., d. 1972. Formulas,
methods, tips, and data for home and workshop. III. Title.
IV. Title: Workshop formulas, tips and data.
TT153.S88   1989
600—dc 19   88-38606
                                                      CIP

1   3   5   7   9   10   8   6   4   2

Published in 1989 by Sterling Publishing Co., Inc.
Two Park Avenue, New York, N.Y. 10016
The material in this book was originally
published in hardcover by Grolier Book Clubs, Inc.,
in "Formulas, Methods, Tips and
Data for Home and Workshop" copyright ©
1979 by Kenneth M. Swezey and Robert Scharff,
copyright © 1969 by Kenneth M. Swezey
Distributed in Canada by Oak Tree Press Ltd.
℅ Canadian Manda Group, P.O. Box 920, Station U
Toronto, Ontario, Canada M8Z 5P9
Distributed in Great Britain and Europe by Cassell PLC
Artillery House, Artillery Row, London SW1P 1RT, England
Distributed in Australia by Capricorn Ltd.
P.O. Box 665, Lane Cove, NSW 2066
Manufactured in the United States of America
All rights reserved

Sterling ISBN 0-8069-6791-9 Paper

Contents

1 Wood: Selection, Finishing, Preservation   1

How You Are Charged for Lumber ● How Wood Is Graded ●
Choosing the Best Wood for the Job ● How Woods Weather ●
How to Use Plywood ● Wood Flooring ● Sanding ● Bleaching ●
Interior and Furniture Stains ● Stains for Outdoor Use ● Wood
Fillers ● Finishing with Varnish ● Finishing with Shellac ●
Finishing with Lacquers ● Linseed Oil Finish ● Solvent for
Finishing Materials ● How to Repair Wood Finishes ● Mildew
Treatment ● Combating Blue Stain ● Preserving Wooden Fence
Posts ● How to Stop "Dry Rot"

2 Paints and Painting   68

Painting House Exteriors ● Causes and Remedies for Paint Failure ●
Which Outdoor Paints to Use Where ● Guide to Outdoor Body and
Trim Colors ● Interior Painting ● Interior Colors and Their
Psychological Effects ● Which Interior Paints to Use Where ● How
to Mix Colors ● How to Select, Use, and Clean Paint-Applicator
Tools ● Facts About Floor Finishes ● Paint Removers

Editor's Foreword

The second edition of the late Kenneth M. Swezey's 1969 original was updated and greatly expanded by Robert Scharff, a long-time friend and associate of Swezey's. This 1989 abridged edition is based on Scharff's 1979 revision.

Swezey drew the materials for the original edition from the huge collection of notes, books, and personal experiences he used in the preparation of magazine articles on chemistry, physics, and the home workshop—and in the writing of his books *After Dinner Science*, *Science Magic*, *Chemistry Magic*, and *Science Shows You How*. Swezey died in 1972.

Robert Scharff, himself a widely known author and editorial director, first met Swezey in 1952, when both men were working on books for McGraw-Hill. Scharff recalls, "Ken Swezey could give you a formula for anything. If he didn't have it in his head, he could work it up for you in an hour. He had more information in his head—and files—than any man I have ever met. I just couldn't see this book die. That's the reason I wanted to update it. It was the best book of its type and I hope I was able to keep it up to Ken's standards."

Preface
to the First Edition

This is a book of practical but often hard-to-find information for anybody who likes to do things for himself. Its purpose is to put at your fingertips the special technique, the needed table, the right formula to help solve all sorts of problems that crop up constantly around the home and in the workshop.

Some of the methods and formulas may save you money. Others may help you do a better job or make a special product you can't buy readymade. Still others may just satisfy your curiosity or enable you to carry out a project you have always wanted to undertake but didn't know quite how to.

As you can see from the table of contents, the book covers an exceptionally wide range. Included, of course, are the everyday basic and more familiar methods, hints, and tables you would expect to find in any comprehensive home and workshop data book. Beyond these, however, are hundreds of lesser known and more specialized techniques, uncommon tables, and useful formulas that have been selected and adapted from technical and professional literature as well as from personal experience, many of which appear in no other book of this type. If, therefore, you can't locate a wanted item by title in the table of contents, don't give up until you have double-checked for it in the index.

One help you should not overlook is the table "Conversions of Common Units," beginning on page 258. In this table—compiled especially for this book—units of weight, area, volume, power, velocity, and so on are listed in simple alphabetical order, with the units you may wish to convert to, and the number you should use to make the conversion, immediately adjacent. Another table in the same chapter will enable you to convert from spoons, cups, and other household measures to more conventional ones. A third table will help you convert from specialized and unusual units, ranging from cubits and furlongs to Angstrom units and light-years.

The formulas in this book are only those that might be actually useful around the home and shop, that are relatively easy to make with home equipment, and that are either better than, or cheaper but just as good as, proprietary products that serve the same purpose.

Most of the basic ingredients needed for preparing these formulas are well-known and are easily obtainable from the local grocery, hardware, paint, or drugstore, or from the supermarket. You may soon discover, however, that many others that were once readily available in such stores have either disappeared or are now sold only in disguise as specialty products under proprietary names and at a considerable markup in price. But don't give up! You can usually still get these products under their own names and at reasonable cost by sleuthing a little among sources that cater to special trades or industries.

Another complication may also at first discourage you. To protect inexperienced persons—especially children—from poisons and other products that may be hazardous if improperly used, federal and state laws now prohibit the sale without prescription of many additional common chemicals that were once freely obtainable in drug and other stores that sell directly to the general public. Again, most of such chemicals can be bought by any responsible adult from chemical supply houses and from dealers to industry or to specialty trades in which the chemicals are routinely used.

Kenneth M. Swezey

Acknowledgments

Below is a listing of the organizations that helped with the preparation of the original and revised editions:

U.S. Army Corps of Engineers
U.S. Bureau of Mines
U.S. Consumer Product Safety Commission
U.S. Department of Agriculture
U.S. Department of Health, Education and Welfare
U.S. Department of the Interior
U.S. Fish and Wildlife Service
U.S. Food and Drug Administration
U.S. Forest Products Laboratory
U.S. Occupational Safety and Health Administration
U.S. Public Health Service
U.S. Secret Service
National Bureau of Standards
N.Y. State College of Agriculture, Cornell University
N.Y. State College of Home Economics, Cornell University
University of Wisconsin, College of Agriculture
N.Y. Zoological Society
Air-Conditioning and Refrigeration Institute
American Dental Association
American Red Cross
American Society of Heating, Refrigeration and Air-Conditioning
    Engineers
National Better Business Bureau
National Board of Fire Underwriters
National Fire Protection Association
National Safety Council
American Brush Manufacturers Association
American Gas Association
American Petroleum Institute
American Plywood Association
Asphalt Roof Manufacturers Association
Best Foods
Bethlehem Steel Corporation
Borden Chemical Company
Calgon Corporation

(Continued)

California Redwood Association
Church & Dwight Company
Commercial Solvents Corporation
Diamond Crystal Salt Company
Dow Chemical Company
E. I. DuPont de Nemours & Company
Eastman Kodak Company
ESB, Inc. (formerly the Electric Storage Battery Company)
Esso, Inc.
Fisher Scientific Company
Ford Motor Company
General Aniline & Film Corporation
Heath Company
Home Ventilating Institute
Honeywell Inc.
International Nickel Company
International Salt Company
Walter Kidde & Company
Knape & Vogt Manufacturing Company
Landers-Segal Color Company
Lead Industries Association
Mallinckrodt Chemical Works
Marble Institute of America
Morton Salt Company
National Flaxseed Processors Association
National Lead Company
National Lime Association
National Paint and Coating Association
Pennsalt Chemicals Corporation
Pittsburgh Plate Glass Company
Portland Cement Association
Pyrofax Gas Corporation
Radio Corporation of America
Rockwell International Corporation
Rose-X Chemical Company
Shell Chemical Company
Small Homes Council
Velsicol Chemical Corporation
Vermont Marble Company
Western Wood Products Association
Wool Bureau, Inc.
William Zinsser & Company

Success and safety in the use of tools or in compounding or using formulas depend largely on the operator's skill and knowledge in handling tools and chemicals. To promote both success and safety, techniques in this book have been described in unusual detail, and precautions in handling chemicals that may be hazardous if improperly used have been explicitly pointed out. These instructions and precautions should be followed faithfully. Because the actual manipulation of the materials and processes described in the book are entirely in the hands of the operator, however, neither author nor publisher can guarantee the results of any instructions or formulas. Therefore each of them expressly disclaims any responsibility for injury to persons or property through their use.

1

Wood: Selection, Finishing, Preservation

HOW YOU ARE CHARGED FOR LUMBER

Lumber is sold by the board-foot measure. A board foot is equal to a piece 1 inch thick and 12 inches square. If you know the board-foot price, you can find the cost of any size or shape of lumber by using this formula (thickness and width are in inches and length is in feet):

$$\frac{\text{Thickness} \times \text{width} \times \text{length}}{12} = \text{board feet}$$

Thus a 2 × 4-inch piece of lumber that is 12 feet long would contain 8 board feet:

$$\frac{2 \times 4 \times 12}{12} = 8$$

Lumber is always quoted at a specified price per M (thousand) board feet. For example, if it was quoted at $220 per M board feet, it would be charged for at the rate of $.22 per foot $\left(\frac{\$220}{1000} = \$.22\right)$. Thus the 8 feet from the formula above would be multiplied times $.22 for a cost of $1.76. The number of board feet in lumber of various sizes and lengths is given in the lumber calculator table on the next page.

LUMBER CALCULATOR

Size in inches	8-foot	10-foot	12-foot	14-foot	16-foot
1 × 2	1⅓	1⅔	2	2⅓	2⅔
1 × 3	2	2½	3	3½	4
1 × 4	2⅔	3⅓	4	4⅔	5⅓
1 × 5	3⅓	4⅙	5	5⅚	6⅔
1 × 6	4	5	6	7	8
1 × 8	5⅓	6⅔	8	9⅓	10⅔
1 × 10	6⅔	8½	10	11⅔	13⅓
1 × 12	8	10	12	14	16
1¼ × 4	3⅓	4⅙	5	5⅚	6⅔
1¼ × 6	5	6¼	7½	8¾	10
1¼ × 8	6⅔	8⅓	10	11⅔	13⅓
1¼ × 10	8⅓	10⁵⁄₁₂	12½	14⁷⁄₁₂	16⅔
1¼ × 12	10	12½	15	17½	20
2 × 4	5⅓	6⅔	8	9⅓	10⅔
2 × 6	8	10	12	14	16
2 × 8	10⅔	13⅓	16	18⅔	21⅓
2 × 10	13⅓	16⅔	20	23⅓	26⅔
2 × 12	16	20	24	28	32
4 × 4	10⅔	13⅓	16	18⅔	21⅓
4 × 6	16	20	24	28	32
4 × 8	21⅓	26⅔	32	37½	42⅔
4 × 10	26⅔	33⅓	40	46⅔	53⅓
4 × 12	32	40	48	56	64
6 × 6	24	30	36	42	48
6 × 8	32	40	48	56	64

It must be remembered, however, that prices are based on *nominal* or original rough sizes rather than *actual* dimensions as sold. In the case of softwoods, the actual thickness and width depend upon whether the pieces are rough-sawed or planed smooth, green or dry. For instance, a green, rough-sawed board 1 inch thick is actually ¾ inch thick if dry and dressed; it is ²⁵⁄₃₂ inch thick if it is green (above 19-percent moisture content) and dressed. If the lumber is grade-marked, the stamp will indicate whether the piece was green or dry when it was dressed to size. The table at the top of page 3 gives the nominal and actual average sizes of commonly used softwood lumber.

NOMINAL AND ACTUAL SIZES OF SOFTWOODS

Nominal (rough) size*	THICKNESSES Actual (inches) Minimum dry**	Dressed green	Nominal (rough) size*	FACE WIDTHS Actual (inches) Minimum dry**	Dressed green
1	3/4	25/32	2	1 1/2	1 9/16
1 1/4	1	1 1/32	3	2 1/2	2 9/16
1 1/2	1 1/4	1 9/32	4	3 1/2	3 9/16
2	1 1/2	1 9/16	6	5 1/2	5 5/8
3	2 1/2	2 9/16	8	7 1/4	7 1/2
4	3 1/2	3 9/16	10	9 1/4	9 1/2
			12	11 1/4	11 1/2

* Thickness sometimes is expressed as 4/4, 5/4, etc.

** Dry lumber has been seasoned to a moisture content of 19 percent or less.

In softwoods, thickness less than 1 inch is charged as a full inch, though in hardwoods the prices vary. The amount of size reduction of hardwoods depends partly on the standards used by the planing mill and partly on the amount of finishing (also called "dressing"). A piece may be dressed on one side only (S1S) or on both sides (S2S) and/or on one edge (S1E) or both edges (S2E). In the accompanying table, it should be kept in mind that the widths of hardwoods vary with various grades.

NOMINAL AND ACTUAL SIZES OF HARDWOODS

Nominal (rough) size	Surfaced 1 Side (S1S)	Surfaced 2 Sides (S2S)
3/8″	1/4″	3/16″
1/2″	3/8″	5/16″
5/8″	1/2″	7/16″
3/4″	5/8″	9/16″
1″	7/8″	1 13/16″
1 1/4″	1 1/8″	1 1/16″
1 1/2″	1 3/8″	1 5/16″
2″	1 13/16″	1 3/4″
3″	2 13/16″	2 3/4″
4″	3 13/16″	3 3/4″

Lumber is also worked or *milled* to produce popular molded shapes for specific purposes, such as for baseboards, doweling, etc. Milled lumber also is dimensioned, but the dimensions may or may not refer to thickness and width. Each shape is dimensioned in a manner necessitated by its usage. When buying milled pieces, you must learn, in each case, what the dealer's dimensions specify (usually, but not always, obvious). Milled lumber is always sold by the *lineal foot* or the piece, based on its length. A lineal-foot measurement, of course, refers to the real length of a board, measured in feet.

HOW WOOD IS GRADED

When a lumber dealer refers to "boards," he means stock less than 2 inches thick and usually more than 6 inches wide. Narrower boards are "strips."

Dimension lumber, also called *framing* lumber, includes structural pieces from 2 to 5 inches thick, used for studs, joists, and rafters. Lumber 5 inches thick or more is *timber.*

Each type is sold in various grades according to the size, number, and kind of defects found in them. Softwoods and hardwoods are graded differently; there is no relation between softwood and hardwood grades.

SOFTWOOD LUMBER GRADES

SELECT

(Lumber of good appearance and finishing qualities)

Suitable for Natural Finishes

GRADE A (also called No. 1 Clear). Free of defects. Because of cost, this grade is not stocked in all lumberyards.

GRADE B (also called No. 2 Clear). Allows a few small defects and blemishes. (A slightly higher category—B & Better—is sold by lumberyards. While not an "official" grade, it contains a few pieces of Grade A, but the majority is Grade B. This is slightly more expensive than Grade B itself.)

Suitable for Paint Finishes

GRADE C. Allows a limited number of small defects or blemishes that can be covered with paint. Some pieces can even take a natural finish.

GRADE D. Allows any number of defects or blemishes that do not detract from a finish appearance, especially when painted.

COMMON

(Lumber containing defects or blemishes which detract from a finish appearance, but which is suitable for general utility and construction use.)

Lumber Suitable for Use Without Waste

NO. 1 COMMON (also called Construction Grade). Good, sound, watertight lumber with tight knots (none larger than 2 inches and rarely on edges) and limited blemishes. No warp, splits, checks, or decay.

NO. 2 COMMON (also called Standard Grade). Allows larger and coarser defects than No. 1, but is considered graintight lumber.

Lumber Permitting Waste

NO. 3 COMMON (Also called Utility Grade). Allows larger and coarser defects than No. 2 and occasional knotholes.

NO. 4 COMMON (also called Economy Grade). Low-quality lumber admitting the coarsest defects, such as decay and knotholes.

NO. 5 COMMON. Practically waste lumber, good only for use as a filler, and then with considerable waste.

HARDWOOD LUMBER GRADES

Hardwood grading is not consistent for all trees, nor in all parts of the country. On the whole, however, the grades are as follows:

FIRSTS: Lumber that is 91⅔-percent clear on both sides; considered the best possible for cabinetwork.

SECONDS: Lumber that is 83⅓-percent clear on both sides; still very good for most cabinetwork.

FIRSTS & SECONDS: A selection that must contain not less than 20-percent firsts.

SELECTS (in alder, ash, beech, birch, cherry, chestnut, mahogany, maple, sycamore, and walnut only): Lumber that is 90-percent clear on one side only (other side not graded). Good for most cabinetwork, with some waste.

SAPS (in poplar only): Approximately the same as select above.

NO. 1 COMMON: One side only, 66⅔-percent clear. With waste, good for interior and less demanding cabinetwork.

NO. 2 COMMON: One side only, 50-percent clear. Okay for painting, some paneling and flooring.

STAINED SAPS (in poplar only): Equivalent to No. 2 common, above.

NO. 3A COMMON: One side only, 33⅓-percent clear.

NO. 3B COMMON: One side only, 25-percent clear.

SOUND-WORMY (in chestnut only): A No. 1 above but with wormholes.

Notes: Hardwoods are supposed to be free of warp, wind, bad splits, and checks. "Clear" refers to the number of clear cuttings that can be obtained.

COMMON HOME-WORKSHOP WOODS

Name of Wood	Hardness	Strength	Stability	Weight	Rot resistance	Split resistance	Working quality for hand tools	Shaping	Turning	Mortising	Planing and Joining	Nailing	Gluing	Sanding	Cost
Alder	medium	weak	G	light	F	F	G	F	F	F	G	G	G	F	medium
Ash, white	medium	medium	E	medium heavy	F	G	P	E	F	F	G	G	F	E	medium
Balsa	soft	weak	G	light	P	E	E	P	P	P	G	E	E	P	low
Basswood	soft	weak	G	light	P	E	E	P	P	P	G	E	E	P	medium
Beech	hard	medium	P	heavy	P	G	F	F	F	F	F	P	E	G	medium
Birch	hard	strong	G	heavy	P	G	P	G	G	G	G	P	F	F	high
Butternut	soft	weak	E	light	F	F	G	G	G	E	F	F	G	F	medium
Cedar, red	soft	weak	G	medium	E	P	G	P	P	F	F	P	G	P	medium
Cherry	medium	medium	G	heavy	F	P	G	E	E	E	E	F	E	E	high
Chestnut	soft	weak	E	light	E	P	G	F	F	F	F	F	E	E	high
Cottonwood	soft	weak	G	light	P	E	P	P	P	G	G	E	E	P	low
Cypress	soft	medium	G	light	E	F	F	P	P	P	G	F	F	F	medium
Elm	medium	medium	P	medium heavy	F	G	F	G	P	G	P	E	F	G	medium
Fir, Douglas	medium	medium strong	F	medium heavy	G	F	F	P	P	G	G	G	G	F	medium
Fir, white		low	G	light	G	G	G	P	P	G	G	G	G	G	low
Gum, red	medium	medium	P	medium	F	G	F	E	E	F	F	G	E	F	medium

Wood														
Hickory	hard	strong	G	heavy	P	F	P	F	G	E	G	P	G	E	medium
Lauan	medium	medium	E	medium	G	P	G	F	G	F	G	G	E	P	medium
Magnolia	soft	weak	F	medium	F	G	G	G	F	P	G	E	E	G	medium
Mahogany	medium	medium	E	medium heavy	F	G	G	E	E	E	G	G	E	G	high
Maple, hard	hard	strong	G	heavy	P	P	P	E	E	E	F	P	F	G	high
Maple, soft	medium	medium	F	medium	F	G	G	F	F	P	P	F	G	G	medium
Oak, red	hard	strong	E	heavy	P	F	P	F	G	E	E	G	G	E	medium
Oak, white	hard	strong	E	heavy	F	F	P	G	G	E	E	G	G	E	high
Pine, ponderosa	soft	weak	G	light	F	P	E	G	G	F	G	E	E	F	low
Pine, sugar	soft	weak	G	light	F	P	E	G	G	F	G	E	E	P	low
Pine, white	soft	weak	G	light	F	P	E	G	G	F	G	E	E	G	low
Pine, yellow	hard	strong	F	heavy	G	G	F	G	G	G	G	F	F	F	medium
Poplar	soft	weak	G	medium	P	G	E	P	P	F	G	E	E	P	medium
Redwood	soft	medium	E	medium	E	F	G	E	G	P	F	G	E	P	medium
Spruce	soft	weak	G	light	F	G	G	G	F	F	G	E	G	G	medium
Sycamore	medium	medium	P	heavy	G	P	G	P	G	E	P	G	G	P	medium
Walnut	medium	strong	E	heavy	F	G	G	G	E	E	G	F	E	E	high
Willow	soft	weak	G	light	G	F	G	F	F	F	F	G	G	G	low

(E = Excellent, G = Good, F = Fair, P = poor)

By looking over lumber grades carefully, you can choose the cheapest one that will do for your purpose. Don't buy the most expensive clear grade if you're going to cover it with paint. On the other hand. a low, knot-filled grade may be fine for rustic paneling.

If you're building a garage or addition to your house, you'll need a high grade that has good strength. Local building codes may specify grades that must be used; check these before starting construction.

CHOOSING THE BEST WOOD FOR THE JOB

Careful shopping will enable you to suit the wood you buy to the job you intend it for. Woods have widely different characteristics. Woods like redwood and cypress stand up well and are easy to work, but they are too soft to take a fine finish. Birch and maple finish beautifully, but aren't easy to work without power tools. They also are more susceptible to moisture damage and decay. The table on pages 6 and 7 will help you choose the woods that have the qualities you need for each job.

Woods that sand smooth and take a high, hard finish are listed as "excellent." Those that require more work and take softer, duller finishes are listed as "good," "fair," or "poor." Strength won't matter much in woods used for paneling, or those that are supported by a framework, but can be very important in structural woods or furniture parts such as table legs. Hardness, or density, can be roughly translated into "dentability." In general the hardest woods make the best cabinets and table tops.

HOW WOODS WEATHER

The accompanying table shows how woods stand up under age and weather. Only those with very high decay resistance should be used.unpainted outdoors. But many lower-rated woods will last well under outdoor conditions if treated with preservative, or if they are varnished or painted. Woods with high shrinkage aren't necessarily a bad choice if you make sure they are dry. "Checking" (small cracks) and "cupping" (warping) are defects found in woods exposed to the weather. How much a wood cups or checks helps determine its suitability for exterior uses, as in house siding.

CHANGES DUE TO WEATHERING

Wood	Resistance to decay	Amount of shrinkage	Color becomes	Conspicuous checking	Cupping
Ash, white	low	medium	dark gray	yes	very high
Aspen	low	medium high	light gray	no	medium
Basswood	low	high	light gray	yes	medium
Birch	low	medium high	light gray	yes	very high
Cedar, red	very high	low	dark gray	no	low
Chestnut	high	medium	dark gray	yes	high
Cottonwood	low	medium high	light gray	yes	very high
Cypress	very high	medium low	silvery gray	no	low
Fir, Douglas	medium	medium	dark gray	yes	medium
Fir, white	low	medium	dark gray	yes	medium
Gum, red	medium	medium	light gray	yes	very high
Hemlock, Eastern	low	medium	light gray	yes	medium
Hemlock, Western	low	medium	light gray	yes	medium
Hickory	low	high	light gray	yes	very high
Larch	medium	medium high	dark gray	yes	medium
Maple	low	high	light gray	yes	very high
Oak, red	low	medium high	dark gray	yes	very high
Oak, white	high	medium low	dark gray	yes	very high
Pine, Eastern white	medium	low	light gray	yes	medium
Pine, ponderosa	low	medium low	light gray	yes	medium
Pine, sugar	medium	low	light gray	yes	medium
Pine, Western white	medium	medium high	light gray	yes	medium
Pine, yellow	medium	medium high	dark gray	yes	medium
Poplar	low	medium	light gray	no	high
Redwood	very high	medium low	dark gray	no	low
Spruce	low	medium	light gray	yes	medium
Walnut	high	medium	dark gray	yes	high

HOW TO USE PLYWOOD

Plywood is made of a number of thin sheets of wood glued together with the grain of the adjacent layers perpendicular. The grain of the two outside plies must be parallel to provide stability. This gives the panel nearly equalized strength and minimizes dimensional changes. The thin layers of wood, called plies, usually are "peeled" from a log as veneer. In some instances the veneer is sliced from the log. The veneer is cut into various lengths, dried, selected or graded, then glued together to make a sheet or panel of plywood.

Both softwood and hardwood plywoods are available. Softwood plywood is extensively used in building construction; hardwood plywood is used for cabinetwork and furniture; both are used for paneling. Softwood and hardwood plywood are classified by grade and type. Grade is determined by the quality or condition of the separate plies and the appearance of the face plies; type refers to the durability of the adhesive bond between the plies.

Softwood Plywood

Softwood plywood is manufactured from several species of wood, of which Douglas fir is the most common. Some of the other species used in significant quantity include Southern yellow pine, Western larch, Western hemlock, Sitka spruce, commercial white firs, Alaska and Port Orford cedar, and California redwood.

SIZE.   Plywood is most readily available in sheets or panels 4 feet wide by 8 feet long. Lengths up to 16 feet are available, but not always stocked. Widths range from 24 to 60 inches, with 48 inches being most common.

THICKNESS.   Plywood is manufactured in thicknesses of ¼ inch to 1⅛ inches. A special ⅛ inch plywood is also available for model making and similar uses. There always will be an odd number of plies, the minimum number being three.

PRODUCT STANDARD.   Construction and industrial plywood is manufactured in accordance with U.S. Product Standard PS 1. American Plywood Association grade-trademarks (shown here) are positive identification of plywood manufactured in conformance with PS 1 and with rigid quality standards of the Association.

TYPES.   Two types of softwood plywood are available: exterior (waterproof) and interior (moisture-resistant); within each type there are several grades.

Exterior-type plywood is used when the wood will come into contact with excessive moisture and water, such as in boats, outdoor fences, combination sheathing and siding for houses, and outdoor furniture. This type of plywood is manufactured with phenolic or resorcinol-type adhesives that are insoluble in water.

Interior-type plywood will withstand occasional wetting during construction, but should not be permanently exposed to the elements. Within the interior-type classification there are two levels of adhesive durability: (1) interior with interior glue, which may be used where the plywood will not be subject to prolonged moisture conditions or extreme humidity and (2) interior with exterior waterproof glue for use where prolonged but temporary exposures to moisture are expected. Because lower veneer grades are permitted for inner plies of interior plywood, however, these panels are not equal in durability to fully exterior plywood and should not be exposed to continuous moisture conditions.

GROUP.   All appearance grades are identified in the APA grade-trademark with a group number that refers to species. Plywood is manufactured from over 70 wood species of varying strength that have been classified under PS 1 into five groups (see table on page 12). Each species within a given group meets a common criterion for that group. The strongest woods are found in Group 1 (the lower the group number, the greater the stiffness and strength). The group number in APA grade-trademarks is based on the species used for the face or back of the panel. Where face and back veneers are not from the same species, the number is based on the weaker group, except for decorative and sanded panels ⅜ inch or less, which are identified by face-species group.

GRADES.   The presence or absence of defects in the face or surface plies determines the grade of the plywood. The quality of the veneer is graded N (best), A, B, C, and D (poorest). N grade is a special-order veneer for use as a natural finish. In A-A grade plywood, for instance, both faces are of A quality; in C-D grade, one face is of C quality and the other of D quality. Only minor surface defects and limited patches are permitted in Grade A quality, and the face must be sanded. Grade B allows some appearance defects and permits more patching than Grade A as long as the surface is sanded smooth. Grades C and D permit knots, knotholes, and some splits, with larger defects permitted in the D grade. Some manufacturers produce plywood with an improved C veneer called C-plugged. A special grade of plywood, which usually has the second ply repaired, is used for underlayment. Only plywood bearing the "underlayment" or "Sturd-I-Floor" grade stamps should be used for that purpose.

The inner plies may be of any grade, although D is commonly used interior type plywood. C is the lowest-grade veneer permitted for exterior type, and defects in the inner plies of marine plywood for boat hulls must be patched and repaired.

CLASSIFICATION OF SPECIES (Softwood and Hardwood)

Group 1	Group 2	Group 3	Group 4	Group 5
Apitong (a),(b)	Cedar, Port Orford	Alder, Red	Aspen	Basswood
Beech	Cypress	Birch, Paper	Bigtooth	Fir, Balsam
American	Douglas Fir 2 (c)	Cedar, Alaska	Quaking	Poplar, Balsam
Birch	Fir	Fir, Subalpine	Cativo	
Sweet	California Red	Hemlock, Eastern	Cedar	
Yellow	Grand	Maple, Bigleaf	Incense	
Douglas Fir 1 (c)	Noble	Pine	Western Red	
Kapur	Pacific Silver	Jack	Cottonwood	
Keruing (a),(b)	White	Lodgepole	Eastern	
Larch, Western	Hemlock, Western	Ponderosa	Black (Western Poplar)	
Maple, Sugar	Lauan	Spruce	Pine	
Pine	Almon	Redwood	Eastern white	
Caribbean	Bagtikan	Spruce	Sugar	
Ocote	Mayapis	Black		
Pine, Southern	Red Lauan	Engelmann		
Loblolly	Tangile	White		
Longleaf	White Lauan			
Shortleaf	Maple, Black			
Slash	Mengkulang (a)			
Tanoak	Meranti, Red (a),(b)			
	Mersawa (a)			
	Pine			
	Pond			
	Red			
	Virginia			
	Western White			
	Spruce			
	Red			
	Sitka			
	Sweetgum			
	Tamarack			
	Yellow-poplar			

KEY TO SYMBOLS

(a) Each of these names represents a trade group of woods consisting of a number of closely related species.
(b) Species from the genus Dipterocarpus are marketed collectively. Apitong if originating in the Philippines, Keruing if originating in Malaysia or Indonesia.
(c) Douglas fir from trees grown in the states of Washington, Oregon, California, Idaho, Montana, Wyoming, and the Canadian provinces of Alberta and British Columbia shall be classed as Douglas fir No. 1. Douglas fir from trees grown in the states of Nevada, Utah, Colorado, Arizona and New Mexico shall be classed as Douglas fir No. 2.
(d) Red Meranti shall be limited to species having a specific gravity of 0.41 or more based on green volume and oven dry weight.

COMMON GRADES OF PLYWOOD

EXTERIOR

Grade (exterior)	Face	Back	Inner plies	Uses
A-A	A	A	C	Outdoors, where appearance of both sides is important
A-B	A	B	C	Alternate for A-A, where appearance of one side is less important; face is finish grade
A-C	A	C	C	Soffits, fences, base for coatings
B-C	B	C	C	For utility uses such as farm buildings, some kinds of fences, etc., base for coatings
303 Siding	C (or better)	C	C	Panels with variety of surface texture and grooving patterns; for siding, fences, paneling, screens, etc.
T 1–11	C	C	C	Special ⅝-inch siding panel with deep parallel grooves; available unsanded, textured, or MDO surface
C-C (plugged)	C (plugged)	C	C	Excellent base for tile and linoleum, backing for wall coverings, high-performance coatings
C-C	C	C	C	Unsanded, for backing and rough construction exposed to weather
B-B Plyform	B	B	C	Concrete forms; reuse until wood literally wears out
MDO	B	B or C	C	Medium Density Overlay—ideal base for paint; for siding, built-ins, signs, displays
HDO	A or B	A or B	C-plugged or C	High Density Overlay—hard surface; no paint needed; for concrete forms, cabinets, counter tops, tanks

(Continued)

COMMON GRADES OF PLYWOOD (continued)

INTERIOR

Grade (Interior)	Face	Back	Inner plies	Uses
A-A	A	A	D	Cabinet doors, built-ins, furniture where both sides will show
A-B	A	B	D	Alternate of A-A, face is finish grade, back is solid and smooth
A-D	A	D	D	Finish grade face for paneling, built-ins, backing
B-D	B	D	D	Utility grade; for backing, cabinet sides, etc.
C-D	C	D	D	Sheathing and structural uses such as temporary enclosures, subfloor; unsanded
Underlayment	C-plugged	D	C[1] and D	For separate underlayment under tile, carpeting
Sturd-I-Floor	C-plugged	D	C[1] and D	For combination subfloor-underlayment under tile, carpeting

[1] Special construction to resist indentation from concentrated loads.

ENGINEERED GRADES. Structural I and Structural II grades have been recently added to the better grades. They are unsanded grades made with exterior adhesives, and stronger woods, and are for use in engineered applications, such as stressed-skin panels, box beams, gusset plates for trusses, etc.

IDENTIFICATION INDEX. This is a pair of numbers separated by a slash in the APA grade-trademark on unsanded grades.

The index number tells you the panel's basic construction capabilities at a glance. The number on the left refers to the maximum recommended spacing in inches for supports when the panel is used for roof decking with face grain across supports. The number on the right refers to the recommended maximum spacing in inches for supports when the panel is used for residential subflooring with face grain across supports. [For example, an index number of 32/16 means the panel can be used for roof decking with supports spaced up to 32 inches "on center" (o.c.) and for subfloors on supports spaced up to 16 inches o.c.] A number "0" on the right of the slash means the panel should not be used for subflooring. No reference to the index number is needed when the panel is to be used for wall sheathing.

SPAN INDEX. The grade-trademarks for APA Sturd-I-Floor and APA 303 plywood siding products contain Span Index numbers indicating the recommended maximum support or framing spans for normal installations. In the case of Sturd-I-Floor, the Span Index gives the maximum floor joist spacing with plywood face grain perpendicular to supports. Spans are given in inches "on center" (o.c.). Typical Sturd-I-Floor Span Indexes are 16 o.c., 20 o.c., 24 o.c., and 48 o.c. For 303 plywood siding, on the other hand, the Span Index gives the maximum stud spacing (or nail column spacings when applied over plywood sheathing) with plywood face grain *parallel* to supports, the most common application. Span Indexes for 303 siding are 16 o.c. and 24 o.c.

Hardwood Plywood

The species used in the face plies identifies hardwood plywood—that is, black walnut plywood would have one or both face plies of black walnut. Some of the more common species used in hardwood plywood are cherry, oak, birch, black walnut, maple, and gum among the native woods; mahogany, lauan, and teak in the imported category. A major difference in the manufacture of softwood and hardwood plywood is the use of a solid "core" or extra-thick middle ply in some hardwood panels.

VENEER-CORE. Veneer-core plywood is manufactured with layers of wood veneer joined in the standard manner. It is intended for such uses as paneling, sheathing, and furniture parts, or when the plywood might be bent or curved.

LUMBER-CORE. Lumber-core plywood contains a thick core made by edge-gluing several narrow strips of solid wood. This core forms the middle section to which veneer crossbands and face plies are glued. Lumber-core plywood is manufactured for specific uses such as tabletops, built-in cabinets, and fixtures and doors where butt hinges are specified.

PARTICLEBOARD-CORE. In this plywood the core is an aggregate of wood particles bonded together with a resin binder. Face veneers are usually glued directly to the core, although crossbanding is sometimes used. Particleboard-core plywood is used in manufacturing furniture and is particularly adaptable for table, desk, and cabinet tops.

SIZE.   Hardwood plywood is most commonly sold in panels 4 × 8 feet, although it is possible to have plywood made in almost any desired size.

THICKNESS.   Hardwood plywood is manufactured in three, five, seven, and nine plies with thicknesses ranging from ⅛ inch to 1 inch. The table shows the most common thickness dimensions for the different number of plies.

Number of plies	Plywood thickness (inches)			
3	⅛	³⁄₁₆	¼	
5	¼	⅜	½	⅝
7	⅝	¾		
9	¾	1		

TYPES.   The following four types of hardwood plywood are available:

1. Type I is manufactured with waterproof adhesives and is used in areas where it will come in contact with water.
2. Type II is manufactured with water-resistant adhesives and is used in areas where it will not ordinarily be subjected to contact with water. However, it can be used in areas of continued dampness and excessive humidity.
3. Type III is manufactured with moisture-resistant adhesives and is intended for use in areas where it will not come in contact with any water. It can be subjected to some dampness and excessive humidity.
4. Technical has the same adhesive specifications as Type I but varies in thickness and arrangement of plies.

GRADES.   Hardwood plywood is manufactured in six specific grades. As in softwood plywood, each face must be specified.

Specialty grade (SP).   This is a plywood made to order to meet the specific requirements of a particular buyer. Plywood of this grade usually entails special matching of the face veneers.

Premium grade (#1).   The veneer on the face is fabricated for matched joints, and contrast in color and grain is avoided.

Good grade (#1).   The veneer on the face is fabricated to avoid sharp contrasts in color and grain.

Sound grade (#2).   The veneer on the face is not matched for color or grain. Some defects are permissible, but the face is free of open defects and is sanded and smooth. It is usually used for surfaces to be painted.

Utility grade (#3).   Tight knots, discoloration, stain, wormholes, mineral streaks, and some slight splits are permitted in this grade. Decay is not permitted.

Backing grade (#4).   This grade permits larger defects. Grain and color are not matched, and the veneer is used primarily as the concealed face. Defects must not affect strength or serviceability of the panel made from it. At the manufacturer's option, this face can be of some species other than the exposed face.

When ordering plywood—either softwood or hardwood—be guided by the following questions:

Do you want veneer, lumber, or particleboard-core plywood?

What thickness will you need?

What panel size will be most economical?

Will you need one or both surfaces finished?

When you have answered these questions, you are ready to order plywood intelligently.

WOOD FLOORING

Softwood finish flooring costs less than most hardwood species and is often used to good advantage in bedroom and closet areas where traffic is light. It might also be selected to fit the interior decor. It is less dense than the hardwoods, less wear-resistant, and shows surface abrasions more readily. Softwoods most commonly used for flooring are Southern pine, Douglas fir, redwood, and Western hemlock.

The table on page 18 lists the grades and descriptions of softwood strip flooring. Softwood flooring has tongued-and-grooved edges and may be hollow-backed or grooved. Some types are also end-matched. Vertical-grain flooring generally has better wearing qualities than flat-grain flooring under hard usage.

Hardwoods most commonly used for flooring are red and white oak, beech, birch, maple, and pecan. The table lists grades, types, and sizes. Manufacturers supply both prefinished and unfinished flooring.

GRADE AND DESCRIPTION OF STRIP FLOORING

Species	Grain orientation	Thickness (inches)	Width (inches)	First grade	Second grade	Third grade
SOFTWOODS						
Douglas fir and hemlock	edge grain flat grain	$^{25}\!/_{32}$ $^{25}\!/_{32}$	$2\frac{3}{8}$–$5\frac{3}{16}$ $2\frac{3}{8}$–$5\frac{3}{16}$	B and better C and better	C D	D –
Southern pine	edge grain and flat grain	$^5\!/_{16}$–$1^5\!/_{16}$	$1\frac{3}{4}$–$5\frac{7}{16}$	B and better	C and better	D (and No. 2)
HARDWOODS						
Oak	edge grain flat grain	$^{25}\!/_{32}$ $\frac{3}{8}$ $\frac{1}{2}$	$1\frac{1}{2}$–$3\frac{1}{4}$ $1\frac{1}{2}$–2 $1\frac{1}{2}$–2	Clear Clear	Select Select	– No. 1 Common
Beech, birch, maple, and pecan*		$^{25}\!/_{32}$ $\frac{3}{8}$ $\frac{1}{2}$	$1\frac{1}{2}$–$3\frac{1}{4}$ $1\frac{1}{2}$–2 $1\frac{1}{2}$–2	First grade	Second grade	–

*Special grades are available in which uniformity of color is a requirement.

Estimating Wood Flooring Requirements

To determine the board feet of flooring needed to cover a given space, first find the area in square feet (length times width). Where there are bay windows or other projections, allowance should be made for additional flooring. Once the square footage of an area is known, refer to the table on pages 20 and 21.

Preventing Cracks in New Wood Floors

Cracks that develop within a few weeks or months in a new, well-laid floor are the result of changes in the moisture content of the wood either before or just after the floor is laid. By taking proper precautions, you can prevent them.

The well-informed manufacturer generally sees that floor stock is properly dried and delivered in good condition to the retailer. The dealer, in turn, will store it under conditions that won't allow it to absorb moisture. Trouble usually starts, however, if the wood is delivered on a damp or rainy day, or if dry wood is laid in a cold, damp house in which the plaster or masonry has not thoroughly dried.

Boards swell when they absorb moisture and shrink when they dry. If flooring contains too much moisture when it is installed, cracks will open up soon after the house is occupied and heated. If, on the other hand, dry flooring is installed in a damp house, what is known technically as "compression set" will take place. As the boards swell, their edges press powerfully against each other, crushing the wood fiber and permanently compressing it; when they dry again, they leave cracks.

The cure for such cracks lies wholly in prevention. The rules are simple, but often overlooked:

1. Make sure the wood is dry when you lay it.
2. Do not lay it in a cold, damp house.
3. To retard moisture absorption, coat the floor with shellac, floor sealer, or varnish as soon as practicable.

HUMIDITY CONTROL.   To keep indoor dampness low enough to prevent swelling of newly laid flooring, experts of the Forest Products Laboratory of the Department of Agriculture recommend that heat be maintained in a house from the time the workmen leave until they return the next workday, even during warm summer weather. If the heating plant has not already been installed, then a temporary stove should be used.

It is also good practice, they say, to open the bundles of flooring so that all surfaces are exposed to the air for at least 4 days. This allows time for the flooring to reach a moisture equilibrium with the air in the heated house before it is laid. The inside temperature should be kept at least 15° F above outdoor temperatures and should not be allowed to cool below about 70° F during the summer or 62° to 65° F when the outdoor temperatures are below freezing. Slightly higher temperatures will do no harm, but severe overheating should be avoided. After the floor has received its coating of protective finish, temperatures should be kept approximately what they will be when the house is occupied.

Besides preventing crack formation in the flooring, such heating will also permit better performance from mechanical sanders. In addition, it will prevent swelling and cracking of other interior woodwork and finish, such as doors, trim, and cabinets.

HOW DRY SHOULD FLOORING BE?   It depends on where you live and to some extent what type of heating system you will use. With conventional heating systems, using warm air or hot water or steam radiators, flooring should be laid at an average moisture content of 8

ESTIMATING FLOORING REQUIREMENTS

Figures below show the number of board feet of various sizes of flooring
required to cover square footage of floor space, as shown in the left most column.

Square feet of floor space	25⁄32 x 3¼	25⁄32 x 2¼	25⁄32 x 1½	½ x 2	½ x 1½	⅜ x 2	⅜ x 1½
10	13	14	16	13	14	13	14
20	26	28	31	26	28	26	28
30	39	42	47	39	42	39	42
40	52	56	62	52	56	52	56
50	65	70	78	65	70	65	70
60	78	83	93	78	83	78	83
70	91	97	109	91	97	91	97
80	104	111	124	104	111	104	111
90	117	125	140	117	125	117	125
100	129	139	155	130	139	130	139
200	258	277	310	260	277	260	277
300	387	415	465	390	415	390	415
400	516	553	620	520	553	520	553
500	645	692	775	650	692	650	692
600	774	830	930	780	830	780	830
700	903	969	1085	910	969	910	969
800	1032	1107	1240	1040	1107	1040	1107
900	1161	1245	1395	1170	1245	1170	1245
1000	1290	1383	1550	1300	1383	1300	1383

ESTIMATING FLOORING REQUIREMENTS (continued)

	25/32 x 3¼	25/32 x 2¼	25/32 x 1½	½ x 2	½ x 1½	⅜ x 2	⅜ x 1½
Called	1 x 4	1 x 3	1 x 2¼	1 x 2½	1 x 2	1 x 2½	1 x 2
Lbs. per 1,000 board feet	2300	2100	2000	1350	1300	1000	1000
Size of nails used	8d	8d	8d	5d	5d	4d	4d
Nail spacing	10 to 12 inches on center			8 to 10 inches on center		6 to 8 inches on center	
No. pieces per bundle	8	12	12	18	18	24	24
To obtain board feet from bundle multiply by	2⅔	3	2¼	3¾	3	5	4

percent in most parts of the United States. This value is about midway between the highest and lowest values the flooring will attain during the different seasons.

The accompanying table will give you an indication of the moisture allowances for both dry and damp regions and for other parts of the country.

RECOMMENDED MOISTURE CONTENT FOR WOOD FLOORING AT TIME OF LAYING
(for dwellings with conventional heating systems)

Climatic region	Moisture content, percent	
	Average	Individual pieces
Semidesert region (Nevada, parts of California, Utah, and Arizona)	6	5 to 8
Damp southern coastal regions (from North Carolina to eastern coast of Texas, and on the southern coast of California)	11	9 to 12
Remainder of United States	8	6 to 9

Exceptions to these figures should be made for dwellings with radiant-heating systems in which heating pipes or coils are placed beneath the floor. Wood for flooring in such homes should be kiln dried and carefully protected from moisture absorption during both storage and installation. Its average moisture content should be about 2 percent lower than that indicated in the table.

TEST FOR MOISTURE CONTENT.   Large lumber manufacturers test the moisture content of their lumber by means of electric moisture meters. You can make your own test with the help of a fairly accurate scale and your kitchen oven.

Cut a small specimen, preferably not smaller than 9 square inches, from the flooring. Weigh it accurately to find its original weight. Dry it in an oven maintained at a temperature of 212° to 221° F until the wood stops losing weight. The lowest weight of the specimen is its oven-dry weight. You can then compute the original moisture content of the wood by this formula:

$$\frac{\text{Original weight} - \text{oven-dry weight}}{\text{Original weight}} \times 100$$

The answer is the moisture content in percent.

SANDING WOOD

Sanding is the most important operation in preparing the wood for a finish. It must be done to remove tool marks and to smooth the surface so that the reflective properties of the finishing materials will accentuate the full beauty of the wood grain. By taking time to do a good job of sanding, using correct procedures and selected grades of abrasives, you can produce a finish of professional appearance and quality.

Sandpaper

The term *sandpaper,* meaning paper coated with abrasive particles, had its birth many years ago, probably when sand was actually used in that way. Today, modern "sandpapers," now called "coated abrasives," are available in a number of different types in several different shapes, sizes, and grades of grit. In choosing sandpaper, it is important to choose the right coating and appropriate fineness of grit.

FLINT.   This old-timer is a soft, yellowish quartz mineral that looks much like sand. It is the cheapest material but cuts slowly and wears out quickly. Its chief usefulness today is for cleaning painted, resinous, or waxy surfaces that would clog any paper and require frequent replacement.

GARNET.   This is the hardest of natural abrasives. Although it is more than twice as expensive as flint paper, it cuts better and lasts five times as long. It is a favorite with woodworkers for fine sanding.

ALUMINUM OXIDE.   This is a hard, tough synthetic mineral made in the electric furnace. Available in the form of sheets, belts, and discs, aluminum oxide paper is fast becoming the most widely used all-around paper.

SILICON CARBIDE.   Another product of the electric furnace, this is the hardest of all common abrasives. Materials coated with it are used in finishing metal, stone, and plastic. The finest grades are used either dry or mixed with water or rubbing oil for polishing varnish, shellac, and lacquer finishes.

What Grit Size to Use

Modern abrasives come in grits as fine as baby powder and as coarse as gravel. The old grading system, using arbitrary numbers from an ultra-coarse 4 up to a super-fine 10/0, is inadequate for the wide range of present abrasives and is being replaced by a system based on mesh sizes that grains must pass through. Leaving out sizes too coarse for smoothing purposes, the accompanying table shows the corresponding numbers for all classifications.

GRADE AND GRIT NUMBERS OF ABRASIVES

	Aluminum oxide or silicon oxide	Garnet	Flint
Super fine	12/0–600 11/0–500 10/0–400	10/0–400 9/0–320 8/0–280	
Extra fine	9/0–320 8/0–280 7/0–240	7/0–240	
Very fine	6/0–220 5/0–180	6/0–220 5/0–180	4/0 3/0
Fine	4/0–150 3/0–120 2/0–100	4/0–150 3/0–120 1/0–100	0
Medium	1/0–80 ½–60	1/0–80 ½–60	½ 1
Coarse	1–50 1½–40	1–50 1½–40	1½ 2
Very coarse	2–36 2½–30 3–24	2–36 2½–30 3–24	2½ 3

In finishing wood, you might use 60 grit for coarse sanding, 80 for smoothing, and 120 to 220 for finishing. On metal, you would probably use no coarser grit than 80 and, in some cases, run up to the very finest. Smoothing paints or other fine finishes, on wood or metal, will require very fine grits. The first coat might be smoothed with 220 grit, the second with 320, and the third with 400. You might use light oil with the last rubbing.

At the other extreme is floor sanding, where 30 grit may be used for removing the old finish, 40 or 50 for smoothing, and 80 or 100 for final sanding and a professional-looking job.

POWER-SANDING GRITS

OLD-FLOOR SANDING GRITS

Floor	Operation	Grade of abrasive paper
Covered with varnish, shellac, paint, etc.	first cut second cut final cut	coarse 3⅓ (20) medium fine 1½ (40) extra fine 2/0 (100)

NEW-FLOOR SANDING GRITS

Species of wood	Operation	Grade of abrasive paper
Hardwood: oak, maple, beech, birch, pecan	first cut second cut final sanding	medium coarse 2 (36) fine 1 (50) extra fine 2/0 (100)
Softwood: pine, fir	first cut second cut final sanding	medium fine 1½ (40) fine 1 (50) extra fine 2/0 (100)

Coated abrasives can also be used for sharpening tools. For average sharpening, the grit sizes will be about the same as the grinding wheels used for the same purpose, say 40 or 50 grit for rough sharpening and 100 or 120 for finishing.

For work on specialized materials such as glass, marble, gems, and plastics, it would be best to consult a textbook on the proper grits for each particular substance.

Closed or Open Coating?

Abrasive papers come in two types of coatings. Closed-coat papers have tightly packed grains that cover the entire surface; open-coat papers have grains that cover only 50 to 70 percent of the surface. The closed-coat cuts faster but is more apt to become clogged when used on soft materials. Use open-coat on soft or gummy woods, paint, and other finishes, and on some soft metals and plastics. Open-coat papers are usually made only in grit 80 (1/0) and finer.

The backing to which the abrasive particles are glued may be paper, cloth, a cloth-paper combination, fiber, or a fiber-cloth combination. For home-workshop work, paper and cloth backings are generally used. The others are used mostly in industrial applications. Cloth and paper backings (except flint) also come in waterproof versions (sometimes called wet or dry) that permit wet sanding.

Paper backing comes in four weights, which are designated as A, C,

D, and E. The A grade includes the fine-grit lightweight papers known as *finishing papers*. The C and D grades, known as *cabinet*, are mediumweight papers with abrasive particles of medium fineness. The E grade, known as *roll stock*, is heavyweight with stiff paper backing and is used only occasionally in handwork.

In cloth backings, the J grade, the lighter of the two commonly available cloth backings, is used for finishing shaped work. The X grade is heavier and stronger and is used for flat or shaped work in power tools. As a rule of thumb, use either cloth or paper backing in a weight light enough to bend as much as necessary without cracking. When cracking occurs, switch from paper to cloth or to the next heavier weight in either type. Since paper backing is the cheapest, use it wherever it will stand up. A general classification and recommendation for grades to be used on various types of work is given in the accompanying table.

RECOMMENDED GRADES OF PAPER

Handwork	Backing	Grit number	Grade number	Word description
Rough sanding and shaping	D	60 or 80	1/2 or 1/0	medium
Preparatory sanding on softwood	A	100 to 150	2/0 to 4/0	fine
Preparatory sanding on hardwood	A	120 or 150	3/0 or 4/0	fine
Finish sanding on softwood	A	180 or 220	5/0 or 6/0	very fine
Finish sanding on hardwood	A	220 to 280	6/0 to 8/0	very fine to extra fine
Dry-sanding sealers and finishes between coats	A	220 to 280	6/0 to 8/0	very fine to extra fine
Wet-sanding sealers and finishes between coats	J or X	220 to 280	6/0 to 8/0	very fine to extra fine
Rubbing down after finish coat	J	280 to 400	8/0 to 10/0	extra fine to super fine

Sandpaper is available in many forms other than the common sandpaper sheets. Most abrasives can be bought in continuous rolls of various widths and backings for use with hand sanders, for sanding in lathes, and for wrapping on special-purpose mandrels. They also come in discs, drums, and belts for use with various types of power sanding tools.

Which Abrasive for What?

The object here is to choose the one that cuts fastest and most efficiently with a given material. The accompanying table will serve as a guide.

ABRASIVES FOR DIFFERENT MATERIALS			
	Aluminum oxide	Silicon carbide	Garnet
Ceramics (to shape and sand)		X	
Floors (to sand)		X	
Gems (to cut and shape)		X	
Glass (to shape and sand)		X	
Leather (to shape and sand)	X	X	
Metals, hard (to shape and sand)	X		
Metals, soft (to shape and sand)	X	X	
Metals, hard (to polish)	X		
Metals (to remove rust and dirt)	X		
Paint (to smooth)	X	X	
Plastics (to shape and sand)		X	
Wood (to hand-shape and sand)			X
Wood (to power-shape and sand)	X		X
Tools (to sharpen)	X		

Other Finishing Abrasives

STEEL WOOL.   Available in rolls or pads, this is familiar to almost everyone as an aid in cleaning food from pots and pans, rust from tools, and paint and varnish from anything in paint-removal jobs. Pads of finer grade are sold in hardware, paint, and craft stores for the final finishing of wood. Steel wool is graded as follows:

No. 3   The coarsest grade, rarely used in finishing work
No. 2   Should be used on rough lumber only
No. 1   The coarsest grade that should be used on furniture
No. 1/0 The most commonly used of all grades for general cleaning and smoothing
No. 2/0 Used for rough smoothing
No. 3/0 The fine grade, often used for final smoothing
No. 4/0 The very fine grade, used for between-coat smoothing
No. 5/0 The extra-fine grade, used for top-coat rubbing
No. 6/0 The super-fine grade, used for top-coat rubbing

PUMICE. This is a time-honored abrasive powder of volcanic origin used for rubbing down the final finish coat. It comes in four grades, with 4/0 the finest and 0 the coarsest. Lubricate it with water or oil.

ROTTENSTONE. A decomposed siliceous limestone, this is softer and finer than pumice and is sometimes used after it to give a higher sheen.

BLEACHING WOOD

To produce blond, champagne, lime, straw, or other popular light finishes, wood must be bleached first. This process removes the natural coloring matter in wood without damaging the fibers. Light-colored, even-grained woods are best for bleaching, though such dark woods as walnut and mahogany bleach successfully. Individual pieces of wood or veneer that are abnormally dark or that contain dark streaks known as mineral streaks may also be bleached to match the surrounding wood. If varnish, stain, or other finishing material is present on wood surfaces to be bleached, it must be removed completely before bleaching is started. Even waxy materials left on the wood by varnish removers may interfere with the action of the bleaching chemicals. A final sanding before bleaching is desirable in such cases.

Knowing the characteristics of the wood to be bleached is important. Some woods bleach easily; others do not.

BLEACHING QUALITIES OF WOODS

Ash (fairly easy)	Lauan, or Philippine (fairly easy)
Basswood (difficult)	Mahogany (easy)
Beech (fairly easy)	Locust (difficult)
Birch (easy)	Magnolia (easy)
Cedar (no)	Maple (fairly easy)
Cherry (difficult)	Oak (easy)
Chestnut (difficult)	Pine, white (no)
Cypress (difficult)	Pine, yellow (no)
Douglas fir (no)	Poplar (difficult)
Ebony (difficult)	Redwood (no)
Gum (fairly easy)	Rosewood (difficult)
Hemlock (no)	Spruce (no)
Holly (easy)	Sycamore (easy)
Korina (easy)	Teakwood (fairly easy)
Lacewood (fairly easy)	Walnut (fairly easy)

In small-scale work, or in bleaching selected areas such as mineral streaks, the bleaching solutions are usually applied with a cloth swab, sponge, or brush. In large-scale production work, they are sometimes applied with a spray gun. The gun should have a glass-solution container, and all metal parts that come in contact with the solution should be of stainless steel or other corrosion-resistant alloy. (*Caution:* Many bleaching chemicals are injurious to the skin and eyes. Therefore goggles, rubber gloves, and aprons should be worn when applying them, particularly those containing oxalic acid. If any is spilled on your skin, wash the part thoroughly under running water. Also, do large bleaching jobs outdoors over bare ground, or protect the floor and surroundings from spilled solutions.)

Commercial Wood Bleaches

These ready-prepared bleaches should be applied as directed by their manufacturer. Many of these are based on commercial hydrogen peroxide and are fairly expensive. They are very powerful and are the only satisfactory bleaches for light tones on dark wood. The best and most thorough-working wood bleaches are the so-called "two-solution" bleaches, although one-solution commercial bleaches are available.

Oxalic Acid Bleach

Oxalic acid, which comes as white crystals, is one of the oldest bleaching agents. It is used where a comparatively mild bleaching action will suffice. Prepare this bleach as needed by dissolving from 3 to 4 ounces of the acid in each quart of hot water. Do this in glass, earthenware, or enameled steel vessels. Several applications may be made, until the desired color is reached. Then neutralize the acid by swabbing the surface with a solution of 3 ounces of borax per gallon of water. Finally rinse with hot water and wipe dry.

Bleach for Walnut

Black walnut may be bleached by first coating with a solution of 6 ounces of sodium bisulfite in 1 gallon of water. After this dries, apply a second coat consisting of 8 ounces of oxalic acid in 1 gallon of water. After this dries, wash with hot water and neutralize with solution of 3 ounces of borax in 1 gallon of water. Rinse with hot water and dry.

GENERAL WOOD-CHARACTERISTIC AND FINISHING TABLE

Wood	Natural color	Grain figure	Stain Type	Stain Color	Weight +	Filler Color	Natural finish	Bleach	Paint
Alder	pink to brown	plain or figured	oil or water	red or brown	none	none	yes	yes	yes
Amaranth	purple	plain or stripe	none	none	8	match wood	yes	no	no
Ash	white to brown	plain	any	any	1.5 to 2	white or brown	yes	yes	yes
Aspen	light straw	plain or stripe	water	amber	none	none	yes	no	yes
Avodire	white to cream	stripe	none	none	8	match wood	yes	yes*	no
Basswood	cream	mild	water	red or brown	none	none	no	yes*	yes
Beech	white to brown	mild	water	red or brown	8	red or brown	no	yes	yes
Birch	cream	mild	any	walnut or mahogany	none or 7	natural or brown	yes	yes	yes
Bubinga	pale red to flesh red	plain to figured	water	red or brown	12 to 14	red or brown	yes	no	no
Butternut	amber and cream	like walnut	water	walnut or oak	12 to 14	medium brown	yes	yes	no
Cedar	red and cream	knotty or stripe	none	none	none	none	yes	no	no
Cherry	red to brown	fine	water	red or brown	6 to 8	brown, red, or black	yes	no	no

Wood	Color	Grain	Filler thinner	Stain color	Filler weight	Filler color			
Chestnut	gray-brown	heavy grain	oils[s]	red or brown	15	red or brown	yes	yes	yes
Cypress	brown and cream	plain or figured	water or oils[s]	red or brown	none	none	yes	no	yes
Ebony	dark brown to black	plain or stripe	water	red or brown	none	none	yes	no	no
Elm	cream to brown	heavy grain	water	red or brown	12 to 14	dark brown	yes	no	yes
Fir (Douglas)	cream	wild	oils[s]	brown	none	none	no	no	yes
Gaboon	golden to pinkish tan	plain or stripe	water	red or brown	none	none	yes	no	no
Gum (red)	cream and red	plain or figured	any	red or brown	none or 4 to 6	match wood	yes	yes	yes
Hemlock	light reddish brown	plain	water or oils[s]	red or brown	none	none	no	no	yes
Hickory	white to cream	straight	water	red or brown	15	brown	yes	yes	no
Holly	white	mild	water	amber	none	none	yes	yes*	yes
Kelobra	brown	plain or stripe	water	dark brown	12 to 14	dark brown	yes	yes	no
Korina	creamy gray	plain or stripe	water	red or brown	12 to 14	red or brown	yes	yes	no
Lacewood	light brown	flake	water	oak	12 to 14	dark brown	yes	yes	no

(Continued)

+ Weight designates number of pounds of filler plastic per gallon of thinner.

* Generally not necessary because of the light color of the wood.

[s] Penetrating oil stain may also be used. Non-grain-raising stains may be substituted for water stains throughout.

GENERAL WOOD-CHARACTERISTIC AND FINISHING TABLE (continued)

Wood	Natural color	Grain figure	Stain Type	Stain Color	Weight +	Filler Color	Natural finish	Bleach	Paint
Lauan	brown to red-brown	stripe	water or oils	red or brown	18	red, brown, or black	yes	yes	no
Locust	golden brown	wild	water or oils	brown	12 to 16	brown	yes	no	yes
Magnolia	light to dark yellowish brown	plain	water or oils	brown	none	none	yes	yes	yes
Mahogany	brown to red-brown	stripe	water	red or brown	12	red, brown, or black	yes	yes	no
Maple	cream	varied	water or oils	maple	none	none	yes	yes	yes
Oak (red)	red to brown	plain or flake	water	light green	15	brown	no	yes	yes
Oak (white)	white to pale brown	plain or flake	water	brown	15	brown	yes	yes	yes
Orientalwood	light brown	stripe	water	amber or brown	12	brown	yes	no	no
Padauk	golden red to crimson	stripe or mottle	none	none	14 to 16	red or brown	yes	no	no
Pine (white)	white to cream	very mild	water or oil	brown	none	none	no	no	yes

Wood	Color	Figure	Stain vehicle	Stain color	Filler weight+	Filler color			
Pine (yellow)	cream to yellow	mild	water or oil	brown	none	none	yes	no	yes
Poplar	white	mild	water or oil	red or brown	none	none	no	no	yes
Primavera	white to yellow	stripe	water	amber	12	natural	yes	yes	no
Redwood	red	mild	oil	red	none	none	yes	no	yes
Rosewood	red to brown	stripe to varied	water	red	12 to 15	dark red to black	yes	no	no
Sapeli	medium brown	stripe	water	red or brown	10	dark brown	yes	yes	no
Spruce	white	plain	water or oil	amber or brown	none	none	no	no	yes
Sycamore	white to pink	flake	water	amber or brown	none	none	yes	yes*	yes
Teakwood	golden brown	plain or figured	water or oil	brown	16	natural or brown	yes	yes	no
Tigerwood	golden brown	stripe	water	dark brown	8 to 12	dark brown	yes	yes	no
Tupelo	pale to brownish gray	plain	water	brown	none to 7	brown	yes	yes	yes
Walnut	cream and dark brown	varied	water	dark brown	12 to 15	brown to black	yes	yes	no
Zebrawood	tan with brown stripe	heavy stripe	water	light oak	12	natural	yes	no	no

+ Weight designates number of pounds of filler plastic per gallon of thinner.

* Generally not necessary because of the light color of the wood.

¹ Penetrating oil stain may also be used. Non-grain-raising stains may be substituted for water stains throughout.

Bleach for French Walnut Finish

This is a two-solution specialty bleach to precede a French or a Huguenot walnut finish, though it may be used with other woods. Make the first solution by dissolving 1 ounce of potassium permanganate in 1 gallon of water. Apply this purplish liquid liberally. While still wet, apply the second solution, which consists of 3 ounces of sodium bisulfite in 1 gallon of water. The purplish tint will vanish and the wood will be considerably lighter than it was originally. Rinse the surface, let it dry, and then sand lightly.

Sodium Hydrosulfite Bleach

A simple bleach can be made by dissolving 3 ounces of sodium hydrosulfite in 1 quart of water. This chemical is commonly used for removing dyes from textiles, and is the color remover supplied with some brands of household dyes (read label). Repeatedly wet the wood with this solution until the desired bleaching is obtained. Rinsing is not necessary.

Bleaching with Laundry Bleach

Ordinary chlorine laundry bleach—a 5- to 6-percent solution of sodium hypochlorite—is the basis for a simple bleach suited to many woods. Mix 8 ounces with a gallon of water. Apply it liberally, then let it dry. Repeat, if necessary, and then rinse.

Bleach for Mineral Streaks

For dark spots in maple, one recommendation calls for the use of 4 pounds of oxalic acid and 4 pounds of sodium hypophosphite per gallon of water, used hot. Neutralize with a solution of 4 pounds of borax in 1 gallon of water. Rinse with hot water, dry, and sand lightly.

Some mineral streaks in oak or other woods cannot be removed with ordinary bleaches. Many finishers paint these out with material tinted to match the surrounding bleached surfaces.

Bleaching Iron Stains in Oak

Oak sometimes becomes discolored with greenish or black stains where it comes in contact with iron in the presence of moisture. These result from the reaction of iron rust with the tannic acid present in oak. Their composition is insoluble black ferric tannate, the coloring matter in some inks.

Oxalic acid will reduce this to the colorless, water-soluble ferrous tannate. Give the surface several applications of a solution of 4 ounces of oxalic acid per quart of hot water. After the stains disappear, wash the wood thoroughly with warm water to remove both the acid and all ferrous tannate that might in time be oxidized back to the colored salt.

Iron stains on oak may be avoided by keeping all uncoated iron or steel off the wet wood.

Bleaching out Bluestain

Unsightly dark stains known as bluestain or sapstain often appear in the sapwood of woods of some species. They are caused by a type of fungi. Sodium hypochlorite laundry bleach (5 to 6 percent), diluted 8 ounces to 1 gallon of water, will reduce this staining if it is not too severe. This treatment is not recommended for oak or poplar.

Removing Glue Stains

Casein and vegetable glue stains can be removed almost entirely by swabbing them with a solution of 1 ounce of oxalic acid in 12 ounces of water. Rinse thoroughly with hot water and dry.

Bleached Effect Without Bleaching

A finish lighter in color than the natural color of the wood can be obtained by first applying a white or light-colored paint of very thin consistency, made with opaque pigments of the desired color. Such paint can be made by mixing enamel undercoater, flat wall paint, or even ordinary house paint with about twice its volume of a mixture of equal parts of boiled linseed oil and turpentine or mineral spirits. Another suitable mixture is wood sealer with enough color-in-oil or color-in-japan to give the required color and opacity. For a fast-drying material, lacquer enamel may be mixed with twice its volume of a clear lacquer.

The coloring material should be spread on the wood with a mop, brush, or spray gun, allowed to stand 5 to 10 minutes, and then wiped with clean rags to remove excess and leave only what sinks into the grain. Lacquer must be wiped immediately after applying, before it has time to harden. Wipe first across the grain and then parallel with the grain. When dry, apply further protective finish, such as clear wood sealer, varnish, or lacquer, as desired.

To Produce a Limed Finish

A limed effect, not quite as light as that produced by bleaching, can be developed by either of the following methods:

1. Mix thoroughly 1 pound of unslaked lime in 2 quarts of water. Apply this mixture to the surface of the smooth wood with a rough cloth, rubbing it into the pores of the grain as you would a wood filler. Wipe off excess by rubbing across the grain with another cloth and allow the surface to dry. Then apply a wash coat of shellac. After this has dried, finish with varnish or lacquer.
2. Mix 1¼ pounds white lead paste with ½ pound of fine silex and apply this filler to the smooth wood as mentioned in the procedure above. After it has set slightly, force the filler into the pores and wipe off excess by rubbing with a rough cloth across the grain. When thoroughly dry, apply a wash coat of shellac. Then finish with varnish or lacquer.

INTERIOR AND FURNITURE STAINS

Stain gives color to wood and enhances the beauty of the grain. No other step in finishing brings about so radical a change in the appearance of the wood. This change in hue or tone is caused by a chemical reaction of a liquid penetrating the surface of the wood and by coloring matter changing the color of a layer of wood near the surface but at the same time allowing the grain to be seen clearly. Staining should leave a transparent effect and should not obscure the surface with opaque material such as pigments.

You have considerable latitude in the selection of stains, for there are hundreds of types and colors. A convenient classification can be made by grouping the stains according to the solvent used in their manufacture, namely, water, oil, alcohol, and lacquer thinner. The stain color or dye can be purchased in dry powder form or in ready-mixed liquid form. Two exceptions are water stain and non-grain-raising stain which, because their solvent is water, are generally sold in a powder form.

Pigment Oil Stains

These oil stains are easy to prepare and use. They work best on soft woods of close grain, such as poplar, gum, and basswood; they have little effect on hardwoods. Their disadvantages are that they dim the grain a little, and they usually need to be sealed with a thin coat of shellac to prevent bleeding.

To promote even absorption, first wipe on the wood a coat of 1 part boiled linseed oil mixed with 3 parts gum turpentine, or 1 pound cut shellac.

MEDIUM FOR ALL COLORS

Boiled linseed oil	6 parts
Gum turpentine	2 parts
Japan drier	1 part

To this mixture, add the desired colors-in-oil, blended thoroughly with a little turpentine. The amount of the colors to be added will depend on the wood to be stained and on the shade desired. Test a stain for color on a sample or inconspicuous spot of the wood on which it is to be used. To see the true color, wait for it to dry.

GENERAL COLORS

Reds: turkey red, rose madder, rose pink, burnt sienna

Yellows: raw sienna, yellow ochre

Browns: burnt umber, vandyke brown, raw umber

Black: lampblack or ivory black

CHERRY

Dark: burnt sienna

Light: burnt sienna	3 parts
raw sienna	2 parts

MAHOGANY

Red: burnt sienna	3 parts
rose pink	2 parts
burnt umber	½ part

Brown: sienna	3 parts
rose pink or maroon lake	1 part
vandyke brown or burnt umber	1 part

MAPLE

Yellow: raw sienna	3 parts
raw umber	1 part

Red: burnt sienna	4 parts
burnt umber	1 part
Reddish honeytone:	
raw sienna	1 part
burnt umber	1 part

OAK

Light: raw sienna	4 parts
raw umber	1 pint
Dark: raw sienna	4 parts
burnt umber	1 part
Antique: raw sienna	8 parts
burnt umber	2 parts
lampblack	1 part
Mission: Ivory black	2 parts
rose pink	1 part

PINE

Pumpkin pine: raw sienna
small amount of ultramarine

Honey pine: yellow ochre
small amount of raw sienna

EBONY

Coach black	20 parts
Prussian blue	1 part

GRAY

Zinc oxide white

Lampblack, to get shade desired

WALNUT

Dark walnut: vandyke brown	6 parts
drop black	1 part
Rich dark brown: burnt umber	4 parts
vandyke brown	1 part
Yellowish brown: burnt umber	3 parts
raw umber	2 parts

| Rich reddish brown: burnt umber | 8 parts |
| burnt sienna | 1 part |

Apply the stain with a brush or cloth. Let it stand 2 or 3 minutes, then rub it with a soft cloth. Let the stain dry for at least 36 hours before smoothing with fine sandpaper or steel wool.

Penetrating Oil Stains

An easy way to make oil stains that will penetrate more deeply into the wood surface is simply to replace up to half of the linseed oil in any of the preceding formulas with the solvent toluol.

Another way to make penetrating stains is to dissolve oil-soluble dyes in a mixture of 5 parts toluol to 1 part painter's naphtha. Ordinarily about 1 ounce of dye is needed for each quart of liquid dye. Because oil-soluble dyes are made in an almost endless variety of trade-named colors, combinations to produce specific effects must be obtained by experiment, or from suggestions by individual dye suppliers. *Caution:* In using penetrating dyes containing toluol, have plenty of ventilation. The vapor of toluol is toxic, and the vapor of both toluol and naphtha is flammable.

Penetrating Spirit Stains

Stain powders soluble in alcohol make penetrating spirit stains. While the manufacturer's instructions should be followed to the letter, most spirit stains are mixed in a manner such as this: Mix 1 ounce of alcohol-soluble powder with 1 quart of hot denatured alcohol. The alcohol can be heated by placing the can in a pail of hot water away from the fire. One pint of white shellac should be added if the stain is to be used as a shading stain. Spirit stains are also available in ready-mixed liquid form with various blended solvent.

Water Stains

Water stains are especially good for hardwoods such as walnut, birch, maple, cherry, rosewood, and mahogany. They do not obscure the grain and they produce clear, rich colors that do not fade or bleed. They are not recommended for use on veneer, however, because they might loosen the glue.

You can get water stains in powder form in standard wood colors at large paint and craft stores or you can compound your own. In the former case, follow the directions on the package for mixing and application; in the latter, follow directions on the next page.

1. Moisten 1 ounce of dry aniline stain powder with hot water and stir to make a smooth paste. Use only soft or distilled water for mixing water stains, as hard water causes a change or loss of color.
2. Add the paste to 1 pint of hot water and stir well. Then add water to make 1 quart. Let stand for 24 hours.
3. Reduce the standard solution with a measured amount of hot water to make any lighter stain required. Test on wood similar to that to be stained. Mark the solution ration on the label.
4. Keep stock solutions of 1 ounce each of black, red, and yellow in 1-quart jars to use in shading new colors. Make a record of each mixture for future duplication.

Before application of water stain, sponge the wood with plain water and then dry it. This will raise tiny "whiskers" that should be removed with 3/0 or 4/0 steel wool or very fine finishing paper. Use a brush to apply the stain freely and evenly with the grain of the wood. Allow to dry slowly and thoroughly, away from heat, so that the wood will not warp or crack. Let it dry at least 24 hours. Then smooth very lightly once more with the finishing paper or steel wool. Be careful in smoothing edges, as it is very easy to remove color at such places.

Although all standard wood finish colors are obtainable in powder form, you may wish to mix your own water stain color or modify the color of a commercial mixture. Actually, with six powder colors, you can make almost any wood color you desire. Starting points for proportions are given in the table on the next page.

Non-Grain-Raising (NGR) Stains

Because water-soluble colors offer the best types of stain except for their grain-raising qualities, finishing manufacturers have developed stains in which powders are dissolved in a solvent other than water. Stains of this kind are known by various descriptive trade terms such as non-grain-raising, fast-to-light, and non-sand. Ready-mixed NGR stains are, of course, more expensive than water stains because of the solvent used. But you can mix your own by following this procedure: Add to 1 ounce of water-soluble stain powder 1 quart of Carbitol or Cellosolve. Keep in glass. Dilute as used with denatured alcohol, but not over 3 parts alcohol to 1 part stain.

NGR stains (sometimes called NFR, for "non-fiber-raising") are generally not recommended for fir, spruce, pine, and other woods that have a great variation in density between spring and summer growth because the resulting grain pattern will probably be too wild.

HOW TO MIX WOOD STAINS

Color*	Yellow (oak)	Orange (maple)	Red (mahogany)	Brown (walnut)	Dark blue	Black**
Sheraton mahogany (light red)		12	5		3	
Medium-red mahogany	2	6	6			3
Red mahogany		9	7		4	
Brown mahogany	2		2	11		1
Dark-red mahogany	2	6	7			
Light walnut		8	1	4		4
Medium walnut		10		4		6
Oriental walnut		3		1		2
Modern walnut	5			8		1
Light oak	1	10			2	
Dark oak	2	10			5	
Golden oak		22	1		3	
Maple	4	10			1	
Honey maple	4	11		1	1	1
Red cherry			12	8		
Brown cherry	2		2	3		
Fruitwood	8	2		1		
Antique brown	2	8		11		1
Antique pine			2	9		1

* Light tints of same color can be obtained by diluting with proper solvent.
** Add dark colors last.

CHARACTERISTICS OF VARIOUS TYPES OF STAINS

	Water stain	Non-grain-raising stain	Penetrating oil stain	Pigment oil stain	Spirit stain
Coloring matter	water-soluble aniline powder	water-soluble aniline powder	oil-soluble aniline powder	pigment colors in oil	alcohol-soluble aniline powder
Solvent	water	carbitol or cellosolve plus alcohol	benzol, turpentine, etc.	benzol, turpentine, naphtha	denatured alcohol
Cost	low	high	medium	medium	high
Application	brush or spray	best sprayed, but can be brushed[a]	brush and wipe with cloth	brush and wipe	spray only
Grain raising	bad[b]	very little[c]	none	none	very little[c]
Clarity	excellent	excellent	fair	excellent	poor
Bleeding	none	none or very little	bad[e]	none	bad[d]
Permanence of color	excellent	excellent	fair	excellent	poor
Effect on top coats	none	possible slight bleeding	bleeds; must be sealed with shellac[e]	none[f]	bleeds[d]
Mixes with lacquer	no	yes	yes	no	yes
Mixes with varnish	no	yes	yes	yes	yes
Drying time	12 hours	10 minutes to 3 hours	24 hours[g]	3 to 12 hours[g]	10 to 15 minutes
Principal use	staining quality hardwoods	same as water stain; also for refinishing	staining softwoods	softwoods; also as a glaze coat or wiping stain	patching and quick work

[a] Some types, factory-mixed in liquid form, dry very quickly and are difficult to brush smoothly.

[b] Water solvent causes wood fibers to lift. Work must be resanded smooth when dry. The addition of up to 25-percent Carbitol or Cellosolve will help correct this fault.

[c] Alcohol solvent absorbs moisture from air, causing slight grain raising in muggy weather.

[d] Refers to own-mix stain. Some factory-mixed stains of the alcohol series are strictly nonbleeding.

[e] Seal with shellac when used under varnish. Do not use under lacquer.

[f] Refers to factory-mixed product, made with specially treated oils to work under lacquer.

[g] Use benzol as solvent for fast drying. Retard drying with turpentine or turpentine substitute.

Tobacco Stain for Pine

To give new pine paneling and furniture an "old pine-finish look," the tobacco-stain method works well.

Break up 1 plug of chewing tobacco in a jar and add 1 pint of clear household ammonia. Cover the jar tightly and let stand for about a week. Wipe surface and end grain of wood with a damp cloth just before applying stain, to ensure even penetration. Strain liquid though a piece of old but clean nylon stocking, and mop several coats of it on the wood with a lintless cloth. Allow to dry 24 hours. Then rub lightly with fine steel wool. Dust with dry cloth and finally with a tack rag.

This stain dries lighter than it appears when wet; it shows up darker again, however, after it has been shellacked, varnished, or waxed.

Stains for Maple

All maple finishes should be clean, thin, and transparent. Sand wood clean with 4/0 finishing paper; sponge with clean water, but avoid touching with the hands; dry; sand clean again with the finishing paper, then use one of the following water-stain formulas. The colors mentioned are standard water-soluble wood stains sold in powder form.

HONEY MAPLE

Canary yellow, concentrated	½ ounce
Orange	¾ ounce
Hot water	1 gallon

AMBER MAPLE
Add to the preceding formula:

Jet black	¼ ounce

COTTAGE MAPLE
Add to the amber maple formula:

Scarlet	¼ ounce

New Stains with Household Dyes

Everyday household dyes used generally for textiles not only can be used to pinch-hit for regular water stains but also to obtain exciting and off-beat decorator color effects on furniture, craft work, and other home projects in wood. If you are tired of such old standbys as oak, walnut, and maple, these dyes will enable you to try your hand with items in rose pink, tangerine, and Kelly green!

If you use Rit dye, dissolve 1 package of a single color, or an equivalent amount of mixed colors, in 1 pint of hot—but not boiling—water. (If you use a different brand, experiment for yourself. Begin by trying twice the concentration of dye ordinarily used for textiles.) Test the color on hidden parts of the wood to be dyed. If the color is too light, add more dye; if too dark, add hot water.

As with all water stains, be sure the wood to be dyed is clean, free of grease, and sanded smooth. Sponge the surface evenly with water and wipe. When thoroughly dry, smooth with 3/0 or 4/0 steel wool or sandpaper. Apply the dye solution, while still warm, with a brush, sponge, or soft cloth. Let dry 24 hours, sand lightly with 4/0 finishing paper, and finish as you would any other water-dyed surface.

STAINS FOR OUTDOOR USE

Stains used for wood shingles, rough siding, outbuildings, and fences are essentially greatly diluted linseed oil paints. In addition to ordinary paint ingredients, they often contain coal-tar creosote to kill microorganisms, and asbestine—a species of hydrated magnesium silicate or talc—as an extender.

On rough wood they are cheaper than paint and sometimes give service twice as long. Unlike stains for interior use, exterior stains contain only pure, finely divided opaque pigments, with iron oxide, chrome, and carbon pigments being the most durable. The following formulations all use the same basic medium with different combinations of pigment and asbestine to vary the color.

MEDIUM FOR ALL COLORS

Raw linseed oil	36 fluid ounces
Coal-tar creosote	16 fluid ounces
Turpentine	16 fluid ounces
Japan drier	8 fluid ounces

To make a stain of any of the following colors grind thoroughly the specified dry pigment and asbestine with one-half of the linseed oil in the above formula, adding the oil slowly and grinding continuously until it is uniformly mixed. Mix together the other ingredients, and then add them, while stirring, to the combined pigments.

DARK RED STAIN

Indian red dry color	14½ ounces
Asbestine	1½ ounces

LIGHT RED STAIN

Venetian red dry color	14½ ounces
Asbestine	1½ ounces

MAHOGANY STAIN

Raw sienna dry color	13 ounces
Asbestine	2½ ounces

DARK BROWN STAIN

Burnt umber dry color	14½ ounces
Asbestine	1½ ounces

BROWN STAIN

Raw umber dry color	14½ ounces
Asbestine	1½ ounces

GOLDEN OAK STAIN

Raw sienna dry color	13 ounces
Asbestine	2½ ounces

GREEN STAIN

Chrome green dry color	15 ounces
Asbestine	¾ ounce

YELLOW GREEN STAIN

Chrome green dry color	11 ounces
Yellow ochre dry color	4 ounces
Asbestine	½ ounce

OLIVE GREEN STAIN

Chrome green dry color	15 ounces
Lampblack	⅛ ounce
Asbestine	½ ounce

(Continued)

GRAY STAIN

Lithopone	9½ ounces
Whiting	4 ounces
Asbestine	2 ounces
Lampblack	⅛ ounce

EMERGENCY SHINGLE STAIN.   To improvise a shingle stain of a special color, mix 1 gallon of outside paint with 1 gallon of turpentine or mineral spirits and 1 gallon of linseed oil.

Natural Wood Finish for Exterior

Owners of houses of Western red cedar, redwood, or other woods of interesting color and grain figure, often desire a durable finish that will preserve the character of the natural wood. Commercially available finishes that form a clear film, however, do not bond well and are susceptible to cracking and peeling. They therefore must be renewed frequently.

The following oil-base penetrating stain was developed by the Forest Products Laboratory of the U.S. Department of Agriculture to overcome this disadvantage. Tests indicate that one application on planed surfaces of bevel siding of redwood or Western red cedar fully exposed to the weather would last at least 3 years before renewal. The finish should last 1 or 2 years longer on siding that receives some shelter. As it merely wears or erodes away, it may then be reapplied without further treatment. The following formula will make slightly less than 5 gallons of finish.

Paraffin wax	1 pound
Zinc stearate	2 ounces
Turpentine or mineral spirits paint thinner	1 gallon
Pentachlorophenol, concentrate, 10:1	½ gallon
Boiled linseed oil	3 gallons

To the foregoing mixture, the following pigments must be added to produce the colors mentioned:

LIGHT REDWOOD

Burnt sienna in oil	2 pints

CEDAR

Burnt sienna in oil	1 pint
Raw umber in oil	1 pint

DARK REDWOOD

Burnt sienna in oil	⅓ pint
Raw umber in oil	⅓ pint
Indian red iron oxide in oil	⅔ pint
Additional turpentine or mineral spirits	1 pint

By varying the proportions of the burnt sienna and raw umber colors-in-oil, other shades may be produced. Raw umber produces a dark brown, burnt sienna gives a red, and Indian red iron oxide gives a darker red. These components contain iron oxide pigments, which are the most durable of all pigments. By using other colors, or smaller amounts of those specified, the life of the present finish will be shortened.

Pentachlorophenol, commonly called "penta," is used widely as a preservative to protect a finish from mildew. It may be obtained at a paint store, lumberyard, or mail-order house. Zinc stearate may be bought at a drugstore.

To prepare the finish, melt the paraffin and zinc stearate in the top unit of a double boiler. Stir until completely melted and combined. Then, with vigorous stirring, slowly add the mixture to the turpentine or mineral spirits. *Caution:* Perform the latter operation outdoors or in a well-ventilated room, and far from sparks or flame. Turpentine and mineral spirits are flammable and their concentrated vapors are not healthful to breathe.

When the mixture has cooled to room temperature, add the penta concentrate and the linseed oil. Then gradually stir in the pigments until the color is uniform.

A single application of the finish by brush or spray is recommended. On a smooth surface, a gallon should cover 400 to 500 square feet; on rough, 200 to 250 square feet. It may be used over other penetrating natural finishes that have been worn until they need renewal. Varnish films must be removed before applying the finish. In good drying weather, it should dry to a low luster within 24 hours.

This finish was designed particularly for siding, but has been used satisfactorily on wood fences, lawn furniture, and sun decks. It does not provide sufficient protection for exterior millwork, such as frames, window sash, and doors, which should be painted.

Penetrating Stain for Rough and Weathered Wood

Simply by doubling the amount of pigment in the dark redwood finish mentioned above, forest products experts of the University of Wisconsin have developed a moisture-resistant, long-lasting, and economical finish for exterior surfaces that had always been difficult to paint.

The new finish is excellent for rough-sawn and weathered lumber with "fuzzy" surfaces. Because of its penetration, it also works well on dense, smooth woods, such as exterior plywood and knotty or flat-grained boards of oak, pine, and fir, from which paint peels. It is an effective finish for wood that has been neglected until the paint has fallen off and the raw wood is exposed to the weather.

One coat of the fortified stain properly applied to rough wood should last 8 to 10 years. Due to less penetration, it should last about 3 years on smooth planed surfaces. It will not blister, crack, peel, or scale, even if moisture penetrates into the wood.

You can make the finish from scratch by adding ⅓ of a pint each of burnt sienna and raw umber in oil, and ⅔ of a pint of Indian red iron oxide, to the formula given for the dark redwood stain in the section "Natural Wood Finish for Exterior," which precedes this section.

You can also make a satisfactory version by thinning premium-quality red barn paint with linseed oil and water-repellent wood preservative. The paint should contain about 55-percent pigment, at least one-third of which should be ferric oxide. The vehicle should contain about 85-percent linseed, soybean, or other "drying" oil. Thin this paint with 2 gallons of boiled linseed oil and 2 gallons of paintable water-repellent wood preservative to a gallon of paint.

Apply only one coat of the fortified stain, at the rate of 200 to 250 square feet per gallon on rough surfaces and 400 to 500 square feet on smooth surfaces, using a brush or spray gun. Apply immediately to rough wood, but let smooth wood weather several months before application. Apply when the wood is dry, and the temperature above 40° F. To prevent lap marks, stain the full length of boards without stopping for more than 5 minutes.

WOOD FILLERS

For a fine finishing job on many woods, a filler should be used after the stain has dried. The purpose of a filler is to close the cells or tiny crevices in open-grained woods. Close-grained woods are often finished without the use of fillers.

Fillers can be obtained in two forms—paste and liquid. Paste fillers, used on open-grained woods, are either semitransparent or opaque; liquid fillers, normally used on close-grained woods, are transparent. In general, fillers should be as transparent as possible so as not to hide the natural color and beauty of the wood. However, opaque fillers have their place in wood finishing when special effects such as two-tone finishes are desired.

If fillers are not used, finishing materials such as varnish, shellac, paint, or lacquer will sink in and produce a rippled effect. Even though several coats of finishing material are applied and rubbed down, the rippled effect is likely to remain. The rubbing down of each coat serves as a substitute for a filler, but this operation is slower than filling the surface before applying the finish.

FILLER MIX REQUIRED FOR VARIOUS WOODS

No filler needed	Thin filler	Medium filler	Heavy filler
Aspen	Alder	Amaranth	Ash
Basswood	Beech	Avodire	Bubinga
Cedar	Birch	Butternut	Chestnut
Cypress	Cherry	Korina	Elm
Ebony	Gum	Mahogany	Hickory
Fir	Maple	Orientalwood	Kelobra
Gaboon	Sycamore	Primavera	Lacewood
Hemlock	Tupelo	Rosewood	Lauan
Holly		Sapeli	Locust
Magnolia		Tigerwood	Oak
Pine		Walnut	Padauk
Poplar		Zebrawood	Teakwood
Redwood			
Spruce			

Paste Fillers

Paste fillers are made of various formulations. They can be purchased in many stain colors as well as in natural (semitransparent) and white. Paste fillers are usually sold under the name of "wood fillers" and in cans of 1, 5, 10, and 25 pounds. One pound will fill about 40 square feet of surface.

Before use, paste fillers should be thinned to the desired consistency with gum turpentine or naphtha, the amount of dilution depending on the size of the pores to be filled. Obviously, large pores require a thicker mix than small ones. Mix only enough filler for the job at hand, as the thinned filler thickens after a few hours and becomes useless. Mixing by exact weight is always good practice. Refer to the table below for mixing proportions for various quantities of filler. The term *heavy mix* does not mean a heavy-bodied material; actually, the consistency is no thicker than varnish.

PROPORTIONS FOR MIXING VARIOUS QUANTITIES OF FILLER

Approximate amount needed*	Paste	Thinner
HEAVY MIX (16-pound base)		
2 gallons	16 pounds	1 gallon
5 pints	5 pounds	2½ pints
2 quarts	1 quart	1 quart
1 pint	1 pound	½ pint
½ pint	½ pound	4 ounces
MEDIUM MIX (12-pound base)		
1 gallon, 3 quarts	12 pounds	1 gallon
3 quarts	5 pounds	3 pints, 5 ounces
2 quarts, 10 ounces	1 quart	2 pints, 10 ounces
1 quart, 5 ounces	1 pint	1 pint, 5 ounces
1 pint, 20 ounces	1 pound	10½ ounces
9 ounces	½ pound	5¼ ounces
THIN MIX (8-pound base)		
1½ gallons	8 pounds	1 gallon
1 gallon	5 pounds	5 pints
3 quarts	1 quart	2 quarts
3 pints	1 pint	2 pints
1½ pints	1 pound	1 pint
12 ounces	½ pound	½ pint

* One pint of thinned filler covers approximately 36 square feet.

The first step in mixing is to spade the unmixed paste with a putty knife, then add a very small amount of thinner and stir. After the first mixing, add increasingly larger amounts of thinner and stir until the mix is the proper consistency. Do not add a lot of thinner at the start, as this makes mixing much harder. Use naphtha for thinning when the filler is to set up quickly for wiping; use turpentine to hold the coat open longer. A small amount of boiled linseed oil can be added to hold the coat open for 30 to 40 minutes. The reverse of this—a very quick setting filler—can be obtained by adding a small amount of japan drier.

The natural paste filler, which is usually light gray, may be colored by adding a small amount of oil stain or colors-in-oil. For changing natural filler to walnut, for instance, add a little raw umber ground in oil or japan drier. Vandyke brown will give a slightly redder color than raw umber. For mahogany, add lampblack and a little raw and burnt sienna. To test tinting, apply the filler to a scrap of stained wood and then a lacquer or varnish coat over it to get an idea of the color obtained when the surface is finished. For green, gray, white, and other colors, follow the same general procedure, except use colors-in-oil. Dry powder colors mixed in turpentine or oil-soluble aniline colors thinned with turpentine are sometimes used for colors in paste fillers. A shade of color may often be had by using a pigment stain or a penetrating wood stain as it comes from the can. Remember that the filler should be approximately the same color as the surface to which it is applied, except when the final finish is opaque. Otherwise, the filler might show through a transparent finish, if the filler is not correctly applied or properly wiped off.

If you wish to prepare your own paste filler, one much-used formula consists of ½ pint of boiled linseed oil, 4 ounces of japan drier, and 1 pint of turpentine. Mix these liquids and then add fine silica until you have a very thick paste that is well mixed. Put the paste through a paint mill, or mix it thoroughly with a paddle and strain through a wire screen. Thin with naphtha or turpentine to a thick brushing consistency. It should be just thin enough to pour out of a pot. Tinting colors should be broken up with turpentine or benzine and strained before adding them to the filler. While in use, the filler should be stirred every few minutes, because the heavy pigment settles rapidly to the bottom. To overcome this, add cornstarch (10 to 20 percent of the weight of the silica used), or add up to 25 percent of asbestine (silicate of magnesia). These materials will keep the filler pigment suspended in the oil.

Liquid Fillers

For close-grained woods like maple and birch, use liquid filler or paste filler thinned to a liquid consistency. Transparent liquid fillers are available in pint, quart, half-gallon, and gallon cans.

Commercial liquid fillers composed of glass oil, hard oil, or other cheap varnishes are not dependable. Some of the cheap fillers bleach out white in time and make a mottled, cloudy appearance under the varnish. Some are brittle and crack easily. However, when made of first-class varnish by a well-known manufacturer, they are excellent.

For mixing liquid filler yourself, the following formula may be used: 1 gallon of good rubbing varnish, 1 quart of turpentine, 1 pint of japan drier, and 2½ pounds of silica. Mix the silica well with a little of the varnish, then add the other liquids and mix them thoroughly. Grind the whole batch through a paint mill, if one is at hand, or mix it with a paddle. After it is thoroughly mixed, let it stand for 2 or 3 days, and then strain through muslin. Thin the mixture to easy brushing consistency with turpentine. Stir the filler occasionally while you are using it to keep the silica in suspension; it may settle to the bottom. It should dry flat, but not dead flat. Use less silica to avoid the dead-flat appearance.

Apply either a paste or liquid filler with a brush or rough cloth, using a circular motion and rubbing it well into the pores. After the surface has dulled over from evaporation of the turpentine, carefully remove excess filler by scraping with the edge of a card followed by wiping the wood across the grain with burlap. After 24 hours, touch up lightly with 6/0 finishing paper.

COVERING-CAPACITY SPECIFICATIONS*

Material	Square feet per gallon	Material	Square feet per gallon
Bleaching solutions	250–300	Spirit stain	250–300
Lacquer	200–300	Shellac	300–350
Lacquer sealer	250–300	Rubbing varnish	450–500
Paste wood filler	36–50 (per pound)	Flat varnish	300–350
Liquid filler	250–400	Paste wax	125–175
Water stain	350–400	Liquid wax	600–700
Oil stain	300–350	Non-grain-raising stain	275–325
Pigment oil stain	350–400	Paint	650–750

* General average—will vary considerably, depending on thickness of coat application to porous or non-porous surface, etc.

WOOD FINISHING WITH VARNISH

Varnish makes an excellent transparent finish on wood; it is unequaled for depth or build and possesses good durability and hardness. It is made by mixing synthetic resins in oil-derived vehicles, along with driers and other chemicals. Since modern synthetic resin varnishes can be formulated to meet specific conditions by changing or mixing to achieve precise differences in hardness, scuff resistance, clarity, and chemical or water resistance, manufacturers are constantly changing products. For instance, one company recently marketed an excellent varnish by combining alkyd and vinyl resins and the result was a product that contained the good properties of both.

While the synthetic varnishes vary as to their formulations, there are certain characteristics of the resins that will help to predict the finish. For example, the polyurethane, acrylic, and vinyl types of varnish produce the clearest finish and show very little color change in the wood tone. On the other hand, phenolic varnish tends to turn yellow more readily in the same manner that natural-resin varnishes do.

Polyurethane varnish has the highest resistance to abrasion and is most resistant to ordinary chemicals and water. For instance, tests show that polyurethane lasts 25 percent longer than first-quality spar varnishes—the old standard for varnish life—in exterior use. It has double the service life of first-grade natural varnishes when used on interior surfaces. While alkyds and phenolics are only slightly less resistant to abrasion and chemicals, they tend to be brittle. For this reason, they will usually scratch "white" and may show a series of fine cracks over a period of time if the wood is subjected to wide variations in humidity.

To be assured of a well-finished surface, purchase the varnish of reliable manufacturers. Never buy a cheap varnish. A small quantity of varnish covers a large area and a cheap grade will never result in a good or lasting finish. The number-one rule of success with synthetic varnishing is to read the container label *very* carefully, since instructions sometimes run counter to much common practice with "older," regular varnishes that were used for a long time.

WOOD FINISHING WITH SHELLAC

Although shellac's popularity as a top-coat finish has decreased in recent years, it is still one of the most convenient, attractive, and useful finishes for the home handyman. It is easy to apply, is ready for a second coat in an hour or two, and may be washed from brushes and rollers with nothing but ammonia in warm water.

Shellac dries to a varnishlike transparent film. It is sold in solid granular form or as a liquid when dissolved in alcohol. The liquid shellac is ready for use and is available in three stages of purification: orange, bleached (or white), and dewaxed. *Orange shellac* consists of partially refined shellac flakes dissolved in alcohol. It has a pronounced reddish brown color and is cloudy in appearance. *White* or *bleached shellac* is a similar solution but is made from bleached resin. *Dewaxed shellac* is usually light in color, but, unlike the other two, it is wax-free and thus perfectly clear.

The three forms are very much alike. However, white (clear) shellac is best for most work and is essential for blond finishes. Orange shellac is used for dark wood or over darkly stained woods. Intermixing white and orange shellac to obtain color effects is not advisable. Should deeper colors be desired to tone a finish where the stain does not seem exactly right, a transparent toner may be used. It can be made by mixing alcohol-soluble powder stain with alcohol and adding it to the shellac as required. The same method can be used to darken lacquer and varnish finishes, using lacquer-soluble and oil-soluble powder respectively. A shellac may be medium or high gloss, depending on the number of coats applied. It may be steel-wooled or rubbed with pumice and oil to a pleasing low sheen.

What "Pound Cut" Means

This term describes the pounds of dry shellac dissolved in 1 gallon of alcohol solvent. For example, a standard 4-pound cut is made dissolving 4 pounds of bleached shellac in 1 gallon of alcohol. (In 1 gallon of 4-pound cut shellac there would be a little less than 3 pounds of dry resin.)

RATIOS TO USE TO THIN SHELLAC

Original cut	Desired cut	MIXING RATIO Alcohol Shellac
5-lb cut	4-lb cut	1 part to 4 parts
5-lb cut	3-lb cut	1 part to 2 parts
5-lb cut	2-lb cut	1 part to 1 part
5-lb cut	1-lb cut	2 parts to 1 part
5-lb cut	½-lb cut	7 parts to 1 part
4-lb cut	3-lb cut	1 part to 4 parts
4-lb cut	2-lb cut	3 parts to 4 parts
4-lb cut	1-lb cut	3 parts to 1 part
4-lb cut	½-lb cut	5 parts to 1 part
3-lb cut	2-lb cut	2 parts to 5 parts
3-lb cut	1-lb cut	4 parts to 3 parts
3-lb cut	½-lb cut	4 parts to 1 part

Thinning

A coat of 4- or 5-pound cut shellac would be too thick to penetrate and to develop a good bond with wood. For most end uses, shellac must be diluted to a 2- or 3-pound cut before application. For French polishing and for a wash coat under stains, it must be diluted to a ½- or 1-pound cut. As a thinner, use only denatured alcohol that is recommended on the label for this purpose.

Storage and Test for Drying

Liquid shellac tends to deteriorate with long storage, so don't buy more than you need at a time. Also don't expose it to heat. Shellac is too old for use when it refuses to dry. If in doubt, test a sample by coating it on a scrap of clean wood. If the shellac dries to a hard film, it is still good. If it doesn't, throw it out. Adding alcohol won't help.

Uses of Shellac

At one time, shellac was one of the most widely used floor finishes. Today, because of the new synthetic varnishes, we seldom see shellacked floors, but shellac is still used for a number of projects.

FURNITURE, WALL PANELING, WOODWORK.   Sand smooth. Apply 3-pound shellac, with full brush, following grain of wood, and with minimum of brushing. After 3 hours sand lightly with extra-fine paper and wipe free of dust. Apply second coat using same technique. Do not sand. Do not put heavy objects on surface for at least 48 hours.

If a semidull finish is wanted, gently burnish second coat with fine steel wool. For a flat finish, rub down with fine powdered pumice and oil. Waxing will increase the water- and wear-resistance of any finish. Let last coat of shellac dry 24 to 48 hours. Then apply paste wax and buff.

RAW WOOD TO BE PAINTED.   On soft wood such as pine, 1 coat of 3-pound cut seals off pores of the wood and prevents finish coat from striking in to leave an uneven finish.

UNDERCOAT FOR VARNISH.   One coat of 3-pound shellac serves as an excellent undercoat for conventional varnishes. Shellac's quick dry shortens finishing cycle and reduces amount of varnish needed. Note: Do not use under urethanes.

SEALING KNOTS AND SAPPY STREAKS IN NEW WOOD.   Apply 1 or 2 coats of 3-pound cut.

WASH COAT UNDER STAINS.   One coat of 1-pound shellac assures uniform surface and controls penetration of stain.

UNDERCOAT FOR WAX FINISH.   Wood that is to have an all-wax finish should first be sealed with a coat of 3-pound cut. This prevents dirt from being ground into the wood.

FRENCH POLISHING.   This is one of the most beautiful and lasting of finishes. Sanded and stained surface must be completely dry. Then wipe on a 1-pound shellac with a soft lintless cloth rolled into a ball. Dip the ball into the shellac and rub on the wood in rapid straight strokes, exerting only light pressure. On drying, rub the wood with 4/0 steel wool or 7/0 sandpaper. The surface can be sprinkled lightly with very fine powdered pumice before sanding. Continuous coats are applied with sanding or steel wooling every third coat until a light glow appears.

At this point add several drops of boiled linseed oil to the shellac mixture and continue application, but with a rotary motion. Add more oil by degrees with subsequent coats until a deeply glowing finish is achieved. Ordinarily eight to twelve coats will be required.

OUTSIDE APPLICATION.   One or two coats of shellac spot seals knots and sappy streaks. Cover with exterior paint for protection against the weather.

WOOD FINISHING WITH LACQUERS

The original "lacquer" is an Oriental product made by Chinese and Japanese artists from the sap of a plant closely related to our poison ivy. Some of the finer Oriental furniture pieces were finished with over 300 coats of these lacquers and have lasted for centuries.

The principal feature of lacquers is the rapid drying (fully hardened in 30 minutes to 2 hours), and there is no dust problem when using lacquers. The film is hard, durable, and waterproof, and won't become soft or sticky at high temperatures. Of all the top finishes, lacquers also darken wood the least. This is especially true when a lacquer lightener is employed, which will leave the wood almost at its sanded color. While most lacquers are sprayed, slower-drying brushing lacquers are available.

The basic lacquer finishing procedure does not differ materially from the basic varnish procedure. It is simply a case of stain, fill, and lacquer, instead of stain, fill, and varnish. The quality of the lacquer finish is dependent upon the spraying or brushing technique.

The best lacquer finishes, from bare wood to final finish, are made as follows:

1. Sponge work with warm water. Add 2 ounces of dextrin per gallon of water if desired. Allow to dry 1 hour before continuing.
2. Sand with fine paper. Dust.
3. Stain with water stain of desired color. Let dry 12 hours.
4. Shellac wash coat (7 parts alcohol to 1 part shellac). Let dry 30 minutes.
5. Sand with fine paper. Dust.
6. Fill with paste wood filler stain. Wipe clean. Let dry 4, 24, or 48 hours, depending on type of filler. Follow manufacturer's recommendations.
7. Spray one coat clear gloss lacquer. Let dry 2 to 4 hours.
8. Scuff with very fine paper or 3/0 steel wool (list continues).

DRYING-TIME SPECIFICATIONS*

Material	Touch	Recoat	Rub
Lacquer	1–10 minutes	1½–3 hours	16–24 hours
Lacquer sealer	1–10 minutes	30–45 minutes	1 hour
Paste wood filler		24–48 hours	
Paste wood filler (quick dry)		3–4 hours	
Water stain	1 hour	12 hours	
Oil stain	1 hour	24 hours	
Spirit stain	zero	10 minutes	
NGR stain	2 minutes	15 minutes	
Penetrating resin finishes	15–45 minutes	3–4 hours	4 hours
Pigment oil stain	1 hour	12 hours	
Pigment oil stain (quick dry)	1 hour	3 hours	
Shellac	15 minutes	2 hours	12–18 hours
Shellac (wash coat)	2 minutes	30 minutes	
Varnish (spar)	1½ hours	18–24 hours	24–48 hours
Varnish (synthetic)	½ hour	4 hours	12–48 hours

* Average time. Different products will vary.

9. Spray second coat of clear gloss lacquer. Let dry 4 hours.
10. Scuff with very fine paper or 4/0 steel wool.
11. Spray third coat of clear gloss lacquer. Let dry overnight.
12. Rub to satin finish.

LINSEED OIL FINISH

A rubbed linseed oil finish requires patience and "elbow grease" to apply, but develops a beautiful, durable, mellow luster on stained or raw wood that many consider the most attractive of all finishes. Although not highly water-resistant, this finish will withstand hot dishes and is less likely to show scratches than a varnish finish. It may be kept in condition just by rubbing on more oil.

Use either straight boiled linseed oil or 2 parts boiled linseed oil diluted with 1 part gum turpentine. Spread the oil liberally over the surface with a thick pad of folded cloth. Allow this to sink in until no more is absorbed. Rub again with the same pad, making an effort to work additional oil into the pores of the wood. Use clean cloths to wipe off surplus oil, allow to dry overnight, and then repeat the whole process. The greater the number of coats, the more attractive and durable the finish will be. For most pieces, a minimum of three coats is recommended. (*Caution:* At the end of the day, burn used rags or store them under water; otherwise they might catch fire spontaneously.)

SOLVENT FOR FINISHING MATERIALS

The following is a summary of the various materials of many solvents or thinners used with various finishing products.

BRONZE POWDERS.   These are not soluble, but are held in suspension by lacquer, varnish, shellac, etc. Best results are obtained by using a special bronzing liquid that can be bought in either a varnish or lacquer formula.

FILLER, PASTE WOOD.   Can be mixed with turpentine, naphtha (benzine), or a half-and-half mixture of turpentine and gasoline.

FILLER, QUICK-DRY.   Same as above. Naphtha usually recommended.

FILLER STAIN.   Same as above. The addition of 20 percent benzol or toluol will ensure better penetration of the stain.

LACQUER.   Usually a blended mixture that can be purchased in fast-, medium-, or slow-drying type, and sold under the general name of lacquer thinner. A standard formula for clear lacquers is butyl acetate 23 percent, ethyl acetate 8 percent, toluol 69 percent. A standard formula for pigmented lacquers is butyl acetate 28 percent, ethyl acetate 29 percent, butyl alcohol 26 percent, toluol 17 percent.

LACQUER SEALER.   Lacquer thinner.

RUBBING COMPOUND.   Can be lubricated with water, soapy water, naphtha, low-test gasoline, or kerosene. It is advisable to follow the manufacturer's recommendations.

STAIN, PENETRATING OIL.   Naphtha, turpentine, benzol, toluol.

STAIN—NON-GRAIN-RAISING.   Special.° Many brands can be reduced with denatured alcohol. Some types reduce with butyl alcohol (butanol).

STAIN, PIGMENT OIL.   Naphtha, turpentine.

STAIN, SPIRIT.   Denatured alcohol.

SHELLAC.   Denatured alcohol. Wood alcohol. Butanol. Denatured alcohol is probably the best, in view of price and workability. It should be no less than 190 proof.

SYNTHETICS.   Special.° Toluol can be used for most products.

VARNISH, OIL.   Turpentine.

VARNISH, SYNTHETIC.   Some synthetic varnishes require special reducers. Many can be thinned with turpentine; others with toluol and other materials.

"Special°" indicates that a special blended solvent is provided by the manufacturer and should be used for best results.

HOW TO REPAIR WOOD FINISHES

Badly worn furniture may require complete refinishing. If, however, it is just soiled from everyday use, or it is marred merely by minor scratches, water marks, cigarette burns, and other local blemishes, it may be wonderfully improved by one of the following treatments.

Cleaning

This may be all that is needed to revive the luster and character of an oil, varnish, or lacquer finish. (Shellac must be given special treatment, which will be described separately.) Here is a cleaning mixture suggested by the College of Home Economics, at Cornell University:

Warm water	1 quart
Boiled linseed oil	3 tablespoons
Turpentine	1 tablespoon

Keep the mixture warm in a double boiler. Rub the finish with a soft cloth dampened with it. Then wipe the surface dry and polish with a dry cloth.

Dullness is difficult to remove from varnish or enamel of poor quality. To increase the luster, apply a thin coat of paste wax and buff well; or use the following mixture:

Boiled linseed oil	2 parts
Turpentine	1 part

Rub this polish well into the surface and buff briskly with a clean dry cloth until the finish is dry and shiny.

White Spots

On oil, varnish, and lacquer finishes, white spots are caused by heat, moisture, or alcohol. In most cases you can remove them by rubbing the finish carefully with a thin paste of finely powdered pumice in light mineral or machine oil.

Rub the mixture over the spot, using your fingertips or a piece of felt. Wipe the surface clean with a dry cloth. To remove any remaining oil, wash the surface with a cloth moistened with detergent suds. If the pumice leaves a dull spot, polish it with rottenstone and oil.

Repairing Shellac

Ordinarily a shellac finish is easily maintained by cleaning with a damp cloth or waxing. For stubborn stains, use mild soap and water. Rinse and dry. Water spots can generally be removed by rubbing gently with a cloth moistened with alcohol. (If the surface is waxed, first remove the wax with turpentine.)

If damage is too severe for this remedy, or the finish is burned or scratched, remove the old film in the affected area with fine sandpaper or pumice and oil. Then apply two or more coats of spray shellac or 3-pound-cut liquid shellac. When dry, buff with No. 00 steel wool until new finish blends with the old.

Scratches

The cleaning solution described above often makes scratches less noticeable. More serious scratches may require further treatment.

Fine scratches can usually be removed by softening the finish and letting it flow together. Use alcohol for shellac, turpentine for varnish, lacquer thinner for lacquer. Dab the solvent on with a fine artist's brush.

Where the stain is damaged, it can be restored with fine-tipped touch-up applicators that come in many colors. Dark woods also respond to repeated rubbing with liquid shoe polish or stain waxes. You might also rub a small amount of oil color into the scratch to color it and then cover with a quick-drying varnish, or mix the varnish directly with the oil color before application. Here are some suggestions for matching colors:

Reds: Turkey red, rose madder, rose pink, burnt sienna.

Yellows: Raw sienna, French ocher.

Browns: Burnt umber, Vandyke brown, raw umber.

Blacks: Lampblack, ivory black.

Walnut: Use either burnt umber or Vandyke brown. Raw umber, a yellowish brown, is sometimes added.

Mission oak: Raw umber.

Brown oak: Burnt umber alone or with a little raw sienna.

Golden oak: Raw sienna, a little burnt umber.

Maple: Burnt sienna for the redder maples; raw sienna for the yellow maples. Mix for blends.

Red mahogany: Turkey red, rose madder, or rose pink; add a little burnt umber or black, if needed.

Brown mahogany: Burnt umber, with a very little red, if needed.

Dark mahogany: Use one of the mahogany reds with black added.

Cherry: Burnt sienna. Add a little burnt umber and one of the mahogany reds, if needed.

Deep Scratches

These can be filled with stick shellac in the same way as for burns (see below). Build up the shellac to the height of the masking tape, then shave it down with a razor blade and polish with fine pumice.

A Temporary Scratch Repair

Do this with a wax crayon of a color to match the finish. Rub in, clean off the excess, then polish with wax. This works especially well on enamel.

Small Dents

These can often be raised by steaming the wood, thus swelling the compressed fibers. Remove the surface wax with turpentine so moisture can penetrate the wood. Lay a blotter over the dent and keep it wet for several hours to saturate the wood.

Apply heat to the dent with an electric iron. Do this by placing a metal bottle cap on the blotter, directly over the dent, and resting the iron on the cap. This concentrates the heat, steaming the dent. If the dent won't swell, remove the finish and try steaming again. If this won't work, use the filling method that follows.

Cigarette Burns, Scars, and Cracks

These need more drastic treatment. If burned, clean out the burn thoroughly, scraping away all damaged fibers with a knife edge or razor blade. Then smooth the wood with a small piece of fine sandpaper or steel wool, feathering the edges into the good wood.

Fill deep scars with wood paste filler or stiff spackling compound until the recess is almost flush with the surrounding surface. Shallow burns can be built up with coats of varnish or shellac, depending on furniture's finish, without the filler.

Mask the area around the scar with masking tape. Cover the filler with stick shellac in a color to match the furniture. Melt the shellac in an alcohol flame and smooth it on with a small spatula. Remove the tape and shave the shellac flush with a razor blade. Rub gently with very fine steel wool, or pumice and oil, to smooth the patch and the surrounding surface. Apply wax or polish.

Instead of using shellac, you may fill large scars with spackling compound mixed with oil color to match the finish. Make the compound a little darker than the finish, however, because it lightens as it dries. When thoroughly dry, smooth down the patch with fine steel wool or very fine abrasive paper. Varnish or shellac.

Removing Silicone Polish

Modern liquid furniture polishes containing silicone compounds are often a blessing to the housewife. These tough chemicals, related to sand, effectively repel water and resist staining and oxidation. Because they also repel the liquids in many present-day paints and varnishes, they can be a bane to the retoucher or refinisher. Every trace of silicone must be removed before the new finish can be successfully applied.

The best way to do this is to wash the surface with a silicone solvent, such as turpentine, xylol, or tuluol. After wiping the surface dry with a clean cloth, wash it again with a fresh cloth. Even after washing, it is best to apply a barrier coat of shellac or other sealer before you apply the final finish.

If you intend to use an old-fashioned oil and resin finish, the washing need not be done. In this case the oil in the finish will dissolve and blend with the silicone.

Tack Rag for Furniture Finishing

In varnishing and enameling furniture and other woodwork, it is important to keep the surface clean just ahead of the brush. A practical means for doing this is to use a so-called "tack rag." This may be purchased or made. To prepare one, use lintless cloth such as an old handkerchief, which is especially good because of its hemmed edges. Dip it in water, wringing quite dry, then sprinkle it lightly with varnish from a brush. Refold and rewring so the varnish permeates the cloth. Keep it rolled in sheet plastic or waxed paper when not in use to prevent drying out. Should this occur, sprinkle with water and wring out again.

MILDEW TREATMENT FOR WOOD

Conditions that favor the growth of surface mold on unpainted wooden parts of buildings and on stored wood are warmth, dampness, and poor ventilation. Because new, unseasoned lumber contains considerable natural moisture, it should be avoided if possible where such conditions prevail.

Under similar conditions, the molds of mildew also feed on the oils and minerals in paint, causing a dirty-looking discoloration. Indoor wood surfaces coated with varnish, enamel, or hard-surfaced paints, if kept reasonably dry, resist these molds fairly well. Softer paints on outdoor surfaces mildew more readily, the molds even penetrating to the wood.

Mildew-resistant paints containing fungicides can be bought readymade, as can fungicides that can be mixed with ordinary paints. Linseed oil paint containing zinc oxide, used as a top coat, also inhibits the mildew fungi.

To prevent and cure mildew on house paint, the Forest Service of the U.S. Department of Agriculture recommends these steps:

1. In warm damp climates where mildew occurs frequently, use a paint containing zinc oxide for top coats over the primer coat. (Zinc oxide, however, makes a paint too brittle for a priming coat.)
2. For mild cases of mildew, use a prepared paint containing a mildewcide (a poison for mildew fungi), or mix a mildewcide in regular paint.
3. Ideally, to cure mildew, remove the mildew from the old paint surface and apply a paint that contains zinc oxide or a mildewcide.
4. To kill the fungi and clean an area for repainting, scrub the paint surface with the following solution:

Trisodium phosphate	6 ounces (¾ cup)
Household detergent	2 ounces (¼ cup)
Sodium hypochlorite, 5% solution (household bleach)	1 quart
Warm water	3 quarts

When clean, rinse thoroughly with fresh water from a hose. Avoid splashing the solution on shrubbery or grass; it may do harm. Repaint with a zinc-oxide paint or one containing a fungicide.

HOW TO COMBAT BLUE STAIN

Blue stain is a blue-black discoloration of wood that may also discolor paint applied over it. Blue stain is caused by certain fungi that grow in sapwood and use part of this wood for their food. It is not decay, although the conditions that lead to its growth may favor decay-producing fungi also. The main condition is an excess of moisture, produced by contact with moist ground or constant exposure to rain, dew, or water vapor.

If it does not penetrate too deeply, blue stain can be removed temporarily by sanding or by treating with a solution of household liquid chlorine bleach. Permanent cure, however, depends on keeping moisture out of the wood. Treat unpainted wood with a water-repellent preservative. Provide protection against excess water and water vapor for other wood.

PRESERVING WOODEN FENCE POSTS

The life of wooden fence posts and other outdoor timber can often be more than doubled by treating them with chemicals that inhibit decay. There are so many possible treatments that it is hard to make a choice. The advertising of commercial or "pattented" preservatives and processes makes the choice harder. Often the products with secret formulas are made to appear less expensive than they really are by recommending such sparing use that they are ineffective. The most common chemicals used as wood preservatives, and their ratings according to various characteristics, are shown on the accompanying table.

WOOD PRESERVATIVES

Preservative	Toxicity	Odor	Color	Paintability	Soil contact	Permeability
Creosote	***	*	*	*	***	***
Penta	***	**	***	***	***	***
Water-soluble preservatives	***	***	**	***	**	**

* = usable   ** = better   *** = best

The two methods that follow on page 66 are simple, proved, and inexpensive ones suggested by the Forest Products Laboratory of the Department of Agriculture.

Cold Soaking

This consists in submerging posts for 1 to 2 days or longer in a solution of pentacholorophenol, or of copper naphthenate in fuel oil. A "penta" solution should contain 5 percent of this chemical by weight. A copper naphthenate water-soluble solution should contain the equivalent of at least 1 percent of copper metal by weight. You can buy both of these preservatives in concentrated solutions, with accompanying directions for proper dilution. This treatment works best with round pine posts that are well seasoned. Posts so treated with the penta solution have averaged more than 20 years of service.

End-Diffusion Treatment

This is a simple and inexpensive method for use on green unpeeled posts. It consists in standing such posts, freshly cut, in a container of a measured quantity of a water-soluble solution of zinc chloride or chromated zinc chloride. These chemicals are cheap, can be bought as dry powder or concentrated solution, and are not dangerous to people or animals.

Use a 15- to 20-percent solution of either. About 5 pounds, or about ½ gallon, is recommended for each cubic foot of post treated. Allow the posts to stand with butts down in the solution until approximately three-fourths of the solution has been absorbed, which may take from 1 to 10 days. Then turn them over and let the tops absorb the rest of the solution. Store at least 30 days before setting in ground.

HOW TO STOP "DRY ROT"

The decay of wood is caused by decay fungi, and these microscopic plants can't work in wood without moisture. Although decayed wood may be dry in the final stages, it is not so while the fungi are doing the damage. For this reason there is actually no such thing as "dry rot."

Often, however, the term is applied to decay that is found in house lumber many feet from the nearest possible source of moisture. When such decay occurs, it is apt to be caused by one of the water-conducting fungi. Between two layers of wood, such as a floor and subfloor, these fungi may produce thick rootlike strands that are capable of carrying moisture for considerable distances. Vapor barriers or ventilation may limit their spread, but may not stop their activity entirely.

The first thing to do to control these fungi is to trace them back to the source of their moisture and cut off the connection. Usually the moisture comes up from the ground, using a brace, frame, wooden concrete form, or a grade stake as a bridge to let the fungus climb from moist soil to a joist or sill. Sometimes a joist is in direct contact with a tree stump that has been left under the house. In other cases the source from which the fungus is bringing its moisture may not be so easily located. These special fungi sometimes get their moisture directly from the soil through strands of mycelium, or vegetative fibers, that may grow a foot or more over the surface of foundation walls, or through cracks in loosely built masonry.

If any wood has already been made useless by the decay, replace it with wood that is sound and dry. If you are sure you have eliminated the sources of moisture that started the decay, replace only the wood that has been weakened. If there is any doubt, it is safer to remove also the apparently sound wood 2 feet in each direction from the part obviously decayed, and to replace it with wood that has been thoroughly impregnated with a preservative (see paragraph on "Cold Soaking" in previous item on preserving fence posts). Before installing the new wood, give all adjacent old wood and masonry surfaces a heavy treatment with a similar preservative.

2

Paints and Painting

PAINTING HOUSE EXTERIORS

The paint on your house will cost less, look better, and be far easier to maintain if you choose and apply it according to a few tried and tested rules. When painting a new wood house or any other outside wood surfaces, there are three recommended steps:

Step 1. Treat with Water-Repellent Preservative

Protect the wood against penetration of rain and heavy dew by applying a water-repellent preservative solution before painting. If you'd rather not do this yourself, you can buy lumber already treated and re-treat cut ends on the job with a preservative solution sold at most paint and building-supply dealers. It is especially important that window sash and trim be treated.

Or you can apply the solution to untreated wood with a brush. Be careful to brush it well into lap and butt joints of trim and siding. Old houses can be treated effectively after paint has been removed. Allow 2 warm, sunny days for adequate drying of the treatment before painting.

Step 2. Apply a Priming Coat

The first or prime coat is the most important coat of paint to be applied to wood. For this coat, and for spot priming bare wood areas when repainting, experts at the U.S. Forest Products Laboratory find that a linseed oil-base paint adheres best to the wood and makes the best foundation for subsequent coats. It may contain lead or titanium pigments, but should not contain zinc oxide, which forms a hard and inflexible film that may crack itself and also crack later paint layers.

Apply the primer thickly enough so you can't see the grain of the wood. If you use ready-made paint, follow the spreading rates recommended by the manufacturer. This rate should be approximately 400 to 450 square feet per gallon with a paint that contains at least 85-percent solids by weight. The prime coat should not be porous, which would permit capillary flow of rain and dew through the paint film.

If the second coat is to be an exterior emulsion or latex paint, a primer of the type just mentioned is still necessary. The primer should be applied both to new wood and to painted surfaces that are badly weathered. It would be extremely unwise to apply emulsion-base paint directly to bare wood or to an undercoat that is chalking or deteriorated.

Step 3. Apply Finish Coats over Primer

For a smooth and durable finish, keep the following points in mind:

- Use a high-quality paint; cheap paints are more costly in the end. Finish coats can be of the linseed oil, alkyd, or latex type.
- Apply two topcoats, particularly to areas that are fully exposed to the weather such as the south side of the house. A two-coat job of low-quality paint may last only 3 years, but a three-coat job with good-quality paint may last as long as 10 years.
- To avoid peeling of one coat of paint from another, apply topcoats within 2 weeks after the primer. Do not prime in the fall and delay topcoats until spring. It is better to treat with a water-repellent preservative and delay all painting until spring.
- To avoid temperature blistering, do not apply oil-base paints on a cool surface that will be heated by the sun within a few hours. Follow the sun around the house.
- To reduce the wrinkling and flattening of oil-base paint and watermarks on latex paint, do not paint late in the evenings of cool spring and fall days when heavy dews frequently form.

Applying today's paints has become such an easy job that the first piece of advice is a warning: Don't spread it too much. When a can of paint says "one gallon covers 400 square feet" it means that the contents will cover that much. It also means don't try to get more than 400 feet, or you'll end up with a coating that is too thin. This is particularly true of the most modern paints that are thicker than ever in the can, but spread more easily than before.

The quickest and easiest exterior painting involves three steps that guarantee complete and uniform coverage:

1. Brush under the edge of the strips, running the brush edgewise.
2. Dip the brush and dab the paint along the face of the strip in patches about 4 inches apart.
3. Brush out the dabs, smoothing the paint lengthwise along the strip. Brush into the preceding "dip" to smooth the joining area. Brush out at the far edge, to produce a "feather" that will accept the next "dip" smoothly.

Where siding meets trim, work paint well into the joint, then pull out the excess by putting the tips of the brush in the joint and stroking away from it. Two or three pulling-out strokes will prevent a deposit of paint in the joint that is too thick and likely to crack.

Most modern house paints are formulated for use on the trim and the body of the house. Therefore, if the trim and the rest of the house are the same color, paint them at the same time and save ladder moving. If the trim is a different color, or if you insist on a special trim paint, it is easiest to do the trim first, because of some tricky techniques involved.

Paint the face of the trim and the edges, if you don't care if a little trim paint slops over on the siding. It is easy to cover it when you do the siding because you can work the brush into the joint more easily when the area the brush rests on is the siding—not that little edge of the trim. In fact, if there should be any reason why you must paint the body before the trim, let the house paint color cover that tiny edge, and use the trim paint only on the flat, easy-to-paint areas of the trim where a roller will save you time.

How to Repaint

A repainted job is only as good as the old paint beneath it. Here are some general rules to observe:

1. Before repainting, wash old, glossy, and unweathered surfaces with a detergent, washing soda, or trisodium phosphate solution, or roughen it well with steel wool to remove contaminants that may prevent adhesion of the next coat. Failure to do this is a common cause of intercoat peeling.

2. Repaint only when the old paint has weathered to the extent that it no longer covers or protects the wood. Where paint is peeling and wood surfaces are exposed, remove loose paint from adjacent areas. Treat with water-repellent preservative and spot prime with the housepaint primer described above. Remove excess chalk or old paint with steel wool. The paint in protected areas of the house may need cleaning only by washing.
3. For the topcoats, use any high-quality exterior paint reputed to give good service.

Other Outdoor Paint Jobs

Besides the wooden clapboard siding of a house, there will probably be wood trim, shingles, porch floors, metalwork, brick, concrete, and other items to be decorated and protected. Each of these may require a different type of paint, varnish, or other coating material.

Shingles of various decorative woods may have a pleasing natural grain that you will want to preserve. These may be coated merely with a clear water-repellent preservative or with a pigmented stain (See Chapter 1). Wood trim, such as window sashes, shutters, and doors, may be given finish coats of colored high-gloss or semigloss exterior enamel.

MASONRY SURFACES.   Brick, cement, stucco, and cinder block can be brightened and protected with a variety of paint products. One of the newest ideas in painting brick is a clear coating that withstands weather yet allows the natural surface of the brick to show through. Cement-based and rubber-based paints, as well as alkyd, vinyl, and emulsion coatings, are also used on many types of masonry. Almost all exterior house paints may be applied to masonry, however, when surface preparations are made properly.

METAL SURFACES.   Iron and steel surfaces should be primed with a rust-inhibiting paint such as red-lead, zinc chromate, or special aluminum paint. Finish coats may be of any good house paint or exterior enamel. Although copper building materials do not rust, they give off a corrosive wash that may discolor surrounding areas and so should be coated with a clear weatherproof varnish. Aluminum, like copper, does not rust in a conventional way, but gets oxidized and stained if not coated.

Porches, floors, and steps are subjected to unusually heavy traffic and so must be coated with a paint designed for durability. You can buy special porch and deck paints that that will stand up well under this hard use. Wooden porches, floors, and steps can be primed with a thinned version of the top coat. Cement and concrete ones may have to be primed with an alkali-resisting paint.

Even though there are a number of different types of paint, selection need not be too much of a problem. First consider the type of surface. Are you painting wood, metal, or masonry? Some paints can be used on all three; others on two. The condition of the surface may also be important. Old chalky surfaces, for example, are not generally a sound base for latex or water-base paints.

Next consider any special requirements. For example, nonchalking paint may be advisable where chalk rundown would discolor adjacent brick or stone surfaces. Or if mildew is a problem in your area, you may use mildew-resistant paint. Lead-free paints may be used in areas where sulfur fumes cause staining of paints containing lead pigments.

Color is a third consideration, but it is mostly a matter of personal preference. Some colors are more durable than others, and some color combinations are more attractive than others. Your paint dealer can help you with decisions on color durability and combinations.

"House paint" is the commercial term for exterior paints mixed with many different formulations. It is the most widely used type of paint. Formulations are available for use on all surfaces and for all special requirements such as chalk or mildew resistance. White is the most popular color.

Exterior paint comes in both oil-base and latex (water-base) types. The vehicle of oil-base paint consists usually of linseed oil plus turpentine or mineral spirits as the thinner. Latex paint contains water as the vehicle thinner; its vehicle consists of fine particles of resin emulsified or held in suspension in water.

Another type of water-base paint has a vehicle consisting of a soluble linseed oil dissolved in water. This paint has the properties of both oil-base and water-base paints.

The advantages of latex paints include easier application, faster drying, usually better color retention, and resistance to alkali and blistering. Also, they can be applied in humid weather and to damp surfaces. Brush and tool cleanup is simpler because it can be done with water.

Many paint dealers custom-mix paints to any shade you have in mind. Custom mixes run a little higher in price than "standard" colors, however. For this reason, check the color cards of several manufacturers to see if you can find a standard shade that suits your fancy and saves you money. Colors can also be tinted, as described later in this chapter.

Estimating Paint Needed

Of the several common methods of computing the amount of paint a house will take, the simplest is this: Multiply the height of the eaves times the linear distance around the house. If there are wings with lower eaves, compute the body of the house and the wings separately, then add.

If the house has gable ends, add 2 feet to the height of the eaves. If it has a gambrel roof, add 4 feet to the height of the eaves.

Do not subtract for windows, unless they are very large, since the paint you save on the area occupied by windows is normally needed for board edges, eaves, soffits, etc.

Roof dormers typically take 100 square feet of paint.

If your house has an overhang no greater than a foot or so, ignore it. More overhang should be computed on the basis of eave-line distance times overhang.

When you have the total square footage, divide it by the number of square feet per gallon given on the label of the paint. This figure varies from product to product, so check labels carefully and remember that square footages are not so much a "boast" about how far the paint will stretch as they are a warning not to stretch too far.

Trim paint is hard to figure in the above manner, since computation of square feet on the irregular shapes and surfaces of trim is just about impossible. However, a gallon of trim paint will take care of the average house. Even if 3 quarts would do it, there is little economy over buying a gallon, and you can always use the leftover paint for touching up. On the other hand, if your best guess is that a gallon won't quite do it, buy a gallon and a quart, and make a deal with the paint store to return the quart if you don't need it.

Floor paint, for porches, terraces, patios, and the like, is simple enough to figure on a pure square-foot basis. For odds and ends such as black wrought-iron railings, carriage lamps, etc., your guess is as good as anyone's. Remember that a little left over, stored away on a shelf in the garage, is excellent insurance against damage that should be touched up.

Causes and Remedies for Paint Failure

When exterior paint fails, not only is it necessary to correct the condition but it is more important to figure out what caused it. Otherwise, it will surely happen again.

(Text continues on page 78)

WHICH OUTDOOR PAINTS TO USE WHERE

	House paint (oil alkyd)	Cement powder paint	Exterior clear finish	Aluminum paint	Wood stain	Roof coating	Trim paint	Porch and deck paint	Primer or undercoater	Metal primer	House paint (latex)	Water-repellent preservative
MASONRY												
Asbestos cement	X										X	
Brick	X	X		X					X		X	X
Cement and cinder block	X	X		X					X		X	
Concrete/ Masonry porches and floors								X			X	
Coal-tar-felt roof						X						
Stucco	X	X		X					X		X	
METAL												
Aluminum windows	X			X			X			X	X	
Steel windows	X			X			X			X	X	
Metal roof	X*									X	X*	

Surface	1	2	3	4	5	6	7	8	9	10
Metal siding	X*		X*		X*			X	X*	
Copper sur-faces		X						X		
Galvanized surfaces	X*		X*		X*			X	X*	
Iron surfaces	X*		X*		X*			X	X*	
WOOD										
Clapboard	X*		X*				X		X*	
Natural wood siding and trim		X		X						
Shutters and other trim	X*				X*		X		X*	
Wood frame windows	X*		X*		X*		X		X*	
Wood porch floor						X				
Wood shingle roof				X						X

X* indicates that a primer sealer, or fill coat, may be necessary before the finishing coat (unless the surface has been previously finished).

GUIDE TO BODY AND TRIM COLORS

And you can paint the trim or shutters and doors as below.

If the roof of your house is	you can paint the body, as below.	Pink	Bright red	Red-orange	Tile red	Cream	Bright yellow	Light green	Dark green	Gray-green	Blue-green	Light blue	Dark blue	Blue-gray	Violet	Brown	White
Gray	White	X	X	X	X	X	X	X	X	X	X	X	X	X	X		X
	Gray	X	X	X	X		X	X	X	X	X	X	X	X	X		X
	Cream-yellow		X	X	X		X	X	X	X							X
	Pale green	X				X	X		X	X							X
	Dark green			X	X	X	X	X	X				X				X
	Putty	X			X	X		X		X			X	X		X	
	Dull red	X		X			X	X	X	X				X			X
Green	White	X	X	X	X	X	X	X	X	X	X	X	X	X	X	X	X
	Gray			X		X	X	X		X						X	X
	Cream-yellow			X	X		X	X	X	X						X	X
	Pale green						X		X								X
	Dark green	X		X	X	X	X	X	X	X	X		X	X			X
	Beige									X	X		X	X			
	Brown	X				X	X	X		X							X
	Dull red					X	X	X		X							X
	White	X	X		X				X		X			X			X
	Light gray	X	X		X				X								X

	White	Cream-yellow	Pale green	Dull red	Brown	Buff	Pink-beige	Gray	Blue
Red									
Cream-yellow	X	X	X		X			X	X
Pale green	X	X	X		X			X	X
Dull red			X	X	X	X	X		X
Brown									
White	X	X	X	X	X	X	X	X	X
Buff	X	X	X	X	X	X	X		
Pink-beige	X	X		X	X	X		X	
Cream-yellow	X	X	X	X	X		X	X	X
Pale green			X		X		X		
Brown	X	X	X	X	X		X		X
Blue									
White	X	X	X		X			X	
Gray	X	X						X	X
Cream-yellow	X	X	X		X			X	X
Blue	X	X	X		X	X		X	X

BLISTERS.   Most exterior paint blisters are caused by moisture. The moisture that creates these blisters comes from a variety of sources. For one thing, water vapor is generated inside the house, from cooking, bathing, and so forth. It will try to migrate outside the house, but when it becomes trapped inside it can push the paint film right off the wall. This will cause blisters, and in the advanced stage, peeling.

The remedy for this paint problem is to provide an escape for the moisture. High moisture areas, such as the kitchen, bath, and laundry rooms, can be equipped with exhaust fans. Even opening windows during high moisture times will remove some of the moisture. Also, you can vent the walls with various commercial products. An example is a miniature, 1-inch-diameter plastic vent. Drill holes through the siding and insert these vents between pairs of studs, about 5 inches below ceiling level and beneath windows. Also, you can buy vents about the size of nails. These are driven in place with a hammer.

Moisture can get behind paint film through cracks or improper openings in the house. Loose or missing caulk, loosely joined window and door frames and corner butts, insufficient flashing, roof damage, and missing shingles are examples. Another prime entry point for moisture is siding that is too close (within 6 inches) to the ground. It sucks up moisture by capillary action.

If the house has cracks or openings, seal them up; if siding is too low, a vapor barrier installed between it and the house foundation will reduce the problem greatly.

When you have blisters or peelings, remove all the loose paint with a scraper and sand down the edges of the remaining "craters" with medium-grade sandpaper. If you have a lot of scraping to do, use the disc sander on your electric drill. Another method is the use of heat to soften the paint, making it easy to scrape off. Never use a blowtorch for this job. Paint and hardware stores sell an electric paint remover that gets hot enough to do its softening job, but not hot enough to start a fire. Some makes combine the heating element and the scraper in a single tool.

ALLIGATORING.   This occurs when the paint has split up into segments and resembles alligator skin. This happens most often when two coats of paint are not compatible, which usually means that they do not swell and shrink at the same rate with changes in temperature. As a result, the top layer of paint develops cracks every which way, to make up for the difference in swell and shrink.

If the cracks in the paint are very fine, you may be able to escape by just repainting with a compatible paint. If not, you'll have to remove the paint to bare wood because the segments will eventually curl up at the edges and flake off, taking off whatever is on top with them.

CHALKING.   Here, pigment washes out of the paint, and onto anything that is below it. There are three causes for this:
1. The paint does not contain adequate binders.
2. Badly weathered surfaces were not primed properly so that the wood absorbs the binders, leaving the pigment to wash away.
3. The paint was applied during freezing weather or below the temperature limit specified on the label.

The answer is proper priming (with a paint that will stick) and painting. If the chalking is really bad, brush it off the surface first. A certain amount of chalking is normal with some oil-base housepaints. It is deliberate in their formulation since the slow, gradual chalking washes away and keeps the surface looking clean. In addition, it prevents undue buildup of paint, as succeeding coats go on.

CRAWLING.   This is characterized by the paint puddling up much as water would on a greasy plate. In fact, the cause is usually grease—a heavy accumulation of oily, greasy dirt, usually in protected areas, such as under the porch or eaves. The solution is simple: wash off all grease and oily deposits.

SPOTTING.   This is characterized by a loss of gloss and color in spots and is commonly caused by paint being spread too thinly—skimping on application. The symptoms may appear right after the paint is applied on up to a few weeks.

There is no real solution to this problem, at least when it occurs over previously painted surfaces. Gradually, the spotting will disappear with age. Do not apply another coat of paint too soon; this can build up an excessively thick paint film that might lead to serious problems.

CRACKING.   When cracking occurs the paint is starting to segment, but is not as pronounced as with alligatoring. The cause is usually having used a paint that has dried to an excessively hard finish and normal expansion and contraction of the house cracks it.

The only sure solution is taking the paint off down to bare wood. If you want to take a chance, you can wire-brush the cracks to remove as much curling-up paint as possible, then repaint.

WRINKLING.   Here, the paint looks as if it were crumpled and then smoothed flat on the wall. The common cause of the problem is the paint is applied too thick and is not properly brushed out. If you have this problem, sand the affected areas smooth with a belt sander using an open-coat sandpaper, such as 60 or 80 grit. Keep the sander moving so you don't make any gouges.

TO PREVENT BLEEDING OF STAIN. When paint or enamel is applied over a surface already treated with oil stain or varnish stain, the oil in the new finish tends to dissolve the stain. This, in turn, discolors the new coating.

To find out if such bleeding will occur on a given project, make a test by painting a small area. The stain may bleed through immediately, but it is better to wait 3 or 4 days before deciding to continue.

If the stain does come through it is best to first remove as much as possible by washing the surface with turpentine or benzine if it is an oil stain, or with denatured alcohol if it is an alcohol stain.

BACK PRIMER FOR UNPAINTED WOOD. On new construction—to help preserve the wood and seal out moisture—it is best to give a priming coat of paint to the back surfaces and edges of siding, plywood panels, and flooring before it is put in place. For such priming give one coat of the same primer that is going to be used on the structure.

Ladder Safety

The most dangerous phase of house painting involves the use of a ladder. For safety's sake observe the following precautions:

1. Make sure that the ladder is not defective. Check the rungs and rails carefully. Any cracked wood or loosened metal should be repaired before the ladder is used. Check any ropes and pulleys also to make sure that they are securely fastened and work properly. Check the locking mechanism to be certain that it works freely. It is a good idea to keep this well oiled at all times.

2. To raise a straight or extension ladder, brace one end against the house foundation, a step, or a curb. Raise the other end and walk in, working the hand alternately rung after rung. Be sure that the ladder is positioned firmly both on the ground and on the top, never against a window or screen or a weak gutter. If the ground is soft or the surface is macadam, install metal cleats at the base. You can avoid ladder pitching by placing a plank under the base or legs, or by driving a stake into the ground, set firmly against the bottom rung. Keep in mind that a stepladder is firmly footed

only when the spreader is fully opened and press-locked. Do not try to climb a step ladder in any other position; it will probably topple or slip.

3. Check the angle of a straight or extension ladder against the wall. It should be set so that its foot is away from the wall one-fourth of the distance to the point of support. Remember that if the base is too far away from the wall, the rungs might not be able to support the weight; if the base is too close to the wall, then the ladder might topple backwards. If you use scaffolding, make sure that it is secure.

4. Always face the ladder when climbing up or down. Hold on with both hands. Carry tools and supplies in your pocket or haul them up with a line. Keep your shoes clean when climbing. It is always wise to scrape off any dirt or mud; corrugated or square rungs add to safety, but not with dirty shoes.

5. Be sure that the paint bucket, tools, and other objects are secure when you are on a ladder or scaffolding. Falling objects can injure persons walking below.

6. Do not overreach when painting. Move the ladder frequently rather than risk a fall. A good rule is to keep your belt buckle between the rails.

7. Lean toward the ladder when working. If you must have both hands free to do a job, then "lock" yourself to the ladder. Slip one leg over a rung and hold the rung below with the heel of your shoe. But keep one hand free, ready to grab the ladder just in case. Never "push off" when painting a spot directly under the ladder—that is, do not shove the ladder away from the wall and let it momentarily "float." It is during this time that a gust of wind could carry the ladder away.

8. Never stand with both feet on the top level. On a stepladder it is wise not to go higher than the second step from the top; on a straight ladder the third step from the top is the highest you should go. If you must go higher, get a longer ladder.

9. Watch out for and avoid any electrical wiring within the area of work. This is especially important if you are using a metal ladder.

10. When painting second roofs, do not rest or place the ladder on the tar or shingles of the first roof. Tar melts and shingles are prone to sliding. Nail a 1 × 2 brace into the roof; this will prevent the ladder's legs from sliding. Always wear rubber-soled shoes when on rooftops.

11. No matter where the job, avoid setting a ladder up in front of a

door—for if someone opens the door, down you go. If you must work in front of a door, then have a helper stand in front of the locked door.

12. If it is necessary to move the ladder a short distance, place your foot against the base and pull on the rungs until the ladder is vertical. Slip your arm through the space between the rungs at about shoulder height and hold the ladder against your side. Use your other hand to brace the ladder. Walk slowly, watching the top (now and then, for you also must watch your step on the ground) to make sure that the ladder remains vertical. To carry a ladder horizontally, lift it at its center of gravity, and put it over one shoulder. Keep the front end raised so that it is at least 5 to 6 feet off the ground.

INTERIOR PAINTING

Many different kinds and formulations of paints and other finishes are available for interior use, and new ones frequently appear on the market. Use the table on pages 84–85 as a general guide in making your selection. For a more specific selection consult your paint dealer. Reputable paint dealers keep abreast of the newest developments in the paint industry and stock the newest formulations. "Dripless" paint is an example of a fairly recent development. It has a jelled consistency in the can, but it loses that form when picked up on a brush or roller and spreads evenly and smoothly. It is particularly convenient when painting a ceiling.

The usual interior paint job consists of painting wallboard or plaster walls and ceilings, woodwork, and wood windows and doors. For these surfaces you need to choose first between solvent-thinned paint (commonly called oil-base paint) and water-thinned paint (commonly called latex paint, but not necessarily latex), and then between a gloss, semigloss, or flat finish. (Enamels, which are made with a varnish, or resin, base instead of the usual linseed-oil vehicle, are included under the broad oil-paint grouping.)

Oil-base paints are very durable, are highly resistant to staining and damage, can withstand frequent scrubbings, and give good one-coat coverage. Many latex paints are advertised as having similar properties.

The main advantages of latex paint are easier application, faster drying, and simpler tool cleanup. The brushes, rollers, and other equipment can be easily cleaned with water. Both oil-base paint and latex paint are now available in gloss, semigloss, and flat finishes. Glossy finishes look shiny and clean easily. Flat finishes show dirt more readily but absorb light and thus reduce glare. Semigloss finishes have properties of both glossy and flat finishes.

Because enamel is durable and easy to clean, semigloss or full-gloss enamel is recommended for woodwork and for the walls of kitchens, bathrooms, and laundry rooms. For the walls of nurseries and other playrooms, either oil-base or latex semigloss enamel paint is suggested. Flat paint is generally used for the walls of living rooms, dining rooms, and other nonwork or nonplay rooms.

Interior Color

Paints are available in a wide range of colors and shades. Dealers usually carry color charts showing the different possibilities. Some of the colors are ready mixed; others have to be mixed by adding or combining different colors.

Color selection is mostly a matter of personal preference. Here are some points to keep in mind in selecting your colors:

1. Light colors make a small room seem larger. Conversely, dark colors make an overly large room appear smaller.
2. Bright walls in a large room detract from otherwise decorative furnishings.
3. Ceilings appear lower when darker than the walls and higher when lighter than the walls.
4. Paint generally dries to a slightly different color or shade. For a preview of the final color, brush a little of the paint on a piece of clean, white blotting paper. The blotting paper will immediately absorb the wet gloss, and the color on the paper will be about the color of the paint when it dries on the wall.
5. Colors often change under artificial lighting. Look at color swatches both in daylight and under artificial lighting.

Psychological Effects of Colors

The colors you select for the various rooms in your home will reflect your personality as well as your good taste. But your color selection will also create an emotional feeling about your home that will help form the opinion your visitors will have about you and your family.

PSYCHOLOGICAL SIGNIFICANCE
Red-Orange.   Heat; stimulation; activity; richness; splendor; dignity.

WHICH INTERIOR PAINTS TO USE WHERE

	Aluminum paint	Casein	Cement-base paint	Emulsion paint (including latex)	Enamel	Flat paint	Floor paint or enamel	Floor varnish	Interior varnish	Metal primer	Rubber-base paint (not latex)	Sealer or undercoater	Semigloss paint	Shellac	Stain	Wax (emulsion)	Wax (liquid or paste)	Wood sealer
FLOORS																		
Asphalt tile																		
Concrete							X									X*	X*	
Linoleum							X									X	X	
Vinyl and rubber							X									X	X	
Wood							X*							X			X	X
MASONRY																		
Old		X	X	X*	X*						X	X*						
New		X	X	X*	X*						X	X*						
METAL																		
Heating ducts	X									X			X*					
Radiators	X									X			X*					

Surface								
STAIRS								
Treads			X	X				
Risers	X*	X*	X	X	X	X*	X	X
WALLS AND CEILINGS								
Kitchen and bathroom		X	X*		X	X	X*	X
Plaster		X	X*		X	X	X*	X
Wallboard		X	X*		X	X	X*	X
Wood paneling		X*	X*	X		X	X*	X*
Wood trim	X*	X*	X	X	X	X	X*	X
WINDOWS								
Aluminum	X		X*	X*		X	X*	X*
Steel	X		X*	X*		X	X*	X*
Wood sill			X*		X	X		X

X* indicates that a primer or sealer may be necessary before the finishing coat, unless the surface has been previously finished.

Pink. Daintiness; gaiety; animation. Slightly stimulating. (Use in masses in bedroom or nursery.)

Yellow–Yellow-Green. Dryness; crispness; relaxation; warmth; light; cheer.

Green-Blue. Coldness; spaciousness; passivity; tranquillity.

Violet, Lavender. Coolness; limpness; dullness; daintiness; reservation; feminity. (Lavender may be used in bedrooms.)

Brown. Warmth.

DECORATIVE USES AND EFFECTS

Red. Stimulating or cheering to the melancholy or lazy; upsetting to the nervous or overactive; attention compelling. (Use in small quantities in dining room, library, kitchen.)

Blue. Soothing to the nervous; depressing to the morose. Inseparable mentally with illimitability—the cold immensity of space, infinity. It has an intellectual appeal. Symbolically, it is the color of truth, which is the result of calm reflection and never of heated argument.

Yellow. In certain hues, the sensation of glory, cheerfulness; in other variations, cowardice, cheapness. Connotes splendor, radiance, vividness. It is of great healing value to the brain. (Use in masses or small quantities, where light is poor.)

Green. Cooling, and productive of extreme reactions. Symbolic of serenity and rebirth; suggestive of hope.

Orange. Associated with life, well-being, energy. (Avoid bright orange in masses.)

Brown (Tan-Golden Brown). Depressing if used alone; best combined with orange, yellow, gold. (Use sparingly to avoid drabness, in living room, library.)

Purple (Plum, Mauve, Orchid). Associated with heroism, or with passion and mystery, pomp, gorgeousness. It has a soothing influence. (Use sparingly in living room, library.)

Black, White, Gray. Intensifies other colors in room.

Light-Reflecting Power of Paint

Colors may be used to give more light or more shadow as your decorative scheme and the type of room requires. The amount of light depends on the quantity of light reflected and absorbed. The more light reflected, the greater the visibility, reading and sewing advantages, etc. The following indicates the relative light-conserving powers (reflection) of colors:

	Percent
White	70–90
Ivories and creams	55–90
Light yellows	65–70
Light buffs	40–56
Light greens	40–50
Medium greens	15–30
Oranges	15–30
Medium blues	15–20
Dark blues	5–10
Medium grays	15–30
Red and maroons	3–18
Medium and dark browns	3–18
Black	1–4

How to Mix Custom Colors

As already mentioned, special colors of interior paint to suit your exact taste can be made in two ways. The first is to blend several different colors of ready-mixed paint. If you do this, be sure to use paints of the same brand and type. Never mix oil-base with emulsion or latex-type paints. Don't mix gloss paint with flat or semigloss, unless you deliberately want to reduce the gloss.

The second way is to tint a light-colored base paint with concentrated colors-in-oil. These may be used with almost all opaque surface coatings except lacquers and those thinned with water. They should not be used in large quantities in flat paints as they may produce glossy streaks.

Colors-in-oil come in both liquid and paste form. If you use the latter, first mix it with enough paint thinner so the mix pours smoothly.

When mixing special colors, be sure you mix enough for the whole job. If you intend to duplicate the color later, note down the amounts of the various colors used. Even if you do this, however, it is seldom possible to duplicate a batch exactly.

HOW TO MIX PAINT COLORS

This table suggests combinations of basic colors from which you can make hundreds of others. The base paint should in all cases have an oil base.

Color	Base paint	Colors-in-oil
Apple green	White	Light chrome green and orange chrome yellow
Apricot	Medium chrome yellow	Venetian red and carmine lake; for light tint, lighten with white
Browns	Venetian red	Ochre and lampblack in proportions according to shades of brown wanted
Café au lait	Burnt umber	Yellow ochre, Venetian red, and white
Canary	Lemon chrome yellow	White
Chartreuse	Lemon chrome yellow	Medium chrome green
Colonial yellow	White	Medium chrome yellow and a touch of orange chrome yellow
Copper	Medium chrome yellow	A little burnt sienna
Coral pink	Vermilion	White and medium chrome yellow
Cream and buff	White	For cream, add ochre. For buffs, also add burnt umber
Crimson	Toluidine red	For very rich hue, add crimson lake
Ecru	White	Ochre, burnt sienna, and lampblack
Electric blue	Ultramarine blue	White and raw sienna
Emerald	Light chrome green	
Fawn	White	Medium chrome yellow, Venetian red, and burnt umber
French gray	White	Lampblack with touch of ultramarine blue and madder lake or carmine
Gray	White	Lampblack to obtain desired shade, plus color, if wanted
Ivy green	Ochre	Lampblack and Prussian blue
Jonquil	White	Medium chrome yellow and touch of vermilion

Color	Base paint	Colors-in-oil
Lavender	White	Ivory black, ultramarine blue, touch of madder lake or carmine
Lemon	Lemon chrome yellow	
Marigold	Medium chrome yellow	White and orange chrome yellow
Maroon	Venetian red	Lampblack
Mauve	Ultramarine blue	White and madder lake
Navy blue	Ultramarine blue	Ivory black
Old gold	White	Medium chrome yellow, ochre, and a little burnt umber
Olive green	Lemon chrome yellow	Prussian blue and lampblack
Peach	White	Pale Indian red and chrome yellow
Pink	White	Any red desired
Plum	White	Indian red and ultramarine blue
Robin's egg blue	White	Prussian blue
Scarlet	Pale English vermilion or any scarlet-toned vermilion reds	
Sea green	White	Prussian blue, raw sienna
Shrimp	White	Venetian red, burnt sienna, and touch of vermilion
Sky blue	White	Prussian blue
Tan	White	Burnt sienna and touch of lampblack
Terra-cotta	Ochre	Venetian red and white, for some shades, also add Indian red
Turquoise	White	Prussian or phthalocyanine blue and pale chrome green
Violet	White	Lake red and ultramarine

Estimating Paint Quantity

To determine the amount of paint needed, measure the square feet of the wall area to be covered. The label usually indicates the number of square feet a gallon will cover when applied as directed.

To get the square feet of the wall area, measure the distance around the room, then multiply this figure by the distance from the floor to the ceiling. For example:

Your room is 12 by 15 feet and 8 feet high. Since 12 + 12 + 15 + 15 = 54 feet, the distance around the room, multiply 54 by the height of the wall—54 × 8 = 432 square feet of wall area.

Deduct the windows and doors that don't require paint. For example, in your room there is one door, 7 feet by 4 feet, and two windows, each one 5 feet by 3 feet. Multiply height by width to get the square feet.

$$7 \times 4 \times 1 = 28 \text{ square feet of door space}$$

$$5 \times 3 \times 2 = 30 \text{ square feet of window space}$$

Add these to get the total amount of space to be deducted from the room size—28 + 30 = 58 square feet. Subtract this from the total: 432 square feet − 58 square feet = 374 square feet of wall area to be painted. If the door is to be painted the same color as the walls, do not deduct the door area.

As mentioned earlier, be sure to buy enough paint to complete the job, especially if you are having colors mixed. Also keep in mind that unpainted plaster and wallboard soak up more paint than previously painted walls and therefore require more paint or primer.

Some paints are guaranteed to give one-coat coverage over all or most colors if applied as directed at a rate not exceeding the number of square feet specified on the label of the paint container.

How to Paint a Room

In general, walls, ceilings, woodwork, and other surfaces to be painted should be clean, dry, and smooth. But read the label on the paint can before you start painting; it may contain additional or special instructions for preparing the surface.

PREPARATION OF NEW SURFACES.   New plaster walls should not be painted with oil-base paint until they have thoroughly cured—usually after about 2 months—and then a primer coat should be applied first. If it is necessary to paint uncured plaster, apply *one coat only* of a latex paint or primer. Latex, or water-base, paint will not be affected by the alkali in new plaster and will allow water to escape while the plaster dries. Subsequent coats of paint—either oil base or latex—can be added when the plaster is dry.

Unpainted plaster picks up and absorbs dirt and is difficult to clean. The one coat of latex paint or primer will protect it.

For new drywall, a latex primer or paint is recommended for the first coat. Solvent-thinned paints tend to cause a rough surface. After the first coat of latex paint, subsequent coats can be of either type.

Clean or dust new surfaces before you apply the first coat of primer or paint.

PREPARATION OF OLD SURFACES.　The first step is to inspect the surface for cracks and mars. Fill small hairline cracks with spackling compound and larger cracks with special patching plaster. Follow the directions on the container label when using the patching material. When the patch is completely dry, sand it smooth and flush with the surrounding surface.

Nailheads tend to "pop out" in wallboard walls and ceilings. Countersink the projecting heads slightly and fill the hole with spackling compound. Sand the patch smooth when it is dry. It is desirable to prime newly spackled spots, particularly if you are applying only one coat.

Next, clean the surface of dirt and grease. A dry rag or mop will remove dust and some dirt. You may have to wash the surface with a household cleanser to remove stubborn dirt or grease.

Kitchen walls and ceilings are usually covered with a film of grease from cooking, which may extend to the walls and ceilings just outside the entrances to the kitchen, and bathroom walls and ceilings may have steamed-on dirt. The grease or dirt must be removed; the new paint will not adhere to it. To remove the grease or dirt, wash the surface with a strong household cleanser, turpentine, or mineral spirits.

The finish on kitchen and bathroom walls and ceiling is usually a gloss or semigloss. It must be "cut" so that the new paint can get a firm hold. Washing the surface with household cleanser or turpentine will dull the gloss, but, for best results, rub the surface with fine sandpaper or steel wool and then wipe the surface to remove the dust.

PAINTING SEQUENCE.　Paint the ceilings first, walls second, then woodwork (doors, windows, and other trim). The place floors occupy in the sequence depends upon what is being done to them. If floors are simply being painted, they are done last; but if they are to be completely refinished, including sanding or scraping, do them first, then cover them with paper or drop cloths while painting the room.

CEILINGS.　When using a roller for ceiling work, brush on a strip of paint around the entire perimeter of the ceiling. Roll the first stroke away from you (don't roll too fast or you will spatter the paint). Slow down as you reach the wall. Ease into the junction of wall and ceiling so as to get as little paint as possible on the wall.

If you are using a latex paint that doesn't show lap marks, paint a narrow strip around the entire perimeter of the ceiling. You'll fill in the center area later with your roller. If you are using an alkyd paint, it is best to work across the narrow dimension of the ceiling. Start in a corner and paint a narrow strip 2 or 3 feet wide against the wall. After loading your roller, roll on a strip of the same width, working from the unpainted area into a still-wet wall-side strip. When you get to the far side of the room, paint the area near the wall with a brush or roller and a paint guard. As you roll along, work backward into the wet edge of the previous strip. Crisscross your strokes to cover the area completely. Light strokes help to eliminate lap marks. It is a good idea to attach a tightly fitting cardboard disc around the handle of the roller to guard against any paint that may drip or run down the side of the roller.

When using a brush, also begin at a corner and paint a strip 2 to 3 feet wide across the ceiling. You may find it easier to brush on the paint and then cross-brush in the opposite direction, but always do the final brushing in the same direction. After you have completed the first strip, do another section about the same width. Continue in this manner until the ceiling is completed. Always work toward a wet edge of the last section to avoid lap marks.

You will find it easier to paint the ceiling if you place a 1½-inch plank of the proper height securely on the treads of two solidly footed, completely opened stepladders. This eliminates constant climbing up and down. An even easier method is to use a long-handled roller, which permits you to paint the ceiling while standing on the floor. You may have to use a ladder only to cut in the edges.

WALLS.   Use the same basic procedure for painting the side walls as you did for the ceilings. When using a brush, start painting in a corner and complete a strip 2 to 3 feet wide from ceiling to baseboard, brushing from the unpainted into the painted area. Flat paint can be applied in wide overlapping arcs. When a few square feet have been covered, "lay off" with parallel upward strokes—that is, make all final brush-off strokes until one wall is completed. Leave the trim and woodwork until all walls are painted.

You can't do a smooth paint job in the corners with a standard 7- or 9-inch roller. Therefore, unless you plan to use a special corner roller, paint the corner, top of the wall next to the ceiling, and the bottom wall next to the baseboard with a wide brush before using the roller. When using any paint other than latex, remember to do this only as you are ready to paint each strip. If the corners are allowed to dry before the inner area is painted, lap marks will show.

To use the roller, start about 3 feet from the ceiling and roll up, then down. Roll across if necessary to fill in spots that you missed with the up and down motions. Always begin a strip by working from the dry area to the wet one.

TRIM AND BASEBOARDS.   When painting a window, adjust it so you can paint the lower part of the upper sash. Then raise the upper sash almost to the top to finish painting it. The lower sash comes next. With the window open slightly at the top and bottom, it can be finished easily. Paint the recessed part of the window frame next, then the frame, and the window sill last. Spatters on the glass can be wiped off when wet, or removed with a razor blade when dry.

When painting a door, do the frame first, then paint the top, back, and front edges of the door itself. If the door is paneled, paint the panels and panel molding first, starting at the top. Keep a clean cloth handy to wipe off any paint that gets on the area surrounding the panels. Paint the rest of the door last, starting at the top.

The baseboards are painted last. A cardboard or plastic guard held flush against the bottom edge of the baseboard will protect the floor and prevent dirt from being picked up in the brush. Don't let paper or drop cloth touch the baseboard while the paint is wet.

Trim work is often painted with enamels and semigloss or gloss paints, which flow on more generously and with much less pressure than flat paints. Completing a small area at a time, brush on the paint with horizontal strokes, then level off with even, vertical strokes. Work quickly and never try to go back and touch up a spot that has started to set.

NATURAL FINISHES FOR TRIM.   Some doors are attractive in their natural finish. However, they will discolor and soil easily unless protected. Your paint dealer can offer suggestions on how to finish and protect your doors. Many kinds of products are now on the market and new ones often appear.

The first step in finishing doors is to obtain the proper color tone. This is usually acquired by staining. However, sometimes no staining is required—the preservative finish is enough to bring out the desired color tone. With new doors, to help you make a decision, you can experiment on the trimmings or shavings.

The next step is sealing. One coat of shellac is usually adequate. When the shellac is dry, the surface should be sanded smooth, wiped free of dust, and varnished. Rubbing the surface with linseed oil, as is done in furniture finishing, provides a nice soft finish but requires more work. Also, surfaces so finished collect dust more readily.

For a natural finish of other interior trim, you need to specify the desired kind and grade of wood at the time of construction. This can add substantially to the construction costs.

Wood Floors and Their Finishes

You may want to refinish your wood floors to complement your paint job. This should be done before you paint.

Complete renewal of the floors requires a thorough removal of the old finish. This can be done by sanding or with paint and varnish remover. Sanding is probably the fastest and easiest method (see Chapter 1). Electric sanders can be rented. Be sure to sand with the grain of the wood until you have a clean, smooth surface. The table on pages 96–98 describes the method of applying the popular floor finishes.

Painting Concrete Floors

Concrete floors can be painted, but it is important to use an enamel that has good alkali resistance. There are good rubber-based, epoxy, and urethane types available. Also available and recommended are latex paints made especially for concrete floors.

Clean dirt and grease from concrete floors before you paint them. Trisodium phosphate is a good cleaner to use.

Slick concrete floors should be roughened slightly before they are painted. To roughen or etch the floor, treat it with a solution of 1 gallon of muriatic acid mixed in 2 gallons of water. (For more details on preparing a concrete floor for paint, see Chapter 4.) After treating, rinse the floor thoroughly and allow it to dry completely before you paint it.

Finishing Radiators and Pipes

1. Clean surface with sandpaper and steel scratch brush. Wipe with clean rags wet with naphtha or mineral spirits to remove all traces of oil and grease.
2. If new and unpainted, radiators should receive a first coat of standard metal primer that should be allowed to dry hard.
3. The finishing coats should be an eggshell or flat finish identical with that on the walls or woodwork of the room. Contrary to an opinion once popular, this type of paint permits the maximum radiation of heat. Aluminum and other metallic paints reduce radiation by reflecting heat into the radiator.
4. Allow the paint to dry completely before turning on the heat. Then bring the heat up slowly over a 12-hour period.

APPLICATOR TOOLS—HOW TO SELECT, USE, AND CLEAN

In order to do a good job with a minimum of trouble, choose the right tools and learn how to handle them properly. When painting your home, outside or inside, you have a choice among three tools: a brush, roller, or sprayer. Which one to use for the painting job you plan depends upon the surface to be painted.

Paint Brushes

The use of a brush assures good contact of paint with pores, cracks, and crevices. Brushing is particularly recommended for applying primer coats and exterior paints. It is also the most effective way of painting windows, doors, and intricate trim work. For spray work, window glass must be masked, a tedious affair for the most part.

SELECTING A BRUSH.   Brush prices vary considerably; the greatest difference between one brush and another lies in the bristle stock, which may be made from either natural or synthetic sources. Natural bristle brushes are made with hog hair. This type of brush was originally recommended for applying oil-base paints, varnishes, lacquers, and other finishes, because natural fibers resist strong solvents.

Synthetic bristle brushes are made from a synthetic fiber, usually nylon. Today's nylon brushes are recommended for both latex (water-soluble) and oil-base paints, because this tough synthetic fiber absorbs less water than natural bristles do, while also resisting most strong paint and lacquer solvents. In addition, nylon bristles are easier to clean than natural bristles.

Brush quality determines painting ease, plus the quality of the finished job. A good brush holds more paint, controls dripping and spattering, and applies paint more smoothly to minimize brush marks. To assure that you are buying a quality brush, check the following factors:

1. Flagged bristles have split ends that help load the brush with more paint, while permitting the paint to flow on more smoothly. Cheaper brushes will have less flagging, or none at all.
2. Tapered bristles also help paint flow and provide smooth paint release. Check to see that the base of each bristle is thicker than the tip. This helps give the brush tip a fine painting edge for more even and accurate work.
3. The fullness of a brush is important too. As you press the bristles against your hand, they should feel full and springy. If the divider

FACTS ABOUT FLOOR FINISHES

Note: The following schedules are for bare floors—either new and sanded, or old with all finish removed and the dust vacuumed. If a stain is used, be sure it is compatible with topcoating. Full drying of finish is important. The time needed varies widely with temperature and humidity. Times given in chart below are approximate.

Preparation	First coat	Wood filler	Second coat	Third coat	Wax
SHELLAC (3-POUND-CUT)					
See Note above; use no oil stain	Brush on uniformly; let dry 2 hours; hand-sand with 2/0 paper; dust	If desired	Let dry 3 hours for recoat, 4 before walking on	Advisable over unfilled woods; sand with 3/0	Apply as directed on container
LACQUER					
See Note above; use no oil stain; apply special primer (optional for oak, required for pine and maple); let dry well	Apply with brush or mohair roller; work fast to avoid lap marks; dry 1 hour; hand-sand with 2/0 paper; dust	No filler required unless pores are very large	Let dry overnight if final coat; for 3rd coat, sand after 3 hours and dust	Reduce: 3 parts lacquer to 1 part thinner	Not essential until wear begins to roughen surface

PENETRATING WOOD FINISH*

See *Note* above	Brush, roll, or swab it on; let penetrate 20 to 30 minutes; wipe off excess; let dry, following directions on label	If desired; usually not used	Same as first coat; let dry according to label directions	Not needed	If desired

VARNISH

See *Note* above	Use 1 part thinner to 8 parts varnish; brush or roll on; let dry; hand-sand with 2/0 paper; dust	Use if smoothest surface is desired	Apply full strength; let dry 24 hours; for 3rd coat, hand-sand and dust	Apply full strength if desired; let dry 24 hours	Immediately, or delay until wear begins to dull surface

POLYURETHANE VARNISH**

See *Note* above	Apply with brush or roller; let dry 6–8 hours; sand with 3/0 paper; use clear to build finish	Use no filler	Use clear for glossy look or to build finish; dry and sand as before	If satin finish is desired, use it for final coat only	Optional

* One-coat method: Swab material on rapidly; keep surface wet for 30 to 60 minutes by adding more material as dry spots appear, then wipe clean and dry. Commercial method: Contractors buff penetrating sealer into the wood with #2 steel wool on a machine, instead of wiping. *Important:* Spread wiping rags to dry outdoors. They're a fire hazard.

** Be sure to read labels of all "plastic" varnishes carefully. Some recommend special fillers. Some have instructions not common to all brands.

(continued)

FACTS ABOUT FLOOR FINISHES (Continued)

Note: The following schedules are for bare floors—either new and sanded, or old with all finish removed and the dust vacuumed. If a stain is used, be sure it is compatible with topcoating. Full drying of finish is important. The time needed varies widely with temperature and humidity. Times given in chart below are approximate.

Preparation	First coat	Wood filler	Second coat	Third coat	Wax

GYM-TYPE FINISH

Preparation	First coat	Wood filler	Second coat	Third coat	Wax
See *Note* above; seal wood with 3-pound shellac; dry 2 hours; sand and dust	Brush on in a smooth even coating	If desired	Apply after 2 hours and before 6 hours; if latter is impossible, wait 48 hours	Not needed	Optional

TWO-COMPONENT VARNISH

Preparation	First coat	Wood filler	Second coat	Third coat	Wax
See *Note* above; use no oil stain	Brush on full strength (for maple, reduce 1 to 4); let dry 3 hours; hand-sand with 2/0 paper; dust	See manufacturer's instructions	Brush on; let dry 4–6 hours; sand and dust before 3rd coat	Required for pine; let final coat dry 48 hours before waxing (cure takes 2 weeks)	As directed on container

* One-coat method: Swab material on rapidly; keep surface wet for 30 to 60 minutes by adding more material as dry spots appear, then wipe clean and dry. Commercial method: Contractors buff penetrating sealer into the wood with #2 steel wool on a machine, instead of wiping. *Important:* Spread wiping rags to dry outdoors. They're a fire hazard.

** Be sure to read labels of all "plastic" varnishes carefully. Some recommend special fillers. Some have instructions not common to all brands.

in the brush setting is too large, the bristles will feel skimpy, and there will be a large hollow space in the center of the brush.

4. Bristle length should vary. As you run your hand over the bristles, some shorter ones should pop up first, indicating a variety of bristle lengths for better paint loading and smoother release.

5. A strong setting is important for bristle retention and maximum brush life. Bristles should be firmly bonded into the setting with epoxy glue, and nails should be used only to hold the ferrule to the handle. Brush size and shape are also important. The choice of a brush width is determined by the amount of open or flat area to be painted. The accompanying table may be used as a guide but should not be considered a limiting factor when selecting a brush.

PAINT BRUSH SIZES

Size (inches)	Application
1 to 1½	Touch-up and little jobs, such as toys, tools, furniture legs, and hard-to-reach corners
2 to 3	Trim work such as sashes, frames, molding, or other flat surfaces; an angular-cut brush helps do clean neat sash or narrow trim work and makes edge cutting easier
3½ to 4	Larger flat surfaces, such as floors, walls, or ceilings
4½ to 6	Large flat areas, particularly masonry surfaces, barns, or board fences

BRUSHING TECHNIQUE. Hold the brush by gripping the wide part of the handle between your fingertips near the metal ferrule. The rest of the handle should be held between your thumb and forefinger, as you would grip a pencil. This is the best way to hold the brush except when working overhead. In this case, wrap your hand around the handle with the thumb resting against the handle's inside curve. Use long, steady strokes and moderate, even pressure; excessive pressure or "stuffing" the brush into corners and cracks may damage the bristles.

Always work toward the "wet edge," the previously painted area, making sure not to try to cover too large a surface with each brush load. When loading the brush with paint, do not dip more than half the bristle length into the paint. Tap the bristle tips lightly against the inside rim of the can to remove excess. Never wipe the brush edgewise against the rim. This removes more paint than necessary, causes the brush to separate or finger, and causes tiny bubbles that make it hard to get a smooth job.

BRUSH CARE.   A good brush is an expensive tool, and it pays to invest the necessary time and effort to take care of it properly. Clean brushes immediately after use with a thinner or special brush cleaner recommended by your paint or hardware store. Use turpentine or mineral spirits to remove oil-base paints, enamels, and varnish; alcohol to remove shellac; and special solvents to remove lacquer. Remove latex paints promptly from brushes with soap and water. If any type of paint is allowed to dry on a brush, a paint remover or brush-cleaning solvent will be needed. Use the following procedure to clean paint brushes:

1. After removing excess paint with a scraper, soak the brush in the proper thinner, working it against the bottom of the container.
2. To loosen paint in the center of the brush, squeeze the bristles between thumb and forefinger, then rinse the brush again in thinner. If necessary, work the brush in mild soap suds, and rinse in clear water.
3. Press out the water with a stick.
4. Twirl the brush in a container so you will not get splashed.
5. Comb the bristles carefully, including those below the surface. Allow the brush to dry by suspending it from the handle or by laying it flat on a clean surface. Then wrap the dry brush in the original wrapper or in heavy paper to keep the bristles straight. Store the brush suspended by its handle or lying flat.

TSP PAINT BRUSH CLEANER.   A strong solution of trisodium phosphate makes an excellent cleaner for old brushes so hardened with paint they are no longer usable. The water should be hot and contain 4 ounces of TSP per quart (*Caution:* Wear rubber gloves and don't spatter the solution on surroundings.) A squat 1-pound coffee can makes a good working container.

Start by pressing the bristles against the bottom of the can to work the cleaner up into the heel of the brush. Separate the bristles with a comb or the edge of a putty knife as the paint softens. Keep dunking the brush and combing it until all the paint has been removed. When the brush is clean, rinse it thoroughly in plain water to remove all the solution. Squeeze out excess water and smooth the bristles to their proper shape. Let dry thoroughly before wrapping for storage.

Paint Rollers

Paint rollers are faster than brushes when working on large, flat surfaces. It has been estimated that rollers are now being used to apply over 75 percent of all interior wall and ceiling paint, and they are also being used in an impressive share of outdoor painting tasks as well.

SELECTING A ROLLER.   It is important to choose the proper type of roller for the particular job to be done. Modern paint rollers are available in various sizes and with handles of different lengths. Many are built so that extensions can be screwed into their handles. This makes it possible to paint ceilings or stairwells as high as 12 feet while standing on the floor, or to paint the floor without stooping. You can enamel a baseboard much faster with a roller than a brush and thus will have to spend less time in an uncomfortable position.

Paint rollers are available in many different shapes, sizes, and "nap" lengths. Some of them are intended for working into corners, some for delicate trim work. There's even one designed specifically for painting posts and columns. Look them over; you can usually tell whether a non-standard roller would be useful by visualizing its performance.

The standard rollers come in a universal core diameter, to fit any roller handle. They come in two lengths—7 and 9 inches. There is a wide range of thickness of the roller pile or nap—actually its length. If you are going to paint a rough surface such as the basement wall, a long nap will work paint into the pores and crevices. But if the job is a smooth wall in the living area, a shorter nap will produce the best results.

ROLLER TECHNIQUE.   Before applying the paint with a roller, first cut in the edges of the wall and hard-to-reach areas with a brush or with an edging roller, taking care not to get paint on the ceiling or the adjacent wall.

Some roller models have a roll that may be filled with paint, which soaks through a perforated backing into the pile cover. However, most rollers used by amateurs are manually loaded from a tilted tray, which usually has a corrugated bottom. Before paint is poured into the roller tray, it should be thoroughly mixed in the can to assure even pigment distribution. The tray should be propped so that about two-thirds of the bottom is covered with paint.

Dip the roller into the tray. Drip it into the edge of the paint, rolling the tool back and forth over the slanting corrugated section of the tray to distribute the paint evenly over the entire surface of the roller and to remove excess paint. If the roller drips when lifted from the tray, it is overloaded. The excess should be wiped off on the dry side of the tilted tray before you begin your stroke.

Apply even pressure when rolling paint on a surface. Even if the general direction of the painting may be downward, make your first stroke upward to avoid dripping. Work up and down first, doing about three strips, then work the roller horizontally to assure even coverage. As you progress, always start in a dry area and roll toward one just painted, blending in the laps.

ROLLER CARE.   Rollers should be thoroughly cleaned after each use. You should use the same cleaning liquids as those recommended for brushes for the various types of coatings. Pour the liquid into a shallow pan and roll the tool back and forth in it. Then roll out the paint and thinner on newspaper. The roller cover can also be cleaned by putting it into a large-mouth jar filled with thinner for water (if you are using a water-thinned paint), and then shaking the jar.

The paint tray should also be cleaned after each use. If you line it with newspaper held in place with masking tape, before use, your cleaning will be much easier. Tin or aluminum foil serves better with water-base paints, since newspapers may disintegrate when wet with water. After the roller has been washed, wipe with a clean dry cloth and wrap in aluminum foil. This will keep it soft until the next time it is used.

DAUBERS.   The first time anyone looks at one of the paint daubers now on the market, he snickers. But after he tries one he is ready to apologize. There are innumerable types of daubers in any good paint store. They are tiny—intended for painting delicate trim and windows. They are gross—intended for painting siding in a single stroke.

Basically, a dauber is a piece of napped fabric fastened to a flat surface, with a handle. The pile or nap is not unlike that on a paint roller. But in operation the dauber slides along the surface, forming a sort of vacuum because of the movement and friction. Like magic, the paint is pulled from the nap, and spread smoothly and uniformly on the surface.

Where does the dauber fit into the world of painting? In the hands of a novice, who finds smooth brush application difficult. And in the hands of any pro who discovers how daubers often do the job more efficiently in many situations, on many surfaces.

Paint Sprayers

Paint sprayers are particularly useful for large areas. Spraying is much faster than brushing or rolling and, although some paint will likely be wasted through overspraying, the savings in time and effort may more than compensate for any additional paint cost. Once you have perfected your spraying technique, you can produce a coating with excellent uniformity in thickness and appearance. In many localities, paint sprayers may be rented on a daily or weekly basis from paint dealers or tool-rental shops.

Surface areas accessible only with difficulty to the brush or roller can readily be covered by the sprayer. All coats can be applied satisfactorily by the spray technique except for the primer coats. Spraying should be done only on a clean surface since the paint may not adhere well if a dust film is present.

Prepreparation of the paint is of critical importance when a sprayer is to be used. Stir or strain the paint to remove any lumps, and thin it carefully. If the paint is lumpy or too thick, it may clog the spray valve; if it is too thin, the paint may sag or run after it is applied. Follow the manufacturer's instructions on the paint label for the type and amount of thinner to be used.

SPRAYER TECHNIQUE.   Before you begin, ask your paint dealer to show you exactly how the sprayer works, and to give you pointers on how to use it to best advantage. For best results:

1. Adjust the width of the spray fan to the size of the surface to be coated. A narrow fan is best for spraying small or narrow surfaces; a wider fan should be used to spray table tops or walls.
2. Before spraying any surface, test the thickness of the paint, the size of the fan, and the motion of the spray gun. Excessive thickness can cause rippling of the wet film or lead to blistering later.
3. Hold the nozzle about 8 inches from the surface to be painted.
4. Start the stroke or motion of the hand holding the sprayer while the spray is pointed slightly beyond the surface to be painted. This assures a smooth, even flow when you reach the surface to be coated.
5. Move the sprayer parallel to the surface, moving back and forth across the area with an even stroke. Spray corners and edges first.
6. Use a respirator to avoid inhaling vapors.
7. Cover everything close to the work area with drop cloths, tarps, or newspapers. The "bounce-back" from a sprayer may extend several feet from the work surface.

CARE OF SPRAYING EQUIPMENT.   Paint-spraying equipment should be cleaned before the paint sets because otherwise it may be difficult or even impossible to remove the hardened paint from the operating mechanisms. With accelerated or catalyst-set types of paint (such as epoxy) now being used, cleaning must usually be done within a matter of minutes. If paints of the latter type are allowed to harden in the operating mechanism, they cannot be removed and valuable parts may have to be discarded.

When spray equipment is to be taken out of service, clean the paint pot thoroughly with an appropriate solvent and wipe it out. Then place clean solvent in the pot and force it through the gun until all paint has been removed.

The nozzles of small pressurized paint containers may be cleaned by turning the can upside down and pressing the valve until only propellant gas comes through the nozzle.

PAINT REMOVERS

Removing Hard Paint and Varnish with Lye

Many homeowners and do-it-yourself enthusiasts have discovered what professional painters and furniture refinishers have known for a long time—that the fastest and cheapest way to remove old, hard, and many-layered coatings of paint and varnish is with a strong solution of every-day household lye. The method can be used successfully on woodwork, metals (except aluminum), and old furniture. In many cases, a lye solution will do a stripping job as well as, or better than, a solvent-type cleaner costing ten to fifteen times as much.

Don't try lye, however, unless you can meet the following conditions:

1. Lye and the softened paint must be flushed off finally with a garden hose or buckets (literally) of water. This means that it must be used over an unpainted concrete floor (say in a garage or a basement) provided with a drain, or outdoors over concrete or dirt where the runoff will not damage grass or plants.
2. Because lye solution works too slowly when cold, it must be used where the air temperature is at least 70° F.
3. As with other strong paint removers, you must wear rubber gloves (the best for this and similar uses are workmen's gauntlet-type canvas gloves coated with neoprene, a synthetic rubber that resists acids, alkalies, and solvent), and protect from spatter any of the surroundings that might be damaged by it.

If you can meet these conditions, here is what you do: Measure 1 quart of cold water into an earthenware crock or an enamel or stainless steel utensil. Do not use aluminum. Dissolve 1 can of household lye in the water, pouring it in slowly and stirring with a stick as you pour.

Next, measure 2 quarts of water into another container of similar material and stir in 4 heaping tablespoons of ordinary cornstarch. Then pour the lye solution into the cornstarch solution, stirring as you do so. The resulting mixture is of a jellylike consistency that helps hold the lye against upright surfaces.

To remove paint or varnish, merely apply the solution to the surface with a scrubbing brush (remember the rubber gloves!). Let stand a few minutes, then flush off with water. If more paint remains, repeat the procedure. When all has been removed, flush off thoroughly with the hose.

When dry, metal surfaces are ready for repainting without further treatment. After thorough rinsing, wood surfaces should be dried with old rags or paper towels and then rinsed with a solution of 1 part vinegar to 1 part water, followed by a final rinse with plain water.

Lye solution will generally darken wood. If this is objectionable, you can lighten it again by applying a household liquid chlorine bleach (Clorox, Rose-X, Purex, etc.) as a neutralizer instead of the vinegar. Rinse finally, as in the other case.

If you prefer a straight liquid to a pasty remover, you can use the lye solution described above all by itself. You can apply it with a wad of cotton waste or cloth tied to the end of a stick. Keep mopping on the solution, as the paint softens, until you are down to the bare wood.

Lye Paste Paint Remover

Except on flat, horizontal surfaces, the paste form of paint remover adheres better and is easier to apply. Here is another type of lye remover, containing soft soap and whiting to lend body and pumice powder to help final removal of the paint:

	Parts
Sodium hydroxide (lye)	10
Soft soap	30
Whiting	20
Pumice powder	10
Water	30

Put the water in an earthenware, enamel, or stainless steel vessel. Dissolve the lye in the water, pouring it in slowly and stirring with a stick. (*Caution:* Observe all the conditions in handling lye mentioned in the preceding section.) Next stir in soft soap. Mix the whiting and the pumice powder thoroughly, and then stir this into the lye and soap mixture until it is uniformly distributed.

Apply thickly with a fiber-bristled brush (lye eats hair!). Let remain until paint has softened down to the wood, then scrape off. Finally wash the surface thoroughly with plain water, and dry with rags or else with a dry mop.

Universal Paint Remover

The following preparation will remove most finishes, including paint, varnish, lacquer, and shellac:

Toluol	1 quart
Paraffin wax	4 ounces
Acetone	1 pint
Denatured alcohol	1 pint

Warm the toluol slightly by placing a pan of it in another pan of warm water. (*Caution:* All the ingredients in this mixture are flammable, so do not mix or use near any open flame. Also mix and use in a well-ventilated room, as the vapors are somewhat toxic.) Melt the wax separately in a double boiler and pour it, stirring, into the warm toluol. Then add the acetone and alcohol and stir until all are combined. Store it in a tightly capped metal or glass container.

To use, shake well and then flow on in a thick coat on the surface to be treated. Do not brush out. Leave undisturbed for about 30 minutes, then test by pressing down one finger into it, using a small rotary motion. If by this test your finger touches bare wood, the remover has done its job; if not, apply more remover and wait until the test is positive. Then remove the softened finish with a putty knife. Before refinishing, wash off any remaining wax with paint thinner or turpentine.

TSP as a Paint Remover

Used in a much higher concentration than for cleaning paint, trisodium phosphate makes an excellent paint remover—one that is easier to handle than lye, yet is cheap and effective if the paint coating is not too thick. Use it in the same proportion as for the cleaning of paint brushes—1 pound of TSP per gallon of hot water. Mop or brush on the solution and let it remain for about 30 minutes, then remove the softened paint with a dull scraper or putty knife. Rinse the clean surface well with plain water, and dry it with rags or a dry mop to prevent excessive raising of the wood grain. (*Caution:* Wear rubber gloves when handling hot concentrated TSP solution, and do not spill it on surfaces from which you do not wish to remove paint.)

TSP Paint Remover for Walls

This paint remover for vertical surfaces is not quite as caustic as one made with lye, but be sure to wash it off with plain water immediately if you get any on yourself or your surroundings.

Trisodium phosphate	1 part
Whiting	2 parts
Water	

Mix the TSP thoroughly with the whiting and add enough water to make a thick paste. Apply with a trowel or putty knife to a thickness of about ⅜ inch. Allow to remain about 30 minutes. Then scrape it off, with the finish beneath it. Rinse with plain water.

Varnish Remover Procedure

1. Apply paint and varnish remover freely with one-way strokes only. Leave until the old surface softens, wrinkles, or becomes blistered.
2. Peel off the material with a flexible putty knife. Wipe the knife on squares of newspaper. Burn all waste promptly, to reduce fire hazard, or keep it in tightly covered metal containers until this can be done.
3. Recoat the surface as often as may be needed.
4. Use No. 2 steel wool and denatured alcohol for the final cleanup.
5. Wash thoroughly with alcohol and burlap or bagging. Wipe dry with clean rags. Use a wooden picking stick on all panel lines and moldings.
6. Carefully use a scratch brush or a fiber brush to clean any carvings that may be present.

Finishing, Plating, and Working Metals

HOW TO BUFF METALWARE

Few workshop operations are as satisfying as buffing. With little effort, dramatic changes take place right before your eyes.

Almost any metal object that was shiny once will respond. Wall-switch plates, decorative copper pots, silverware, door knobs and knockers, andirons, and golf clubs can all be restored to their original brilliant finish.

The process of buffing involves three operations. The first is *polishing,* which, surprisingly, is the term for a coarse preliminary operation done with a specially prepared polishing wheel. This removes the pits and scratches and prepares the surface for the next operation, *cutting down.* This is actually buffing with sharp buffing compounds that remove the smaller imperfections and leave the metal bright. *Coloring* is the final buffing, done with soft compounds, to bring out the natural color and luster of the metal.

TYPES OF BUFFS AND COMPOUNDS FOR VARIOUS MATERIALS

MATERIAL	FOR CUTTING		FOR COLORING	
	Wheel	Compound	Wheel	Compound
Iron, steel, other hard metals	spiral sewed	emery or stainless	cushion	stainless
Brass, copper, aluminum, soft metals	spiral sewed	tripoli	cushion or loose	stainless or rouge
Brass or copper plate		Do not cut.	loose, cushion, or flannel	tripoli or rouge
Solid and plated gold or silver		Do not cut.	flannel	natural rouge or jewelers' rouge
Nickel or chrome plate	spiral sewed	stainless	cushion or loose	stainless

Selecting Wheels

Buffing wheels are made in various types for different operations. Before buying, consult the table shown on page 111 to determine the wheel diameter and thickness best suited to the horsepower and speed of your motor.

Spiral-sewed wheels are stitched in a continuous circle from center to face, making them hard and well suited to cutting down. Cushion-sewed wheels have only two or three rows of stitching to provide a resilient, cushioning effect. Softest are the loose wheels, which are joined by a single circle of stitching around the arbor hole. Loose wheels are also made in flannel.

Preparing and Using a Polishing Wheel

Mount several spiral-sewed wheels on a dowel and roll them in liquid glue poured on waxed paper. Smooth out blobs of glue with fingers and hang wheel to dry for 24 hours. Then sand smooth to remove loose or projecting threads.

To apply powdered grit, roll wheel again through abrasive, such as

No. 280 grit silicon carbide. Roll wheel back and forth without pressing until entire surface is coated. For fast work, make a second wheel using a coarser grit, such as No. 120.

When glue dries, scrape off loose abrasive and tap face of wheel with ball end of ball peen hammer to produce hundreds of tiny cracks, making the wheel flexible enough to follow contours. Ink an arrow on one side of the wheel so you can always mount it to turn in the same direction. Also mark on it the grit size. Properly made, an abrasive wheel will give long service.

This wheel cuts fast. Rust disappears almost immediately; pits and scratches take a little longer. After a good working over with abrasive wheel, metal is bright and smooth and ready for cutting down and coloring.

Cutting-down and coloring wheels are made by applying stick buffing compounds to uncoated wheels. Mark wheels with the compound used on them and use them only with that compound.

BUFFING AND POLISHING SCHEDULES

Material	Method of working (Note: s.f.p.m. means surface feet per minute)
Aluminum	Polish at 5,500 s.f.p.m. using Nos. 80, 120, and 180 grits. All wheels over 120 grit should be well greased. Buff at 7,500 s.f.p.m., using tripoli for the first buffing and finishing with red rouge.
Brass	Polish at 6,000 s.f.p.m. using Nos. 80, 120, and 180 grits. The 80 grit is necessary only for rough coatings. Buff with tripoli or emery at a speed of about 5,500 s.f.p.m.
Cast iron	Use grits 120, 150, and 180. The two coarser grits can be run dry. Buff at 7,500 s.f.p.m. Buff with 220 to 240 grit silicon carbide applied to a greased rag wheel.
Copper	Same schedule as brass. Fine-grit wheels should be greased. Avoid heavy pressure since copper heats quickly and holds heat longer than other metals.
Lacquered surfaces	Use a lacquer suitable for buffing. Buff at 6,000 s.f.p.m., using any reliable brand of lacquer buffing compound.
Nickeled surfaces	Buff at 7,500 s.f.p.m. using tripoli and lime. A perfect finish is necessary if the work is to be chromium plated.
Plastic	Polish with 200 grit silicon carbide. Buff with 400 and 500 grit silicon carbide on greased wheels. Finish with red or green rouge.
Steel	Polish at 7,500 s.f.p.m., using aluminum oxide grits Nos. 90 and 120 dry and No. 180 greased. Buff with tripoli or a very fine grit aluminum oxide. For a mirror finish, buff with green rouge. For satin finish, buff with pumice on a Tampico brush.

Buffing Techniques

Knowing what wheel to use with what compound on what material is only half of your buffing education. The other, equally important, half is knowing how to use your equipment. Here are some tips:

1. Protect your eyes with safety goggles or a face shield.
2. Leave your necktie in the closet; it is dangerous around a buffing wheel.
3. Wear gloves unless the work is so small or delicate that gloves are impractical. Much heat is generated when buffing and the work often becomes uncomfortably hot.
4. Wear a shop coat and hat to catch the dust that will settle on you.
5. Hold work firmly against the buffing wheel slightly below the spindle center and move it up and down—up to get the maximum cut, and down to blend the cuts together.
6. Never take your eyes off the work, not even for a moment. The fast-moving wheel can snatch the work away from you, especially when it strikes an edge.
7. Inspect the work frequently while cutting. When the many fine lines and scratches are blended out, you are ready for coloring.

BUFFING WHEEL SELECTION TABLE FOR VARIOUS SIZE MOTORS

RECOMMENDED WHEEL THICKNESS

Motor size	4-inch diameter	6-inch diameter	8-inch diameter	10-inch diameter
⅙–⅛ hp	1	½		
¼ hp	1½	1	½	
⅓ hp	2½	2	1½	½
½ hp	3	2½	2	2

FORMULA FOR CALCULATING SURFACE FEET PER MINUTE (S.F.P.M.)

(Ideal buffing speed is 5,000 s.f.p.m.)

$$\frac{\text{diameter of wheel in inches}}{4} \times \text{r.p.m. of spindle} = \text{s.f.p.m.}$$

Example:

$$\frac{\text{6-inch diameter wheel}}{4} \times 3{,}450 \text{ r.p.m.} = 5{,}175 \text{ s.f.p.m.}$$

COLORING METALS WITH CHEMICALS

The chemical coloring of metals ought to be more popular in home workshops than it is. In most cases the process is simple, and the results range from pleasing to spectacular.

Before applying any of the following formulas, be sure the metal to be treated is absolutely clean. If lacquered, remove this finish with a lacquer solvent or a heavy-cutting buffing compound. Unlacquered brass, copper, and aluminum can be cleaned by rubbing with a good metal polish. Wash in hot water with a strong detergent and follow with a hot-water rinse.

Many of the processes are simply artificially induced corrosion. Others etch the metal bare. To prevent continued action, rinse them in very hot water. Brass, copper, and aluminum objects can then be waxed or coated with a clear metal lacquer. Colored steel tools and hardware should be coated with oil.

Caution: When using the processes described below, you may be working with acids, lye, or other caustic materials. Protect your skin against spills or splashes with rubber gloves, longs sleeves, and an apron. Wear shop eye goggles. Since heat is required in many cases, you may have to work in the kitchen. In this case, keep chemicals away from food, utensils, and countertops. A final safety note: *Always add acid to water, not the reverse.*

Black on Brass

Dissolve 1 ounce of copper nitrate in 6 ounces of water and apply to the brass. Then heat the brass to change the copper nitrate to copper oxide, which produces a permanent black finish.

Instead of heating, you may apply this solution over the copper nitrate coating.

Sodium sulfide	1	ounce
Hydrochloric acid, concentrated *(Caution:* caustic)	½	ounce
Water	10	ounces

This changes the coating to black copper sulfide.

Dull Black on Brass

Dissolve copper scraps in concentrated nitric acid diluted with an equal amount of water in a glass container. (*Caution:* Nitric acid is extremely caustic.) Immerse brass object in solution until desired depth of black has been produced. Remove and wash well with water. If desired, the coating can be given a sheen by rubbing with linseed oil.

Golden Matte on Brass

Immerse in a solution of 1 part concentrated nitric acid (remember that nitric acid is caustic) in 3 parts water in a glass container. Rock the solution gently. Wipe the object clean under running tap. When dry, protect the surface with wax or lacquer.

Antique-Green Patina on Brass

Potassium bitartrate (cream of tartar)	3 ounces
Ammonium chloride	1 ounce
Copper nitrate	7½ ounces
Sodium chloride (table salt)	3 ounces
Water, boiling	13 ounces

Dissolve the salts in the boiling water and apply the hot solution to the brass with a piece of sponge or rag mounted on a stick. When the desired effect has been attained, wash and dry.

As another method, paint the object daily for 3 or 4 days with this solution:

Copper carbonate	3 ounces
Ammonium chloride	1 ounce
Copper acetate	1 ounce
Potassium bitartrate	1 ounce
Strong vinegar	8 ounces

Yellow-Orange, Blue, Red-Brown on Brass

You can get yellow through bluish tones by immersing the object in the following solution. Increase the concentration for bluish tone.

Sodium hydroxide (lye, *caustic*)	½ ounce
Copper carbonate	1 ounce

Hot water	24	ounces

Get red-brown shades by brief dip in this solution:

Copper carbonate	¼ ounce
Household ammonia	7½ ounces
Sodium carbonate (Washing soda)	¼ ounce
Water, near boiling	48 ounces

Cold-rinse the object and dip for a moment in dilute sulfuric acid (*caution:* caustic). Experiment for different shades.

Black on Copper

Potassium or sodium sulfide	¼ ounce
Household ammonia	1½ ounces
Water	32 ounces

Do not heat this solution, as heat will drive off the ammonia gas.

Light Matte on Copper

Use same treatment as for golden matte on brass, above.

Antique-Green Patina on Copper

Use same treatment as for similar finish on brass, above.

Yellow-Green Patina on Copper

Swab the object for a few days with a mixture of equal parts of sugar, salt, and strong vinegar. Don't immerse the metal. Crush the salt and sugar to a fine powder before mixing the solution.

Bright Blue on Copper

Lead acetate (*Caution:* poison)	½ ounce
Sodium thiosulfate (hypo)	1 ounce
Water	32 ounces

Immerse the object in this solution for about 15 seconds.

Bronze on Copper

Ferric nitrate	1½ ounces
Potassium thiocyanate	½ ounce
Water	32 ounces

Use this solution hot. Heat the metal object by first immersing it in hot water. Then dip in the hot chemical solution until the color is satisfactory. Rinse in running water and dry in breeze of a fan.

Red-Bronze to Brown on Copper

Sulfurated potassium (liver of sulfur)	½ ounce
Sodium hydroxide (lye)	¾ ounce
Water	32 ounces

Use this solution hot and dip the object in it.

Concentration and temperature of the solution, metals alloyed with the copper, and time of immersion will cause differences of color.

Steel-Gray on Aluminum

Zinc chloride	8 ounces
Copper sulfate	1 ounce
Water, boiling	32 ounces

Immerse the objects until desired tone is obtained. Rinse in a 2-percent solution of lye (*Caution*) in water, then thoroughly in clear water.

Near-White and Matte Colors on Aluminum

A soft-etched, imitation anodized finish may be produced on aluminum by dipping it in a solution of 1 tablespoon or more of lye to a pint of water. To color the aluminum, then dip it in a solution of household dye. (*Caution:* Be careful with the lye—caustic.)

Black on Iron and Steel

Heat red-hot and dip in heavy engine or linseed oil. Most cast irons, etched or blasted, will become bluish-brownish or blackish if soaked or painted with a solution of 6 tablespoons of tannic acid in 1 pint of water.

This formula is also good:

Copper sulfate	2 ounces
Concentrated nitric acid	4 ounces
Denatured alcohol	10 ounces
Water	24 ounces

Dissolve the copper sulfate completely in the water. Then stir in the nitric acid (*caution:* corrosive) and the alcohol. Apply this solution uniformly to the metal and allow to air dry. If not black enough, apply again. When dry, rub on a coat of linseed oil.

Brown on Iron and Steel

The following is an old formula for coloring the outside of gun barrels. It is especially popular because the ingredients can usually be obtained at the drugstore.

Copper sulfate	¾ ounce
Mercuric chloride	1 ounce
Concentrated nitric acid	½ ounce
Denatured alcohol	1 ounce
Tincture ferric chloride	1 ounce
Tincture ethyl nitrate (sweet spirits of nitre)	1 ounce
Water	25 ounces

Dissolve the copper sulfate and the mercuric chloride in the water, then stir in the other ingredients in the order named. Apply the solution uniformly with a pad of glass wool and expose to the air for 24 hours. Then wash in hot water, dry in air, and wipe with linseed oil. (*Caution:* nitric acid, caustic; mercuric chloride, poison.)

Blue on Iron and Steel

Ferric chloride	2 ounces
Antimony chloride	2 ounces

| Gallic acid | 1 ounce |
| Water | 5 ounces |

Dissolve in the order given, and apply the same as the last formula. (*Caution:* Antimony chloride, poison.)

Antiquing Copper

When the natural color of copper or a highly polished finish is inappropriate, it is a simple matter to give it a more subdued "antique" or French finish.

Dissolve about 1 cubic inch of potassium sulfide (liver of sulfur) in 1 pint of water. Add 6 drops of household ammonia. Clean the copper thoroughly to remove all dirt and grease, and rapidly swab on the solution. The metal will gradually darken to black. With a cloth or toothbrush and clear water, rub off the outer black deposit immediately. If the metal is not then a deep brown-black, clean thoroughly and repeat the process. Wash well and dry with a cloth.

With a very fine steel wool, rub to bring out the tone desired. The less rubbing, the deeper the tone. Excessive rubbing will restore the copper to its natural color. It is at this point that recessed parts can be left dark, while high parts are brightened to the amount desired. A smooth surface can be given an attractive mottled appearance by judicious use of steel wool, some spots being left darker than others.

The finish should be protected either with clear metal lacquer or by several coats of good-quality wax, each left to harden and then polished.

Apart from embossing, peening, crimping, and other worked effects that are set off by the treatment, considerable variation on a smooth surface is possible by scratch-brushing, sandpapering, or rubbing with coarse steel wool before treatment. The deeper the scratches, the more dark tones will remain, and the more "grain" and the deeper the tone the finish will have.

ANNEALING AND PICKLING COPPER AND ITS ALLOYS

When being shaped, copper, brass, and other alloys of copper become work-hardened and must be softened by annealing. They also become dirty and covered with an oxide, and must be cleaned, or "pickled," in an acid bath. During forming, annealing and pickling may be done in a single operation. When forming is completed, only pickling is necessary.

Annealing

Heat piece to dull red over a Bunsen burner, gas stove, or with torch. Move the piece in the flame to bring it slowly and evenly up to annealing temperature. Holding it with copper tongs or tweezers, slide it gently into pickling solution, avoiding splash. The solution will anneal (by quickly cooling it) and clean the metal at the same time. Remove the piece with tongs and rinse it under warm water.

Pickling Solution

To make pickling solution for copper and alloys, mix 1 part concentrated sulfuric acid with 9 parts water. (*Caution:* Always pour the acid into the water, and not vice versa. Do not spill on skin or clothing, as acid is extremely caustic.) Mix and use in a glass or earthenware container. Cover when not in use and keep in a well-ventilated place, as concentrated fumes from it may rust nearby articles of iron and steel.

When object is completely formed, and does not have to be softened again, place in solution without heating. Let remain 5 to 10 minutes, then remove with tongs, rinse, and dry with paper towels.

CLEANING METAL FOR PLATING

Before metals can be plated, all grease, corrosion, and scale must be removed so the plating solution can make perfect contact with the bare solid metal. Grease can be removed by organic solvents, such as a combination of 1 part trichloroethylene and 1 part naphtha, or by washing in a hot solution of washing soda or trisodium phosphate. (*Careful:* Avoid breathing fumes; wear rubber gloves.) After degreasing, you can remove corrosion and scale from silver, copper, and copper compounds by dipping the objects in the pickling solution described above. From iron and other base metals, you can do so by using a weaker solution: ½ part sulfuric acid to 9½ parts water (mixing and using, of course, with the same precautions).

PLATING WITHOUT ELECTRIC CURRENT

Thin films of nickel or silver can readily be plated on copper or brass without the use of an external source of current, simply by local chemical or electrolytic action. These films are not as durable as those made by regular electroplating, but they may serve on objects that will not be subjected to hard use.

Plating with Nickel

When moistened with water, the following mixture will cause a plating of nickel to be formed on copper or brass:

Nickel ammonium sulfate	60 parts
Powdered chalk	35 parts
Powdered magnesium metal	4 parts

Mix the powders thoroughly, and apply to the previously cleaned metal with a cloth pad kept wet with water. Zinc dust may be substituted for the magnesium powder if a little tartaric acid is added to the mixture.

Plating with Silver

Silver may similarly be plated on copper or brass with the help of one of the following formulas:

FORMULA 1

Silver nitrate	1 part
Salt (not iodized)	1 part
Potassium bitartrate (cream of tartar)	14 parts

Mix these ingredients thoroughly in a glass or ceramic vessel. Apply to the cleaned metal with a damp cloth pad. Keep the powder dry until immediately before use, as moisture causes it to decompose in the presence of light. (*Caution:* Silver nitrate is poisonous and corrosive and produces an indelible stain on the skin, cloth, and other materials. So be careful not to spill it; also wear rubber gloves when applying it.)

FORMULA 2

Salt (not iodized)	12 parts
Potassium bitartrate (cream of tartar)	7 parts
Powdered chalk	10 parts
Silver nitrate	4 parts

Mix salt, potassium bitartrate, and chalk thoroughly, and then mix in the powdered silver nitrate. Apply as in Formula 1, being sure to observe the precautions, and store the remaining powder in well-stoppered bottles.

FORMULA 3

This formula is a solution, in which small objects can be immersed:

Silver nitrate	15 parts
Potassium hydroxide	15 parts
Water	50 parts

Dissolve the silver nitrate in half the water and the potassium hydroxide in the other. Use glass vessels for mixing and do not spatter either solution on yourself or your surroundings, as both are poisonous and caustic. Until ready to use, keep both solutions in opaque glass or plastic bottles with corrosion-resistant stoppers (do not use rubber stoppers on the silver nitrate bottle).

When ready to use, mix the solutions in equal quantity in a glass or plastic container, and immerse the well-cleaned object to be plated in the resulting combination, using a slight motion to remove air bubbles. Leave it for several minutes. Then remove, wash, dry, and buff lightly.

ELECTROPLATING

The plating of copper, chromium, silver, gold, or other superior metals on baser metals by means of an electric current can make a fascinating hobby, or even a profitable small business. To do a first-rate plating job with different metals on different sizes and types of objects requires special equipment, plus a knowledge of techniques and of handling extremely corrosive and poisonous chemicals that cannot be adequately described in a few pages. If you would like to investigate further, consult a book on electroplating, or write to a manufacturer or dealer in electroplating supplies.

To Copper Plate Nonmetallic Objects

You can do this in a simple acid bath. The process is relatively safe and uncomplicated. By means of this process, you can encase small objects of wood, plaster, plastics, ceramics—or even baby shoes—in a novel and permanent sheath of metal.

First of all, you will need a source of regulated direct current—one that will deliver up to about 6 volts at up to 5, 10, or more amperes, depending upon the size of the object to be plated. This can be a storage battery, a battery charger, or a transformer-rectifier low-voltage power supply such as is used in radios. In any case, a rheostat must be connected in series with the output of the power supply and the tank electrodes to regulate the voltage. To check the current and voltage, an ammeter must be connected in series with the rheostat and a voltmeter connected in parallel with the tank terminals.

The plating tank should be large enough to handle your work. Allow at least 6 inches from the object to be plated to the anode plates, and at least 1 inch from the anodes to the tank sides. You can make it yourself from wood lined with sheet lead or sheet rubber, or you might use a one-piece rectangular glass fish tank or a container made of polyethylene.

Be sure that the finish on the object to be plated is as perfect as you can make it, as any flaws in the surface will be more conspicuous in the final metal coating.

To make the surface conductive you can coat it with copper bronzing powder held in place with thinned-down lacquer. Mix about 1 ounce of this powder with ¾ ounce of clear lacquer thinned with about 6½ ounces of lacquer thinner. Before applying this, test it on a piece of material similar to that of the object. When dry, a finger touched to the surface should show some of the copper powder. If it doesn't, add more thinner and test again.

Good electrical contact with the surface can be ensured by drilling several tiny holes in inconspicuous spots in the work and wedging in them one end of the copper wires from which the object will be suspended, afterwards touching these spots with a brush dipped in the bronzing mixture. Then spray the mixture over the whole surface.

Make the plating solution, or electrolyte, by dissolving 27 ounces of copper sulfate crystals in enough warm water to make a gallon, using a glass or plastic stirrer. Then gradually and carefully stir in 6½ ounces by weight (about 3½ fluid ounces, by measure) of concentrated sulfuric acid. (*Caution:* Always add acid to the water, and not vice versa. Do not spill on skin or surroundings as it is extremely corrosive.) Increase or decrease the quantities proportionately to make enough solution to fill your tank.

With the tank filled, place two copper or brass rods across the top, about 1 inch away from the sides. Hang from these rods (by copper wires, or by bending one end and hooking it over the rods) strips of copper sheet having an immersed area at least equal to the area to be plated. These are the anodes and should be connected to the positive lead from the current source. Connect the negative lead to a "buffer," consisting of a small piece of copper or brass, suspended from a wooden bar across the center of the tank. Turn on the current and adjust the rheostat until the voltage is between 0.75 and 2 volts. Then connect the wires attached to your object to the negative lead and suspend it also from the center bar.

If plating is taking place properly, the lacquered surface will take on a pinkish glow. The buffer sheet may be removed as soon as this happens. After 15 minutes, remove the work and inspect it carefully. Color should be a light shade of pink. If it is darkish pink, the plate is "burning." In this case, the burned areas must be removed and the object recoated with the conductive coating. You must reduce the voltage and begin again. If the color is right, continue plating until about ⅟₃₂ inch of metal (determined by caliper comparison) has been deposited.

For best plating, keep the temperature of the solution from about 77° to 80° F and agitate the object frequently. Professional platers generally keep the solution moving about the objects being plated by connecting a mechanical agitator to the rod on which they are hung or by bubbling air through the solution.

After plating, the work can be finished by very light and careful filing, buffing, and polishing. If desired, it may then be lacquered.

Note: Baby shoes can be electroplated by the same method. First, remove all wax and polish from the shoes with lacquer thinner. To stiffen the shoes, submerge them for 12 hours in lacquer diluted with an equal amount of lacquer thinner. Cover the container in which this is done to prevent evaporation. Then remove the shoes, let them dry for 1 hour, shape them, and let them dry for another 36 hours. Apply the bronzing mixture, suspend the shoes in the center of the tank by means of copper wires, and plate as described above.

ALLOYS THAT MELT AT LOW TEMPERATURES

Certain alloys of lead, tin, and bismuth have a lower melting point than that of any one of these metals. This curious fact was discovered by the famous Isaac Newton more than 250 years ago. Not long after that, a German chemist, Valentin Rose, and a French physicist, Jean Darcet, produced combinations of the same metals that have still lower melting points.

These and similar alloys are used today to make fusible links in automatic sprinklers, safety plugs for steam boilers, special electrical fuses, and other heat-triggered safety devices. They are also used for making molds and casts of wooden or other objects that might be damaged by molten metals of higher temperature.

Their low melting temperature makes such alloys especially useful to the home mechanic who would like to cast small metal objects but has no blast furnace. Because they have the unusual property of expanding when they cool, they make particularly sharp impressions. If he is a practical joker, the home mechanic can use them, too, to make fusible parts in spoons or other tableware. These parts will melt away when an unsuspecting friend tries to stir coffee or other hot liquid with the trick implements.

Here are the approximate formulas and melting points for the original alloys, all parts being measured by weight:

Alloy	Bismuth	Lead	Tin	Melting point, °F
Newton's	5	3	2	201
Rose's	8	5	3	200
Darcet's	2	1	1	199

As Darcet's alloy contains equal parts of lead and tin, you can make it rather easily by melting regular half-and-half solder, and mixing into this melt an equal weight of bismuth.

More recent investigators have found that by substituting cadmium for part of the tin, the melting point of low-melting alloys can be lowered still further. The following are two common examples:

Alloy	Bismuth	Lead	Tin	Cadmium	Melting point, °F
Wood's	4	2	1	1	149
Lipowitz's	15	8	4	3	154

In making fusible alloys, the lead and bismuth are generally melted together first. Then the tin is added and stirred until melted and mixed. Cadmium, which comes in sticks, may catch fire if heated too hot in the open air. So add this metal by holding a stick of it in tongs and stirring it into the other molten metals that are kept just hot enough to melt the cadmium.

Alloy for Making Exact Castings

Most metals shrink when they solidify from a melted state; bismuth, contrariwise, expands. By combining bismuth in different combinations with tin and lead, low-melting alloys that shrink, expand, or do neither, on cooling can therefore be produced.

An alloy that melts at 248° F and maintains its same dimensions when cold can be made by combining 57 percent bismuth with 43 percent tin. This alloy is used in making master patterns in foundry work and for soldering lead, tin, and zinc foils.

SOLDERS AND SOLDERING

The term "soldering" generally means "soft soldering," a method of joining two metals together with an alloy of relatively low melting point, usually composed of tin and lead.

Types of Solder

Common soft solder comes in bar, ribbon, and wire form. Wire solder may be solid or it may be tubular with a core of either acid or rosin soldering flux. Bar solder is used with heavy irons and blow torches on plumbing and large sheet-metal work, while ribbon and wire solder are used with light irons on electrical wiring and other small jobs.

When solder is designated by numbers, the first number represents the proportion of tin, the second of lead. A 40–60 solder, for instance, means a solder with 40 percent by weight of tin and 60 percent by weight of lead. One of the commonest solders for all-round use is 50–50, or "half-and-half." Soft solders for gold and silver and for copper and brass sheet generally contain more tin and melt at a lower temperature. Solders containing more lead are better for lead plumbing, but require more heat. Pewter is soldered with a special alloy to which bismuth has been added to lower the temperature below that of lead and tin alone.

So-called "liquid solders" or "cold solders," which are recommended by their manufacturers for joining all types of materials, are usually not really solders at all, but are cements or glues fortified with aluminum or other metallic powder. Although such preparations may be useful for sealing off small holes to stop leaks and for other minor patching jobs, they should not be used where real solder is required. They do not make a metal-to-metal bond, they are not electrically conductive, and they may disintegrate in the presence of organic solvents or at temperatures considerably below the softening point of lead–tin solders.

Need for Fluxes

For the solder to adhere firmly to the metals to be joined, the surfaces must be completely free of oxide. Because oxides form on most metals at room temperatures, and almost immediately when heated by a soldering iron, a coating material must be used that will remove the film already present and protect both solder and metal from further oxidation. Such a material is called a soldering "flux," from a Latin word meaning "to flow."

Except for electrical work, the fluxes most commonly used for soft soldering are solutions or pastes that contain zinc chloride or a mixture of zinc and ammonium chlorides. The heat of the soldering operation evaporates the medium containing the chloride flux. The flux then melts and partially decomposes with the liberation of hydrochloric acid, which dissolves the oxides from the metal surfaces. The fused flux also forms a protective film that prevents further oxidation.

Acid Fluxes

The fluxes just mentioned, called "acid fluxes," come in both liquid and paste form, and as the core in acid-core wire solders. Zinc chloride and ammonium chloride (sal ammoniac) are also used dry, in the form of cake or powder.

A good liquid zinc-chloride flux can be made simply by adding scraps of zinc to hydrochloric acid until no more zinc dissolves. The resulting solution should be diluted with an equal amount of water before using.

A liquid flux that combines both chemicals can be made by dissolving 2½ ounces of zinc chloride and 1 ounce of ammonium chloride in 6 ounces of water.

To make a paste-type flux, dissolve 1 teaspoon of zinc chloride and 1 teaspoon of ammonium chloride in 4 teaspoons of hot water. Then stir in thoroughly 3 ounces of petroleum jelly, heating the combination until it boils. Let cool before use.

A small stiff brush is useful in applying either liquid or paste. When the liquid flux is applied, the soldering operation should follow immediately. The paste-type flux can remain on the work for as long as an hour before soldering, owing to its lesser activity at room temperature. At soldering temperatures, however, one type is as active as the other, and once heat has been applied, soldering should be continued without delay. Otherwise, salt deposits will be formed, which will make subsequent soldering difficult.

After soldering, excess flux should be removed immediately by using a large swab and hot water.

Rosin Fluxes

Because acid fluxes do have a corrosive action, they should not be used in soldering electrical connections or on other types of work where the last traces of flux cannot be removed after the job has been completed. For such jobs, a noncorrosive flux is necessary. Rosin is the most commonly used flux of this type, and is the only flux known to be noncorrosive in all soldering applications. Rosin may be mixed with alcohol in varying proportions to obtain any desired consistency. Paste rosin flux also can be made by using petroleum jelly as a base.

Other Fluxes

Palm oil, olive oil, or rosin, or mixtures of these, have been recommended as suitable fluxes for pewter. Tallow is often used by plumbers in wiping lead joints. These mild fluxes are not corrosive, but for the sake of cleanliness and appearance are generally removed with naphtha or other organic solvent after soldering.

Soldering Irons

Soft soldering is generally done with a copper-headed tool called an "iron." Nonelectric soldering irons that must be heated by a torch or other means come in sizes from ¼ pound to 5 pounds. Electric irons are more popular today and are generally used wherever an electric circuit is available. They range from 25 to 300 watts.

In wiring radio or other electronic kits, the 25-watt size is the largest recommended for making connections to printed circuit boards, while the 50-watt size may be the largest ever needed for making chassis connections. A 150- to 200-watt iron will do for most home sheet-metal work, with the 300-watt size being required for only the heaviest jobs.

Soldering guns, which heat up almost instantly on the pull of a trigger, are used widely in electrical work; but many consider them too heavy and less convenient than a small regular iron for extensive kit wiring. Some soldering guns are available that are cordless; that is, they don't need to be plugged into an electrical outlet for operation.

Tinning the Iron

Before a soldering iron can be used, one or more faces of its tip must be filed smooth and coated with solder, or "tinned." For most work, the iron should be tinned on all four faces. For work where the iron is held under the object to be soldered, only one face should be tinned—the face to be held against the object. If all four sides were tinned in this case, solder from the top of the iron would flow down the sides and drip off the bottom. Untinned sides will prevent this flow.

To tin an iron, follow these steps:

1. File the tip faces bright while the iron is cold.
2. Plug iron into outlet (or heat over a burner, if nonelectric). As the iron heats, rub flux-core solder (or flux followed by solder) over the tip faces every 15 or 20 seconds. As soon as the iron is hot enough, the solder will spread smoothly and evenly over the faces. The purpose of this caution is to coat the copper before it gets hot enough to oxidize.

3. As soon as the tinning is completed, wipe the tip with a rag or a paper towel while the solder is still molten. This will expose a mirrorlike layer of solder on the tip faces.

Soldering a Joint

First of all, the area to be soldered must be absolutely clean. If it is dirty or greasy, clean it with a solvent cleaner. If it is heavily oxidized, clean the surface with abrasive cloth until it is bright. Make sure the parts to be soldered are rigidly supported, so they won't move while the solder is setting.

Apply the proper flux to the entire surface to which the solder is to adhere. Too much flux, however, will interfere with soldering.

Heat the soldering iron to the proper temperature. Test this by touching solder to the tip: if it melts quickly, the iron is nearly hot enough. Then heat the metal to be joined hot enough with the iron so that solder touched to it will flow into the joint. If the metal is not hot enough to vaporize the rosin and to cause the solder to take its place, the result will be a "cold-soldered" joint held together feebly and non-conductively by rosin, rather than strongly by solder.

Hard Soldering

Hard solders are distinguished from soft solders in that they have much higher melting points and form joints of much higher strength. They are used for joining such metals as copper, silver, and gold, and alloys such as brass, German silver, and so on, which require a strong joint and often solder of a color near that of the metal to be joined. When used to join common metals, hard soldering is generally called "brazing," and the lower-melting alloys are known as "spelter."

There are three general types of hard solders: precious-metal alloy solders or "silver solders," common brazing solders, and aluminum brazing solders. Because of their high melting points, hard solders cannot be applied with a soldering iron, but require the use of torches, furnaces, or dipping tanks.

PRECIOUS-METAL SOLDERS.   Silver solders for use with a torch are supplied in the form of wire and powder. They consist of alloys of silver, copper, and zinc, and have melting points ranging from about 1,200° to 1,600° F. Solders containing gold are used primarily for joining gold and gold alloys, and usually are alloys of gold with copper, silver, and zinc. Gold solders are generally designated by karat numbers to indicate the fineness, or karat number of the alloy with which they should be used. Soldered joints in platinum or platinum alloys may be made with fine gold or the higher karat gold alloys.

COMMON BRAZING SOLDERS. These are generally supplied in granular, lump, rod, or wire form. They are made from different combinations of copper, zinc, and tin, and have melting points from about 1,400° to 1,980° F.

ALUMINUM BRAZING SOLDERS. These are used almost exclusively by industry. They consist of special, and usually proprietary, alloys of aluminum and must be obtained from manufacturers of aluminum alloys.

FLUXES FOR HARD SOLDERING. For most purposes, borax, or mixtures of borax with boric acid, is a good flux for the precious metal and ordinary brazing solders. The chloride fluxes used for soft soldering would vaporize immediately under the high temperatures of hard soldering, and so cannot be used here.

PROPANE TORCHES

Propane torches operate on a simple principle. The torch tank is filled with propane, a liquified petroleum gas. The propane remains in a liquid state because it is under pressure. When the valve on the burner assembly is opened, propane is released through the fuel orifice. With reduced pressure, the propane converts to a gas, which burns readily when mixed with air.

The burner assembly unit screws onto the top of the propane tank. It can be tightened by hand; a wrench should not be used. The unit is produced under rigid quality-control standards and is thoroughly flame-tested at the factory. Caution should be exercised to prevent dropping material particles down into the center-inlet valve area. Such particles could wedge the valve pin into the open position preventing normal cylinder-valve closure upon separation of the cylinder and appliance.

Lighting the Torch

If using a match, light the match and twirl or rotate it approximately 180 degrees to create a full flame. Turn the valve-control knob to the ON position as far as it will go. Hold the match to the burner at the top of and slightly behind the tip. Never hold the match directly in front of the burner tip. The force of the escaping propane will usually blow out

SOLDERING TABLE

This table will help you determine what kind of solder to use and when to apply it. For the metals listed along the top of the table, you can use the solders and fluxes shown in the left-hand column and noted for use by Xs.

	Aluminum	Chrome plate	Copper or bronze	Galvanized iron or steel	Silver and silver plate	Stainless steel	Steel
Stainless steel solder and flux (solder flows freely on contact with heated metal)		X			X	X	X
General-purpose acid-core solder (flows freely on contact with heated metal)			X	X			
All-purpose resin-core electrical solder (solder flows freely on contact with heated metal)			X				
Aluminum brazing alloy and flux (flux becomes a clear liquid)	X						
Silver solder and flux (flux becomes a thin, clear liquid and forms dull red)					X	X	X

Note: Metals with Xs in the same horizontal column can be joined.

the match. When the torch is lit, use the control knob to adjust the desired flame.

To light the torch with the sparklighter, place the cup of the sparklighter against the end of the burner. Incline the sparklighter about 30 degrees. Turn the valve-control knob to the ON position as far as it will go. Actuate the sparklighter. Use the control knob to adjust to the desired flame. Always allow the torch to warm up before using it in an inverted or upside down position.

PROPANE-TORCH BURNER TIPS AND USES

Job	Precision-burner tip	Pencil-point burner tip	Brush-flame burner tip	Flame spreader	Chisel-point soldering tip
Soldering small fittings or connections		X			
Soldering jewelry or very tiny wires	X				
Soldering electrical connections					X
Soldering flat surfaces					X
Soldering over large areas			X		
Soldering gutters		X			X
Starting threaded pipe joints		X			
Thawing pipes		X	X		
Sealing soil pipes		X			
Removing paint			X	X	
Removing putty		X			
Bending metal		X	X		
Metal sculpturing		X			
Laying asphalt tile			X	X	
Thawing frozen locks		X			
Loosening screws, nuts, bolts		X			
Lighting charcoal		X	X		
Auto body leading		X			
Removing brake linings			X	X	
Separating exhaust pipes, auto body springs		X			
Plywood sculpturing					X
Glass working		X	X		
Antiquing wood			X	X	

Soldering with a Propane Torch

You can use a propane torch to solder by the direct (open) flame method or the indirect (enclosed) flame method. The latter is usually preferable, where practical.

When using the direct method, select the burner tip best suited to the size of the job. The standard pencil-point tip, for example, is excellent for small fittings and connections. When larger areas are involved, the brush-flame tip is more efficient.

To solder by the indirect method, attach the chisel-point soldering tip to the standard pencil-point burner. Before using the chisel point, the copper tip must be tinned with solder. If the tip is not tinned, oxides will form on it and interfere with the transfer of heat to the workpiece.

When using the chisel point, press one of the flat surfaces against the work and move the tip along as the solder flows onto the workpiece.

Always use a small flame when soldering with the chisel-point tip. A large flame shortens the life of the tip and often makes it necessary to retin the soldering copper frequently.

After lighting the torch, wait about 30 seconds, until the tip hisses when it comes in contact with the flux.

To tin the copper tip, file while cool, and sandpaper or steel wool each flat side of the tip until it presents a metallic sheen. Heat the tip until the soldering copper begins to darken. Rub either solder covered with flux or flux-core solder over each flat side of the tip. Remove excess solder with steel wool or by flicking off excess solder onto a non-combustible surface. (Be careful . . . it's hot!)

Don't dip the soldering tip into the flux. Instead, use a small brush to dab the flux directly onto the part you are soldering. Apply the torch to the area to be soldered. Hold solder to area being joined and wait until temperature of material is hot enough to melt solder. It should flow smoothly over surface. End of solder flow should blend into material with a feathered edge. It should not be abrupt or "puddled" or with cleavage on the interface.

SOLDERING COPPER TUBING AND PIPE FITTINGS. A variety of plumbing jobs can be accomplished quickly and easily with a propane torch and burner attachments. Soldering or "sweating" copper tubing and fittings is a simple task with a Turner Torch. You can install water lines and repair appliances, such as washers, dryers, refrigerators, and hot water heaters, avoiding costly service charges.

"Sweat"-type fittings are widely used when making joints and connections in copper tubing. They are a quick, inexpensive, and sure means of making a joint.

First, cut the tube to the desired length with a hacksaw (32 teeth to the inch) or a disc cutter. Be sure the ends of the tube are cut square and excessive burrs are removed. Wirebrush or sandpaper the end of the tube and the inside of the fitting. Apply flux liberally to both cleaned areas and fit the tube into the joint. Apply an open flame evenly around the circumference of the fitting. As the fitting heats, be sure to move the flame back and forth to prevent overheating. When the fitting is hot enough to melt solder, remove the flame and apply solder to the edge of the fitting where it meets the tube. Continue heating until solder flows completely around the joint. Don't apply torch flame directly to solder joint. Allow heat to move from surrounding area to area being soldered, indirectly.

Wipe off excess solder and flux. Slightly reheat the connection in order to help the solder permeate the metal. Remove the flame and continue to feed solder to make certain the joint is filled. Allow the connection to cool for a moment, then remove surplus solder from around the edges with a wire brush or metal scraper.

When soldering small fittings, use the standard pencil-point burner tip. For larger fittings, use the brush flame and be especially careful to heat the entire circumference of the fitting. The flame will envelop the area to be worked.

SAFETY TIPS. Like many other tools, propane torches are safe when used properly. If abused, they can be dangerous. Follow these simple precautions for safe torch storage and operation:

1. Do not let unignited propane escape from the torch near any possible source of ignition.
2. Never store propane tanks in a confined, unventilated space, such as a closet, or any area where the temperature may exceed 120° F. Do not store in a room for habitation.
3. Never use a flame to test for propane leaks.
4. Never use a tank with a leaking valve or other fitting. If in doubt, test by brushing a generous amount of liquid detergent over the suspected area and check for bubble formations.
5. Never lay a torch down unless the gas flow has been shut off. If maintaining a pilot flame during work pauses, use a rack or stand for the torch and keep it away from combustible materials.
6. Don't start fires. Be very careful when working near combustible materials and use asbestos shields when necessary.
7. Never solder a container that holds or has held flammable fluids or gases unless the container has been totally purged of these mate-

rials. If in doubt as to the previous contents of a container, thoroughly purge it. Be sure any container you work on is well vented.
8. Propane consumes oxygen and generates toxic fumes; therefore, use torch only in a well-ventilated area.
9. Avoid breathing vapors and fumes generated during torch usage. Provide ventilation that will move vapors away from work area.

MAPP GAS TORCHES

While it looks a great deal like the propane torch, the MAPP gas torch designed for home use is not an ordinary outfit. The gas in the cylinder is called MAPP (a trademark of Airco, Inc.), and the regulator and burner heads are different to suit the new compound.

MAPP gas gets hotter than propane, and thus makes metal brazing possible. The flame temperature of MAPP will be about 3200° F, depending on the particular torch used. This is up to 500° F or so hotter than most propane torch units. Even if you use MAPP only for propane torch jobs, you can probably save money because you heat more rapidly.

While the MAPP gas torch is designed as a heating torch that produces the higher temperatures needed for brazing and aluminum welding, the torch can be used for such jobs as flame hardening, melting, burning off paint, removing old putty, softening brittle tile, replacing damaged tile, leveling tile, etc.

Brazing or hard soldering, silver soldering, and aluminum welding, because of the structural superiority of the joints they produce, make the MAPP gas torch a useful home-repair tool. Garden tools, lawnmowers, toys, fences, metal furniture, and many more items can be given new life with brazing repair.

Brazing

Brazing is a process in which metals are joined with metal with the use of a wirelike rod. The brazing rod may be stainless steel, aluminum alloy, nickel silver, or a bronze alloy, and may be bare or coated with flux. The material and type depend on the materials to be brazed. When the metals to be joined are heated (generally to cherry red) and the brazing rod applied, the rod material melts and flows into the joint to make a strong weldlike bond.

A WORD OF CAUTION: If you are not familiar with brazing procedures, study the manual that comes with the torch. Practice the

SOLDERING AND BRAZING RODS FOR MAPP GAS TORCHES

	Aluminum	Chrome plate	Copper	Copper or bronze	Galvanized iron or steel	Silver and silver plate	Stainless steel	Steel
Stainless steel and flux (solder flows freely on contact with heated metal)		X				X	X	X
General-purpose acid-core solder (solder flows freely in contact with heated metal)				X	X			
All-purpose resin-core electrical solder (solder flows freely on contact with heated metal)			X					
Aluminum brazing alloy and flux (flux becomes a clear liquid)	X							
Silver solder and flux (flux becomes a thin, clear liquid and forms dull red)					X	X	X	X
Aluminum bare brazing rod (brazing rod puddles on contact with heated metal)	X				X			

Flux-coated nickel-silver brazing rod (brazing rod flows freely on contact with heated metal)   X   X   X   X   X

Flux-coated bronze brazing rod (brazing rod flows freely on contact with heated metal)   X   X   X   X   X

Copper-phosphorous brazing rod (brazing rod flows freely on contact with heated metal)   X

Note: Metals with Xs in the same horizontal column can be joined.

USES FOR SOLDER OR BRAZING RODS:

Aluminum: for strength in joining sheets, sections, etc.

Chrome plate: for trim when on steel, brass, copper or nickel alloys (not on die castings)

Copper: for electrical equipment

Copper or bronze: for fittings, tubing, utensils, etc.

Galvanized iron or steel: for cans, buckets, tanks, eavestroughs, etc.

Silver and silver plate: for jewelry, flatware, etc.

Stainless steel: for appliances, kitchen equipment, or wherever strength is needed

Steel: for utensils, pipes, sheets, tool sheets, motors, etc.

procedures, and always make absolutely sure the bond is sound before you put into use any device where the repair, if poorly made, could result in a safety hazard.

SAFETY TIPS.   Since a MAPP gas torch produces more heat and will be used for a greater variety of jobs than a propane torch, safety precautions beyond those for propane—such as not refilling or incinerating the empty cylinders, not working around flammable or explosive materials, and not working in poorly ventilated areas—are necessary.

1. Wear protective glasses to protect eyes from sparks or metal splatters.
2. Do not use a MAPP gas cylinder with conventional propane torch regulators and burner heads.
3. Some MAPP torch units require special handling to use in a tipped position. Be sure to check instructions for the particular unit.
4. Never use a flame to check for torch leaks. Periodic leak checks should be made with soapy water. Bubbles indicate a gas leak.
5. Respect hot metal. Handle heated parts with clamps or pliers.

WHICH METAL GAUGE MEASURES WHAT?

This is a question that can sometimes baffle experts as well as laymen. When the wire and sheet-metal industries were young, systems of thickness gauging were devised by, and often named after, individual manufacturers. In an attempt to establish greater uniformity, the United States and the British governments, late in the last century, established national standards. Because even these did not fit all the conditions in the manufacturing of iron and steel sheets, manufacturers jointly set industrial standards for such sheets. To complicate things still further, the dozen or so different metal-thickness gauges that were developed during this time have been variously assigned several times that many names and abbreviations.

To help you find your way through this maze, upcoming pages provide the names and abbreviations for the most commonly used gauges, indicate what the gauges are used for, and list the thicknesses associated with the gauge numbers. A separate table giving additional information on copper wire can be found on pages 286 and 287.

AMERICAN WIRE GAUGE (AWG), or
BROWN AND SHARPE (B&S). This should cause you little
trouble. It is the gauge commonly used in the United States for copper,
aluminum, and resistance wires; also for copper, aluminum, and brass
sheets.

BIRMINGHAM WIRE GAUGE (BWG), or
STUBS' IRON WIRE GAUGE. An old gauge still used in the
United States for brass wire, and used to a limited extent in Great
Britain.

STEEL WIRE GAUGE (SWG, StlWG, A [steel]WG), or
WASHBURN AND MOEN (W&M), or
AMERICAN STEEL AND WIRE CO'S GAUGE, or
ROEBLING GAUGE.   The gauge usually used in the United States
for iron and steel wire. Watch out for the abbreviation SWG, as that is
also one of the abbreviations for the British standard wire gauge.

BRITISH STANDARD WIRE GAUGE, or
STANDARD WIRE GAUGE (SWG), or
NEW BRITISH STANDARD (NBS), or
ENGLISH LEGAL STANDARD, or
IMPERIAL WIRE GAUGE. Since 1883 this has been the legal
standard of Great Britain for wires of all metals. It is a modification of
the Birmingham wire gauge.

United States Standard Gauge (US)

This gauge for sheet iron and steel was adopted in 1893 by an Act of
Congress, and was formerly the legal standard for duties. It is a weight
gauge based on the density of wrought iron at 480 pounds per cubic
foot. As originally interpreted, a gauge number in this system represented a fixed weight per unit area. Steel, however, weighs about 9½
pounds more per cubic foot than wrought iron, and so a steel sheet
would have a smaller thickness under this system than a wrought iron
sheet of the same gauge number. In the face of this discrepancy, some
manufacturers make sheets according to weight, others according to
thickness, while still others settle on a compromise thickness of their
own. In any case, however, thicknesses will not vary greatly from those
shown in the table on pages 138 and 139. If you are in doubt about
gauge number, order your sheet metal by actual thickness.

COMPARISON OF SHEET-METAL AND WIRE GAUGES

Dimensions are expressed in approximate decimals of an inch.

Gauge	AWG B&S	Birmingham or Stubs BWG	Steel wire gauge	British Imperial NBS SWG	United States Standard US
0000000	—	—	0.4900	0.500	0.5000
000000	0.5800	—	0.4615	0.464	0.4688
00000	0.5165	0.500	0.4305	0.432	0.4375
0000	0.4600	0.454	0.3938	0.400	0.4063
000	0.4096	0.425	0.3625	0.372	0.3750
00	0.3648	0.380	0.3310	0.348	0.3438
0	0.3249	0.340	0.3065	0.324	0.3215
1	0.2893	0.300	0.2830	0.300	0.2813
2	0.2576	0.284	0.2625	0.276	0.2656
3	0.2294	0.259	0.2437	0.252	0.2500
4	0.2043	0.238	0.2253	0.232	0.2344
5	0.1819	0.220	0.2070	0.212	0.2188
6	0.1620	0.203	0.1920	0.192	0.2031
7	0.1443	0.180	0.1770	0.176	0.1875
8	0.1285	0.165	0.1620	0.160	0.1719
9	0.1144	0.148	0.1483	0.144	0.1563
10	0.1019	0.134	0.1350	0.128	0.1406
11	0.0907	0.120	0.1205	0.116	0.1250
12	0.0808	0.109	0.1055	0.104	0.1094
13	0.0720	0.095	0.0915	0.092	0.0938
14	0.0641	0.083	0.0800	0.080	0.0781
15	0.0570	0.072	0.0720	0.072	0.0703
16	0.0508	0.065	0.0625	0.064	0.0625
17	0.0453	0.058	0.0540	0.056	0.0563
18	0.0403	0.049	0.0475	0.048	0.0500
19	0.0359	0.042	0.0410	0.040	0.0438
20	0.0320	0.035	0.0348	0.036	0.0375
21	0.0285	0.032	0.0318	0.032	0.0344
22	0.0254	0.028	0.0286	0.028	0.0313
23	0.0226	0.025	0.0258	0.024	0.0281
24	0.0201	0.022	0.0230	0.022	0.0250
25	0.0179	0.020	0.0204	0.020	0.0219
26	0.0159	0.018	0.0181	0.018	0.0188
27	0.0142	0.016	0.0173	0.0164	0.0172
28	0.0126	0.014	0.0162	0.0148	0.0156

COMPARISON OF SHEET-METAL AND WIRE GAUGES (continued)

Dimensions are expressed in approximate decimals of an inch.

Gauge	AWG B&S	Birmingham or Stubs BWG	Steel wire gauge	British Imperial NBS SWG	United States Standard US
29	0.0113	0.013	0.0150	0.0136	0.0141
30	0.0100	0.012	0.0140	0.0124	0.0125
31	0.0089	0.010	0.0132	0.0116	0.0109
32	0.0080	0.009	0.0128	0.0108	0.0102
33	0.0071	0.008	0.0118	0.0100	0.0094
34	0.0063	0.007	0.0104	0.0092	0.0086
35	0.0056	0.005	0.0095	0.0084	0.0078
36	0.0050	0.004	0.0090	0.0076	0.0070
37	0.0045	—	0.0085	0.0068	0.0066
38	0.0040	—	0.0080	0.0060	0.0063
39	0.0035	—	0.0075	0.0052	—
40	0.0031	—	0.0070	0.0048	—

TWIST DRILL SIZES

Above ½ inch, drills are available in fractional sizes only. Three sets of drills are commonly used for smaller sizes. One set is based on wire-gauge sizes—ranging from 80, the smallest, to 1, the largest. Letter sizes begin where wire-gauge sizes end. Fractional-size drills range from 1/64 inch to ½ inch, increasing by steps of 1/64 inch. The table on page 142 includes all three sets. Notice that every drill is of a different size except the E and the ¼-inch drills.

CUTTING SPEEDS FOR DRILLS

The most efficient cutting speed for drills varies with the material being worked, the rate of feed, and the cutting fluid used. Carbon-steel drills lose their temper at about one third to one half the temperature of high-speed drills, and so must be run slower. If they are used within their heat range, however, they will cut just about as well and last just about as long as their high-speed relatives. The table at the top of page 141 suggests conservative speeds for both types of drills under highly controlled industrial use and in ordinary hand use in the home shop. In hand work, the operator must be governed, of course, by the immediate action of the drill and be ready to adjust the speed accordingly.

HOW SHEET METALS ARE MEASURED AND PURCHASED

Sheet metals are measured and sold in the United States in the following manner:

Metal	How measured	How purchased	Characteristics
Aluminum	decimal thickness	24 × 72-inch sheet or 12 or 18 inches by linear foot	pure metal, or stronger and more ductile alloys
Copper	gauge number (Brown & Sharpe or American Wire Gauge) or by weight per square foot	24 × 96-inch sheet or 12 or 18 inches by linear foot	pure metal
Brass	gauge number (B & S or AWG)	24 × 76-inch sheet or 12 or 18 inches by linear foot	copper and zinc alloy
Cold-rolled steel sheet	gauge number (US Standard)	24 × 96-inch sheet	oxide removed and cold rolled to final thickness
Black annealed steel sheet	gauge number (US Standard)	24 × 96-inch sheet	hot-rolled mild steel with oxide coating left on
Galvanized steel	gauge number (US Standard)	24 × 96-inch sheet	mild steel plated with zinc
Tin plate	gauge number (US Standard)	20 × 28-inch sheet 56 or 112 to a package	mild steel plated with tin
Expanded steel	gauge number (US Standard)	36 × 96-inch sheet	Metal is pierced and stretched to produce diamond-shape openings.
Perforated steel	gauge number (US Standard)	30 × 36-inch sheet 36 × 48-inch sheet	Here design is cut in sheet and many designs are available.

Note: The actual thickness of steel sheet may be a shade less than that indicated by the United States Standard Gauge number, but it is close enough for most practical purposes. The reason for this difference is given in the following discussion of wire and sheet-metal gauges.

	SAFE DRILLING SPEEDS FOR MILD STEEL (RPM)			
Drill size (in inches)	Industrial use (with machine feed and copious lubrication)		Home-shop use (with hand feed and intermittent or no lubrication)	
	Carbon	High-Speed	Carbon	High-Speed
1⁄16	1830	6110	920	3060
3⁄32	1220	4075	610	2050
1⁄8	920	3060	460	1530
3⁄16	610	2040	310	1020
1⁄4	460	1530	230	760
5⁄16	370	1220	180	610
3⁄8	310	1020	150	510
1⁄2	230	764	115	380

SAFE DRILLING SPEEDS FOR OTHER METALS

To find the safe drilling speed for any of the following metals, just multiply the number of rpm in the table above by the number given after the metal below. For example, to find the safe drilling speed for aluminum, under home-workshop conditions and using a 1⁄4-inch high-speed drill:

$$760 \text{ rpm} \times 2.5 = 1900 \text{ rpm}$$

Die castings (zinc base)	3.5
Aluminum	2.5
Brass and bronze	2.0
Cast iron, soft	1.15
Malleable iron	.85
Cast iron, hard	.80
Tool steel	.60
Stainless steel, hard	.30
Chilled cast iron	.20
Manganese steel	.15

NUMBER, LETTER, AND FRACTIONAL DRILL SIZES

Diameter	Decimal equivalent	Diameter	Decimal equivalent	Diameter	Decimal equivalent	Diameter	Decimal equivalent
80	0.0135	49	0.073	20	0.161	I	0.272
79	0.0145	48	0.076	19	0.166	J	0.277
1/64	0.0156	5/64	0.0781	18	0.1695	9/32	0.2813
78	0.016	47	0.0785	11/64	0.1719	K	0.281
77	0.018	46	0.081	17	0.173	L	0.290
76	0.02	45	0.082	16	0.177	M	0.295
75	0.021	44	0.086	15	0.18	19/64	0.2969
74	0.0225	43	0.089	14	0.182	N	0.302
73	0.024	42	0.0935	13	0.185	5/16	0.3125
72	0.025	3/32	0.0938	3/16	0.1875	O	0.316
71	0.026	41	0.096	12	0.189	P	0.323
70	0.028	40	0.098	11	0.191	21/64	0.328
69	0.0292	39	0.0995	10	0.1935	Q	0.332
68	0.031	38	0.1015	9	0.196	R	0.339
1/32	0.0313	37	0.104	8	0.199	11/32	0.34375
67	0.032	36	0.1065	7	0.201	S	0.348
66	0.033	7/64	0.1094	13/64	0.203	T	0.358
65	0.035	35	0.11	6	0.204	23/64	0.359
64	0.036	34	0.111	5	0.2055	U	0.368
63	0.037	33	0.113	4	0.209	3/8	0.375
62	0.038	32	0.116	3	0.213	V	0.377
61	0.039	31	0.12	7/32	0.21875	W	0.386
60	0.04	1/8	0.125	2	0.221	25/64	0.3906
59	0.041	30	0.1285	1	0.228	X	0.397
58	0.042	29	0.136	A	0.234	Y	0.404
57	0.043	9/64	0.1406	15/64	0.2344	13/32	0.4063
56	0.0465	28	0.1405	B	0.238	Z	0.413
3/64	0.0469	27	0.144	C	0.242		
55	0.052	26	0.147	D	0.246		
54	0.055	25	0.1495	1/4	0.250		
53	0.0595	24	0.152	E	0.250		
1/16	0.0625	23	0.154	F	0.257		
52	0.0635	5/32	0.15625	G	0.261		
51	0.067	22	0.157	17/64	0.2656		
50	0.07	21	0.159	H	0.266		

TAP DRILL SIZES (Fractional)

Nominal size	Commercial tap drill	Nominal size	Commercial tap drill	Nominal size	Commercial tap drill
1/16—64	3/64	24	Q	27	27/32
72	3/64	27	R	15/16—9	53/64
5/64—60	1/16	7/16—14	U	12	55/64
72	52	20	25/64	1—8	7/8
3/32—48	49	24	X	12	59/64
50	49	27	Y	14	15/16
7/64—48	43	1/2—12	27/64	27	31/32
1/8—32	3/32	13	27/64	1 1/8—7	63/64
40	38	20	29/64	12	1 3/64
9/64—40	32	24	29/64	1 1/4—7	1 7/64
5/32—32	1/8	27	15/32	12	1 11/64
36	30	9/16—12	31/64	1 3/8—6	1 7/32
11/64—32	9/64	18	33/64	12	1 19/64
3/16—24	26	27	17/32	1 1/2—6	1 11/32
32	22	5/8—11	17/32	12	1 27/64
13/64—24	20	5/8—12	35/64	1 5/8—5 1/2	1 29/64
7/32—24	16	18	37/64	1 3/4—5	1 9/16
32	12	27	19/32	10	1 21/32
15/64—24	10	11/16—11	19/32	1 7/8—5	1 11/16
1/4—20	7	12	19/32	2—4 1/2	1 25/32
24	4	16	5/8	3—3 1/2	2 23/32
27	3	3/4—10	21/32	10	1 29/32
28	3	12	43/64	2 1/8—4 1/2	1 29/32
32	7/32	16	11/16	2 1/4—4 1/2	2 1/32
5/16—18	F	27	23/32	8	2 1/8
20	17/64	13/16—10	23/32	2 3/8—4	2 1/8
24	I	12	23/32	2 1/2—4	2 1/4
27	J	7/8—9	49/64	8	2 3/8
32	9/32	12	51/64	2 3/4—4	2 1/2
3/8—16	5/16	14	13/16	8	2 5/8
20	21/64	18	53/64	8	2 7/8

TAP DRILL SIZES (Machine Screw)

Nominal size	Commercial tap drill	Nominal size	Commercial tap drill	Nominal size	Commercial tap drill
0—80	$\frac{1}{64}''$	44	37	10—24	25
1—56	54	6—32	36	28	23
64	53	36	34	30	22
72	53	40	33	32	21
2—56	50	$\frac{7}{30}$	31	12—24	16
64	50	32	31	28	14
3—48	47	36	$\frac{1}{8}''$	32	13
56	45	8—30	30	14—20	10
4—32	45	32	29	24	7
36	44	36	29	16—18	3
40	43	40	28	20	$\frac{7}{32}''$
48	42	9—24	29	22	2
5—36	40	30	27	18—18	B
40	38	32	26	20	D

Note: The tap drills listed will produce approximately 75-percent full thread. The sizes given are National Form. National Fine (N.F.) comprises a series formerly designated as A.S.M.E. pitches and S.A.E. sizes and pitches. National Coarse (N.C.) comprises a series of former A.S.M.E. pitches and U.S. Standard sizes and pitches.

CUTTING FLUIDS FOR DRILLING AND COUNTERSINKING

Cutting fluids applied at the point of contact between a drill or other cutting tool and the work perform several jobs at once. They reduce heat that would otherwise soften and ruin the cutting edge of a tool by direct cooling and by reducing friction. In this way they permit faster cutting speeds. They also help prevent the sticking of chips to tool or work.

Unfortunately there is no ideal cutting fluid that will serve all purposes. Many of the best cutting lubricants are not good coolants. On the other hand, water is probably the best coolant there is, yet on most materials it has almost no lubricating action.

The table on the next page shows recommended cutting fluids for use with specific materials.

CUTTING-FLUIDS GUIDE

Material	Type of cutting fluid
Aluminum and its alloys	Kerosene, kerosene and lard oil, or soluble oil
Brass and bronze	None
for deep holes	Kerosene and mineral oil, lard oil, or soluble oil
Copper	Mineral-lard oil and kerosene, soluble oil, or none
Monel metal	Mineral-lard oil or soluble oil
Mild steel	Mineral-lard oil or soluble oil
Tool steel or forgings	Sulfurized oil, mineral-lard oil, or kerosene
Cast steel	Soluble oil or sulfurized oil
Cast iron	None
Wrought iron	Soluble oil
Malleable iron	Soluble oil or none
Stainless steel	Soluble oil or sulfurized oil
Manganese steel	None
Titanium alloys	Soluble oil or sulfurized oil

Soda–Soap Cutting Fluid

One of the cheapest lubricant-coolants used for turning and milling steel is a soda–soap mixture you can make yourself. Here are the ingredients:

Sal soda (washing soda)	1½	ounces
Lard oil	3	fluid ounces
Soft soap	3	fluid ounces
Water, enough to make	1	gallon

Dissolve the sal soda in the water, which should be warm to make solution easier. Then stir in the soft soap and finally the lard oil. Boil slowly for about ½ hour, with occasional stirring. If the solution smells bad, you can correct this by stirring in about 3 ounces of unslaked lime.

CUTTING SPEEDS AND RPM FOR METALS ON A LATHE

Cutting speed is the distance the piece you are working on moves past the cutting point in 1 minute, as measured around the circumference of the piece.

		Diameter and RPMs			
Metal	Cutting speed (surface feet per minute)	½ inch	1 inch	1½ inches	2 inches
Tool steel	50	400	200	133	100
Cast iron	75	600	300	200	150
Low-carbon steel	100	800	400	266	200
Brass	200	1600	800	533	400
Aluminum	300	2400	1200	800	600

HOW TO CLEAN FILES

Immerse the files for several minutes in a dilute solution of sulfuric acid made by adding about 1 ounce of the concentrated acid to 4 ounces of water. (To prevent violent spattering, be sure to add the acid to the water and not vice versa. Wear rubber gloves and use a glass dish or pan.) This treatment will etch the embedded iron and steel particles so they may be removed by a stiff wire brush. Next wash the files well in plain water and then coat them slightly with machine oil or penetrating oil diluted slightly with gasoline. Wipe off the excess.

Lead and brass filings lodged in the teeth can best be removed with a stiff brush.

Aluminum filings can be removed quite easily by soaking the files in a warm lye solution. The aluminum is eaten away by this, while the hydrogen gas generated in the process helps to throw out the metal particles. When using lye, again wear rubber gloves and do not spill any on your clothes or surroundings as this chemical and its solution are very caustic. After treatment, wash the files well and oil as before.

SELECTION OF GRINDING WHEELS

ABRASIVE.   Fused alumina for materials of high tensile strength; silicon carbide for those of low tensile strength.

GRAIN SIZE.   Fine grain for hard and brittle materials, small area of contact, and fine finish; coarse grain for soft, ductile materials, large areas of contact, and fast cutting. The number that designates grain size represents the number of openings per linear inch in the screen used to size the grain—8 to 10 is very coarse; 12 to 14, coarse; 30 to 60, medium; 70 to 120, fine; 150 to 240, very fine; 280 to 600, flour sizes.

GRADE.   Hard wheels for soft materials; soft wheels for hard materials. The smaller the area of contact, the harder the wheel should be. Grade is often designated by letters: E to G, very soft; H to K, soft; L to O, medium; P to S, hard; T to Z, very hard.

GRINDING WHEEL SELECTION

Work	Abrasive	Grit	Grade	Bond
Aluminum (surfacing)	aluminum oxide (white)	46	soft	vitrified
Aluminum (cutting-off)	aluminum oxide	24	hard	resinoid
Brass (surfacing)	silicon carbide	36	medium	vitrified
Brass (cutting-off)	aluminum oxide	30	very hard	resinoid
Chisels (woodworking)	aluminum oxide	60	medium	vitrified
Coat Iron	silicon carbide	46	soft	vitrified
Copper (surfacing)	silicon carbide	60	medium	vitrified
Copper (cutting-off)	silicon carbide	36	hard	rubber
Cork	aluminum oxide (white)	60	soft	vitrified
Cutters (moulding)	aluminum oxide	60	medium	vitrified
Drills (sharpening)	aluminum oxide (white)	60	medium	vitrified
Glass (grinding)	silicon carbide (green)	150	hard	vitrified
Glass (cutting-off)	silicon carbide (green)	90	hard	rubber
Glass (cutting-off)	diamond	60	medium	copper
Leather	silicon carbide	46	soft	vitrified
Plastic	silicon carbide	60	medium	rubber
Rubber (hard)	silicon carbide	46	medium	resinoid
Saws (gumming)	aluminum oxide	60	medium	vitrified
Steel (soft)	aluminum oxide	60	medium	vitrified
Steel (high speed)	aluminum oxide (white)	60	soft	vitrified
Tile (cutting-off)	silicon carbide	30	hard	resinoid
Tubes (steel)	aluminum oxide	60	hard	rubber
Welds (smoothing)	aluminum oxide	36	hard	vitrified
Wood (hard)	silicon carbide	30	soft	vitrified

GRINDING WHEEL SPEED

Type	Surface feet per minute
Chisel grinding	5,000 to 6,000
Cutlery wheels	4,000 to 5,000
Cut-off wheels	6,000 to 8,000
Cut-off wheels (rubber, shellac, resinoid)	9,000 to 16,000
Cylindrical grinding	5,500 to 6,500
General grinding	5,000 to 6,500
Hemming cylinders	2,100 to 5,000
Internal grinding	2,000 to 6,000
Knife grinding	3,500 to 4,500
Snagging, off-hand grinding (vitrified wheels)	5,000 to 6,000
Snagging (rubber and resinoid wheels)	7,000 to 9,500
Surface grinding	4,000 to 6,000
Tool and cutter grinding	4,500 to 6,000
Wet tool grinding	5,000 to 6,000

Note: To determine the number of revolutions per minute required, divide the surface speed in feet per minute by the circumference of the wheel you are using (measured in feet or fractions of a foot). You can find the circumference directly with a cloth tape, or calculate it by multiplying the diameter (also measured in feet or fractions of a foot) by 3.1416.

STRUCTURE.   Close grain spacing for hard and brittle, for small area of contact, and for fine finish; wide grain spacing for soft, ductile materials, for large area of contact, and for rapid removal of stock. Numerals are sometimes used to indicate spacing: 0 to 3, close; 4 to 6, medium; 7 to 12, wide.

BOND.   Resinoid, rubber, and shellac wheels are best for a high finish. Vitrified can be used for speeds up to 6,500 surface feet per minute; rubber, shellac, or resinoid for speeds above that.

SPARK TEST FOR METALS

Metal particles thrown off by the grinding wheel appear as dull red streaks until combined with oxygen to form a spark. The sparks caused by different metals vary, and afford a useful index in distinguishing the metal. Three things should be observed in testing metals in this manner:

GRINDING WHEEL SPEEDS IN RPM

	RPM FOR STATED SURFACE FEET PER MINUTE (SFPM)							
Diameter of wheel	4000 sfpm	4500 sfpm	5000 sfpm	5500 sfpm	6000 sfpm	6500 sfpm	7000 sfpm	7500 sfpm
1	15,279	17,189	19,098	21,008	22,918	24,828	26,737	28,647
2	7,639	8,594	9,549	10,504	11,459	12,414	13,368	14,328
3	5,093	5,729	6,366	7,003	7,639	8,276	8,913	9,549
4	3,820	4,297	4,775	5,252	5,729	6,207	6,685	7,162
5	3,056	3,438	3,820	4,202	4,584	4,966	5,348	5,730
6	2,546	2,865	3,183	3,501	3,820	4,138	4,456	4,775
7	2,183	2,455	2,728	3,001	3,274	3,547	3,820	4,092
8	1,910	2,148	2,387	2,626	2,885	3,103	3,342	3,580
10	1,528	1,719	1,910	2,101	2,292	2,483	2,674	2,865

1. The color of the spark, both as it leaves the wheel and as it explodes.
2. The shape of the explosion as the metal particle ignites.
3. The distance from the wheel at which the explosion occurs.

The diagram on page 150 shows the general spark effect obtained with different metals, but it is best to get a first-hand impression by testing known pieces of metal.

HACKSAWS—HAND AND POWER

The hand hacksaw is a cutting tool essential in metal work. Satisfactory results require care and intelligence in blade selection and use, the same as with other tools. Hand hacksaw blades come in 10- and 12-inch lengths and are held in frames having the required tensioning adjustment.

The blade should be taut but not overstrained. A properly strained blade when "thumbed" gives a clear humming note that, once heard, is readily remembered. After a few cuts with a new blade, the tension should be checked and slightly increased. Rigidity of the work is equally important. If possible, the work should be locked securely in a vise and positioned to engage the maximum number of saw teeth during the cut. In cutting sheet metal, for example, it is preferable to saw along the flat surface.

Use a coarse tooth blade (14 or 18 teeth per inch) to cut thick work;

SPARK TEST FOR METALS

Length and thickness of spark streams depend on variables such as the metal, grinding pressure, and hardness and condition of wheel. Grind at point on wheel that allows long spark stream for comparison of colors near wheel and at stream end. "Forked" spurts branch only once from single spark. "Repeating" sparks branch and rebranch. Sparks from manganese and carbon steel are hard to tell apart. Some cast iron produces smaller stream than shown, with fewer spurts. Tungsten carbide creates small stream, orange to light orange, with no spurts. (For practice, grind known test samples.)

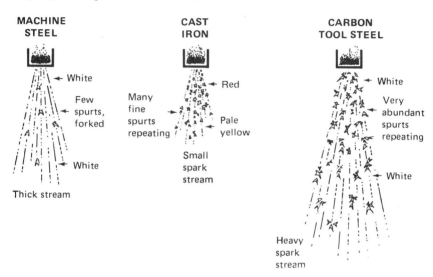

MACHINE STEEL — White / Few spurts, forked / White / Thick stream

CAST IRON — Red / Many fine spurts repeating / Pale yellow / Small spark stream

CARBON TOOL STEEL — White / Very abundant spurts repeating / White / Heavy spark stream

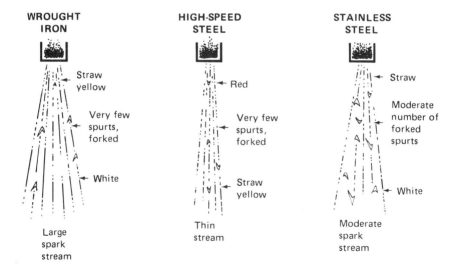

WROUGHT IRON — Straw yellow / Very few spurts, forked / White / Large spark stream

HIGH-SPEED STEEL — Red / Very few spurts, forked / Straw yellow / Thin stream

STAINLESS STEEL — Straw / Moderate number of forked spurts / White / Moderate spark stream

this increases cutting efficiency and chips are removed more effectively. Use a fine tooth blade (24 or 32 teeth per inch) to cut work of thin section; this reduces risk of teeth straddling the work, striping, or breaking the blade.

Teeth should point away from the handle so that the blade will cut on the forward stroke. The cutting stroke, using the same motion as in filing, should be long, steady, and sufficiently firm to assure a cut rather than a slide. The pressure should always be lifted on the return stroke to

MATERIAL CUTTING TABLE FOR HAND HACKSAW BLADES

Material	Type	Teeth per inch
Aluminum	solids	14
Angles	heavy	18
Angles	light	24
Babbitt	heavy	14
Brass	solids up to 1 inch	18
Brass pipe	heavy	24
Brass tubing	light	24
Bronze	solids up to 1 inch	18
BX cable	heavy	24
BX cable	light	32
Cable	heavy	18
Cast iron	up to 1 inch	18
Channel	heavy	18
Channel	light	24
Copper	solids up to 1 inch	14
Drill rod	over ¼ inch	18
Drill rod	No. 30 to ¼ inch	24
Drill rod	No. 30 and smaller	32
General-purpose cutting	heavy	18
Iron pipe	heavy	24
Metal conduit	light	24
Sheet metal	over 18 gauge	24
Sheet metal	under 18 gauge	32
Steels	¼ to 1 inch	18
Steels	¼ inch and under	24
Tubing	over 18 gauge	24
Tubing	under 18 gauge	32

prevent dulling the teeth. Forty to fifty strokes a minute should be the maximum.

It should be kept in mind that there is a great variety of blades for every kind of material and service.

Like hand hacksaw blades, power hacksaw blades are used for cutoff work. They are thicker, wider, and longer to fit various machines, and they cut off stock on a fast, production basis.

Power blades are held in heavy-duty, mechanically driven machine frames. They are fed into the work by mechanical or hydraulic means. Correct blade tension is obtained by using a torque wrench. The tension

MATERIAL CUTTING TABLE
FOR POWER HACKSAW BLADES

Material	Teeth per inch	Strokes per minute	Feed pressure
Aluminum alloy	4–6	150	light
Aluminum, pure	4–6	150	light
Brass castings, hard	6–10	135	light
Brass castings, soft	6–10	150	light
Bronze castings	6–10	135	medium
Cast iron	6–10	135	medium
*Carbon tool steel	6–10	90	medium
*Cold-rolled steel	4–6	135	heavy
Copper, drawn	6–10	135	medium
*Drill rod	10	90	medium
*High-speed steel	6–10	90	medium
*Machinery steel	4–6	135	heavy
*Malleable iron	6–10	90	medium
Manganese bronze	6–10	90	light
*Nickel silver	6–10	60	heavy
*Nickel steel	6–10	90	heavy
Pipe, iron	10–14	135	medium
Slate	6–10	90	medium
*Structural steel	6–10	135	medium
Tubing, brass	14	135	light
*Tubing, steel	14	135	light

*Use cutting compounds or coolant.

should be checked after one or two cuts and the blade tightened slightly as it stabilizes in position on the machine mounting pins.

Successful power hacksawing depends on choosing the right type of blade for the material to be cut, plus the right combination of teeth per inch, speed in strokes per minute, and feed in square inches per minute. The figures in the table on page 152 are offered as starting suggestions and may be altered as specific materials and operating conditions require.

CUTTING METAL WITH A SABER SAW

Because of the high speeds, cutting metal or abrasive materials with a wood-cutting saber saw blade will almost instantly dull it. Good metal-cutting blades are made of high-speed steel (HSS). They work best in a

METAL-CUTTING SABER SAW BLADE-SELECTOR TABLE

Teeth per inch	Material to be cut	Comments
6 (HSS)*	aluminum, copper, brass, laminates, compositions	heavy cutting in plate or tubing; sample maximum cut: ½ inch in aluminum plate
10 (HSS)	same as above	general cutting with smoother finish than above
14 (HSS)	aluminum, brass, bronze, copper, laminates, hardboard, mild steel, pipe	general cutting with smooth finish; maximum in steel: ¼–½ inch depending on manufacturers' specifications
18 (HSS)	same as above	for lighter materials: maximum cuts about ⅛ inch
24 (HSS)	sheet metal, light-gauge steel, thinwall tubing, Bakelite, tile, etc.	finest-tooth blade offered by some makers
32 (HSS)	thin-gauge sheet metals, thinwall tubing, metal trim	wave-set blade cuts fine kerf; maximum in steel: ¹⁄₁₆ inch for typical hacksaw jobs

*High-speed steel

saber saw with a variable-speed or two-speed feature, where you can run at a slower speed. Refer to the table on page 153 for the right tooth-per-inch blade to use for common metal-cutting and abrasive-material-cutting projects with a saber saw.

Tungsten carbide, one of the hardest materials known, is now used to make saw blades that are long lasting and that will easily cut materials that other blades won't, including things like files, glass bottles, ceramic tile, etc. The cut-anything blades are made by bonding hundreds of tiny carbide particles on the cutting edge of the blades.

The "carbide grit" blades are available two ways for hacksaws: a regular-style blade with carbide on the edge, and a "rod saw" blade, which is a wire coated with carbide all around. Eyes at the end of the coated wire are used to fasten it in the blade frame. This type cuts in any direction.

Carbide grit blades for saber saws come in fine, medium, and coarse grit. Refer to the table below for suggestions on selection for typical tough cutting jobs.

CARBIDE GRIT SABER SAW BLADE-SELECTOR TABLE

Material to be cut	Fine grit	Medium grit	Coarse grit
Fiberglass, reinforced plastics	good	good	best
Ceramic tile, slate, cast stone	best	good	—
Asbestos cement, nail-emnail-em bedded wood, plaster with nails	—	—	best
Chalkboard, clay pipe, brick	good	best	—
Stainless steel, trim, sheet metal to 18 gauge, ducting counter top materials, tempered hardboard	best	—	—

TEMPERING TEMPERATURES FOR STEEL

After hardening, steel is given a heat treatment that increases its toughness without reducing its hardness. As the steel heats up a film of oxide forms on its surface. The color of this oxide is an indication of the steel's temperature. This table gives the temperatures judged by color and colors for tempering:

Degrees centigrade	Degrees Fahrenheit	High temperatures, judged by color	Degrees centigrade	Degrees Fahrenheit	Colors for tempering (color of oxide film)
400	752	red heat, visible in the dark	221.1	430	very pale yellow
474	885	red heat, visible in twilight	226.7	440	light yellow
525	975	red heat, visible in daylight	232.2	450	pale straw-yellow
581	1075	red heat, visible in sunlight	237.8	460	straw-yellow
700	1292	dark red	243.3	470	deep straw-yellow
800	1472	dull cherry red	248.9	480	dark yellow
900	1652	cherry red	254.4	490	yellow-brown
1000	1832	bright cherry red	260.0	500	brown-yellow
1100	2012	orange-red	265.6	510	spotted red-brown
1200	2192	orange-yellow	271.1	520	brown-purple
1300	2372	yellow-white	276.7	530	light purple
1400	2552	white welding heat	282.2	540	full purple
1500	2732	brilliant white	287.8	550	dark purple
1600	2912	dazzling white (bluish white)	293.3	560	full blue
			298.9	570	dark blue

4

Masonry, Plastering, Roofing, Paneling, and Flooring

HOW TO MIX CONCRETE FOR DIFFERENT JOBS

Properly made concrete is a strong and versatile building material made by combining portland cement and sand with pebbles, crushed stone, or other aggregate, and enough water to cause the cement to set and to bind the whole mass solidly together.

In mixing concrete the most important proportion to remember is that between cement and water. As long as a mix is workable, the amount of aggregate may be varied considerably. For a given strength of concrete, the ratio between cement and water, however, is fixed. The relationship between strength of concrete and the relative quantities of water and cement is expressed more definitely by concrete experts:

For given materials and conditions of handling, the strength of the concrete is determined primarily by the ratio of the volume of the mixing water to the volume of cement as long as the mixture is plastic and workable.

In other words, if 6 gallons of water are used for each sack of cement in a mixture, the strength of the concrete at a certain age is already determined. The only extra provision is that the mixture is plastic and workable and the aggregates are strong, clean, and made up of sound particles. More water will mean less strength and less water greater strength.

Following this principle, the modern practice is to state the amount of mixing water for each sack of cement to produce "pastes" of different strengths. Common combinations are 5-gallon paste, 6-gallon paste, and 7-gallon paste, to be selected according to the type of work to be done.

To help choose pastes and make trial mixes for different types of jobs, the table on page 158 shows proportions recommended by the Portland Cement Association.

Choosing Materials

Portland cement is sold in sacks of 94 pounds each, or 1 cubic foot in volume. It should be free from all lumps when used. If it contains lumps that cannot be pulverized between thumb and finger, don't use it.

Water should be clean and free of oil, acid, or alkali. As a general rule, you can use any water that is fit to drink.

Aggregates are classified as fine or coarse. Fine aggregate consists of sand or other solid and fine material including rock screenings. Suitable sand will contain particles ranging uniformly in size from very fine up to ¼ inch.

Coarse aggregate consists of gravel, crushed stone, or other materials up to about 1½ inches in size. Material that is sound, hard, durable, and free from foreign matter is best for making concrete.

The maximum size of coarse aggregate depends on the kind of work for which the concrete is to be used. Aggregate up to 1½ inches, for example, may be used in thick foundation walls or heavy footing. In ordinary walls, the largest pieces should never be more than one fifth the thickness of the finished wall section. For slabs the maximum size should be approximately one third the thickness of the slab. Coarse aggregate is well graded when particles range uniformly from ¼ inch up to the largest that may be used on the kind of work to be done.

ALLOWANCE FOR MOISTURE IN THE AGGREGATES.   Most sand or fine aggregates contain some water. Allowance must therefore be made for this moisture in determining the amount of water to be added to the mix. You can easily determine whether sand is damp, wet, or very wet by pressing some together in your hand. If the sand falls apart after your hand is opened, it is damp; if it forms a ball that holds its shape, it is wet; if the sand sparkles and wets your hand, it is very wet. If the sand is bone dry—an unusual condition—you should use the full 5, 6, or 7 gallons of water called for in the table.

HOW TO SELECT PROPER CONCRETE MIX

KINDS OF WORK	ADD U.S. GALLONS OF WATER TO EACH SACK BATCH IF SAND IS			SUGGESTED MIXTURE FOR TRIAL BATCH*			MATERIALS PER CU. YD. OF CONCRETE*		
	Very wet	Wet (average sand)	Damp	Cement, sacks	Aggregates Fine cu. ft.	Coarse cu. ft.	Cement, sacks	Aggregates Fine cu. ft.	Coarse cu. ft.
5-Gallon paste for concrete subjected to severe wear, weather or weak acid and alkali solutions									
One-course industrial, creamery and dairy plant floors, etc.	3½	4	4½	1	2	2¼	*Maximum size aggregate ¾ in.* 7¾	15½	17½
6-Gallon paste for concrete to be watertight or subjected to moderate wear and weather									
Watertight floors, such as industrial plant, basement, dairy barn; watertight foundations; driveways, walks, tennis courts, swimming and wading pools, septic tanks, storage tanks, structural beams, columns, slabs, residence floors, etc.	4¼	5	5½	1	2½	3½	*Maximum size aggregate 1½ in.* 6	15	21
7-Gallon paste for concrete not subjected to wear, weather or water									
Foundation walls, footings, mass concrete, etc., for use where watertightness and abrasion resistance are not important.	4¾	5½	6¼	1	3	4	*Maximum size aggregate 1½ in.* 5	15	20

* Mixes and quantities are based on wet (average) aggregates and medium consistencies. Actual quantities will vary according to the grading of aggregate and the workability that is desired for each job.

Measuring Materials

All materials, including water, should be measured accurately. For measuring water, a pail marked on the inside to indicate quarts and gallons will prove handy. On small jobs a pail may also be used for measuring cement, sand, and pebbles. In mixing 1-sack batches merely remember that 1 sack holds exactly 1 cubic foot. Sand and pebbles are then conveniently measured in bottomless boxes made to hold exactly 1 cubic foot or other volumes desired.

If you can buy concrete aggregates in your community by weight, you may assume, for purpose of estimating, that a ton contains approximately 22 cubic feet of sand, or about 20 cubic feet of gravel. For closer estimates on local aggregates, consult your building material dealer.

How to Obtain a Workable Mixture

A workable mixture is one of such wetness and plasticity that it can be placed in the forms readily, and with light spading and tamping will result in a dense concrete. There should be enough portland cement mortar to give good dense surfaces, free from rough spots, and to hold pieces of coarse aggregate into the mass so that they will not separate out in handling. In other words, the cement-fine aggregate mortar should completely fill the spaces between the coarse aggregate and ensure a smooth, plastic mix. Mixtures lacking sufficient mortar will be hard to work and difficult to finish. Too much fine aggregate increases porosity and reduces the amount of concrete obtainable from a sack of cement.

A workable mix for one type of work may be too stiff for another. Concrete that is placed in thin sections must be more plastic than for massive construction.

Mixing and Placing the Concrete

Mixing should continue until every piece of coarse aggregate is completely coated with a thoroughly mixed mortar of cement and fine aggregate. Machine mixing is preferable, if you have the equipment available, and should continue for at least 1 minute after all the materials have been placed in the mixer.

The concrete should be placed in the forms within 45 to 60 minutes after mixing. It should be tamped or spaded as it goes into the form. This forces the coarse aggregate back from the face or surface, making a dense concrete surface.

How to Estimate Materials Required

The accompanying table will give you the approximate quantities required for 100 square feet of concrete of a given thickness. Actual quantities used may vary 10 percent, depending upon the aggregate used. It is good practice to provide 10 percent more fine and coarse aggregates than estimated, to allow for waste.

ESTIMATING MATERIALS FOR CONCRETE									
		PROPORTIONS							
Thick-		1:2:2¼ mix			1:2½:3½ mix			1:3:4 mix		
ness of con-crete, in.	Amount of con-crete, cu. yd.	Cement, sacks	Aggregate Fine, cu. ft.	Coarse, cu. ft.	Cement, sacks	Aggregate Fine, cu. ft.	Coarse, cu. ft.	Cement, sacks	Aggregate Fine, cu. ft.	Coarse, cu. ft.
3	0.92	7.1	14.3	16.1	5.5	13.8	19.3	4.6	13.8	18.4
4	1.24	9.6	19.2	21.7	7.4	18.6	26.0	6.2	18.6	24.8
5	1.56	12.1	24.2	27.3	9.4	23.4	32.8	7.8	23.4	31.2
6	1.85	14.3	28.7	32.4	11.1	27.8	38.9	9.3	27.8	37.0
8	2.46	19.1	38.1	43.0	14.8	36.9	51.7	12.3	36.9	49.3
10	3.08	23.9	47.7	53.9	18.5	46.2	64.7	15.4	46.2	61.6
12	3.70	28.7	57.3	64.7	22.2	55.5	77.7	18.5	55.5	74.0

ESTIMATING TRANSIT-MIX NEEDS. When estimating the amount of transit-mix concrete needed for a given project, multiply the length and width in feet by the thickness in inches and divide by 12 to get the cubic footage. You'll need a yard of concrete for each 27 cubic feet.

It may pay you to figure your job so you use enough concrete to get the best price. In some areas, 2 yards bought separately cost more than 3 yards taken at one crack, which works out to an appealing 33 percent discount on the latter.

How to Prevent Concrete from Sticking to Forms

To prevent concrete from sticking to wooden forms, the forms must be treated with a suitable oil, varnish, or other coating material. This oil should also prevent absorption of water from the concrete.

Almost any light-bodied petroleum oil will do. Fuel oil is satisfactory for use with normal gray concrete except in very warm weather, when it should be thickened with 1 part petroleum grease to each 2 parts oil.

When making pastel-colored concrete or concrete using white portland cement, use white mineral oil to prevent staining.

Before applying oil, be sure the form is clean and smooth. Rough wood surfaces may cause the concrete to stick. Apply the oil evenly with a brush, spray, or swab. Wipe off excess so it does not soften or discolor the concrete.

Several coats of shellac applied first to plywood is better than oil alone in preventing moisture from raising the grain and so marring the finished surface of the concrete. Forms that are to be used repeatedly should be coated with asphalt paint, varnish, or several coats of boiled linseed oil rubbed in and allowed to dry. Forms so coated may be used just as they are, or oiled as usual for extra ease in removal.

If oil is not available, wetting the forms with plain water just before placing the concrete may help prevent absorption and sticking, but this method is not so effective and should be used only in an emergency.

FINISHING CONCRETE

Concrete can be finished in many ways, depending on the effect desired. Walks and floors may require screeding only to proper contour and height. In other cases you may wish to give surfaces a broomed finish or trowel them smooth. Here are the basic operations in finishing horizontal slabs:

Screeding

The term "screed" comes from an old Anglo-Saxon word meaning "strip" or "band." To the cement mason, screeds are the side strips of a concrete form that mark the height at which the concrete is to be leveled off. Screeding, then, is simply leveling off the concrete by drawing along it a straight-edged or contoured board whose ends ride on the screeds.

Screeding should be done just as soon as possible after the concrete has been dumped and spread—before free water in the concrete has had time to rise to the surface, or "bleed." This is one of the most important rules of successful concrete finishing. *Screeding or any other operation performed on a concrete surface when bled water is present may result in subsequent severe scaling, dusting, or crazing.*

Do your screeding with a "strikeboard," which can be simply a 2×4 or 2×6, a foot or so longer than the width of the form. The working edge should be straight, unless you are making a walk or other surface that you want higher in the middle to provide better drainage. In the latter case, contour the edge as desired.

Move the strikeboard back and forth across the concrete with a sawing motion, advancing it a short distance along the length of the slab with each motion. Keep a surplus of concrete against the front face of the strikeboard as a supply to fill depressions as the board is moved forward.

Floating

If you want a smoother surface than that obtained by screeding, the surface should be worked sparingly with a "float." This can be a flat rectangle of wood, 12 to 18 inches long and 3½ to 4½ inches wide, provided with a handle on its upper face. Use the float to remove high or low spots or ridges left by the strikeboard, also to embed the coarse aggregate so the surface is smooth enough for subsequent troweling. This operation must be done immediately after screeding, being careful not to overdo it and so bring an excess of water and mortar to the surface. Concrete is often floated a second time, after the surface water has disappeared and just before troweling.

Troweling

If a dense, smooth finish is desired, floating must be followed by steel troweling at a time after surface water has disappeared and the concrete has hardened enough so that no fine material and new water will be worked to the top. This step should be delayed as long as possible, but not so long that the surface is too hard to finish properly. Troweling should leave the surface smooth, even, and free of marks and ripples. If there are wet spots on the surface, do not trowel these spots until the water has been absorbed, has evaporated, or has been mopped up. Never sprinkle dry cement on such spots to take up the water; this will only produce a surface that will later scale off.

Brooming

A nonskid surface can be produced by brushing or brooming. The brushed surface is made by drawing a soft-bristled push broom over the slab just after it has been steel-troweled. For coarser textures, a stiffer bristled broom may be used.

CURING CONCRETE

The first requirement for strong, high-quality concrete is the proper proportion between water and cement; the second, and more often neglected, requirement is proper curing.

Concrete hardens because of a chemical reaction between cement and water. This reaction starts as soon as they are mixed and causes the concrete to set solid in a matter of hours. Hardening, however, does not stop with this setting. If you do not let the concrete dry out, it will continue to harden for about a month. Tests have shown that if you keep concrete warm and moist during a curing period as long as 28 days, it will be more than twice as strong as it would have been if you had kept

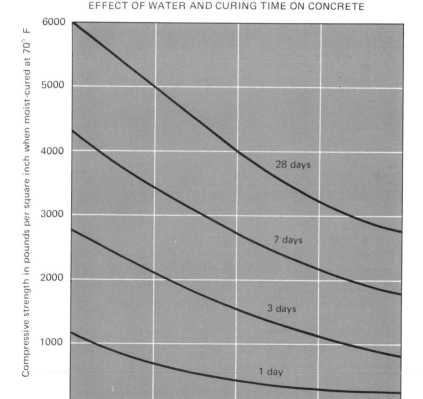

EFFECT OF WATER AND CURING TIME ON CONCRETE

Compressive strength in pounds per square inch when moist-cured at 70° F

28 days

7 days

3 days

1 day

Gallons of water per sack of portland cement

it that way only 3 days. Concrete that is allowed to dry before it is fully cured is relatively soft, porous, and of poor appearance.

For concrete to cure thoroughly, it must be protected so that little or no moisture is lost during the curing or hardening period. Newly placed concrete must not be allowed to dry out too fast and so must be protected from the sun and from drying winds. This may be done in the beginning with burlap or canvas coverings kept constantly wet.

One method of moist curing that is applicable to horizontal surfaces after the concrete has become surface hard is called "ponding." This is accomplished by building an earth dike around the edges of the concrete slab and keeping the slab covered with an inch or so of water. Another method that may be used under the same conditions is to first wet the surface thoroughly with a fine spray of water and then keep it covered during the entire curing time with a sheet of plastic film. The plastic sheet should be large enough to cover the width and edges of the slab. If several sheets must be used, lap them at least 12 inches. Weight down the joints and edges to keep the sheets moisture-tight and in place.

The barest minimum of curing time should be 3 days, although 14 days would make the concrete much stronger. A curing period of 28 days at 70° F is considered standard for greatest strength.

How the proportion of water to cement and the length of proper curing both affect the strength of the resulting concrete is shown in the graph on the preceding page.

CONCRETES FOR SPECIAL PURPOSES

Air-Entrained Concrete

By adding to the concrete mix a small amount of a chemical called an air-entraining agent, billions of microscopic air bubbles are formed in the resulting concrete. These change the basic structure of the concrete, making it more workable during mixing, laying, and finishing, and stronger and more durable after it has set. Air-entrained concrete also has superior resistance to scaling caused by alternate freezing and thawing as well as that caused by salts used to melt snow and ice.

You can buy ready-mixed air-entrained concrete from producers in the colder parts of the country. Or you can buy cement by the bag with the air-entrained chemical already incorporated in it. This is designated as Type 1A portland cement, and the bag is so labeled. Less water should be mixed with air-entrained concrete than with ordinary concrete for an otherwise similar mix.

Lightweight Concrete

Normal portland cement concrete weighs about 145 pounds per cubic foot. By using special lightweight aggregates, concrete can be made weighing only 40 to 110 pounds per cubic foot. Such concretes are used for concrete blocks, for filler material where high strength is not necessary, for fireproofing steel, and for concrete that can be nailed. Lightweight concretes possess good insulating properties and they also have good fire-resistance, especially those made from burned clay or shale.

Aggregates for lightweight concrete are produced by crushing pumice, infusorial earth, lava, or tufa, a porous rock formed as a deposit from springs or streams. Others are made from cinders, by burning clay and shale, and by expanding molten slag with steam.

Because lightweight aggregates vary in their uses and mixing proportions, buy them only from reliable dealers who understand their characteristics and can give you definite instructions for making concrete with them.

Another type of lightweight concrete can be made by adding a chemical compound to standard concrete. This compound causes a gas to form in the mix, expanding it and thus reducing its weight.

Porous Concrete

This concrete, through which water can easily pass, can be made by omitting sand and using coarse aggregate only. Such concrete is frequently used for drain tile, in which the mix proportions are 5 parts pea gravel by weight to 1 part cement. The maximum-size particle in the pea gravel should be ⅜ inch and the smallest ³⁄₁₆ inch. Porous concrete is put in place without much tamping, since tamping tends to over-consolidate it and so reduces its porosity. If cured for about 7 days under conditions recommended for standard portland cement concrete, the compressive strength of porous concrete should be at least 1,000 pounds per square inch.

Grout

This is a special sand-cement mortar made for such uses as sealing cracks, sealing the joints of precast pipe, and filling the space between the bed plates of machinery and foundations. The primary requirement of grout is that it should not shrink. To meet this requirement, mortar used for grouting should be as dry as possible. Shrinkage can also be reduced by prolonged mixing and by the addition of a small amount of aluminum powder.

Aluminum powder mixed in concrete causes the concrete to swell. Thus, by blending in just the right amount, the natural shrinkage of a mortar can be balanced. Only extremely small amounts of aluminum are needed; one teaspoon per sack of cement has been found satisfactory in many cases. The aluminum powder should be mixed thoroughly with fine sand first, because unmixed powder tends to float. One pound of sand–aluminum powder mixture should contain enough aluminum for a batch of mortar that you can place completely within 45 minutes after mixing.

Watertight Concrete

This must be as dense as possible and moist-cured for a longer period than would be necessary if watertightness was not important. Here are the main requirements:

1. Do not use more than 6 gallons of water per sack of cement.
2. Use aggregates that are sound and of low porosity.
3. Place the concrete properly and compact it thoroughly.
4. Keep the concrete moist and at a temperature of more than 50° F for at least 7 days.

The most effective way to prevent the passage of water through concrete is to sandwich a membrane of waterproof material between two concrete layers. On horizontal surfaces the method ordinarily used is to first coat the surface to be waterproofed with hot roofing asphalt. This can be applied with a mop as soon as the concrete surface is dry enough to allow the hot asphalt to stick. One layer of roofing felt is placed on this coating while it is still hot. The felt is then mopped with hot asphalt and a second layer of felt is applied, which is then also coated with asphalt.

On vertical surfaces a thick coat of fibrous tar or asphalt cement is troweled on, and a layer of flexible tar or asphalt-treated burlap is embedded in this coat.

On both horizontal and vertical surfaces, the membrane should be protected with an outer coating of 3 inches of concrete or 1 course of brick.

Waterproofing compounds are sometimes added to the concrete mix or applied as a surface wash to the finished concrete. As they do not affect the strength, setting, or curing of new concrete, and may also be applied to old concrete, the washes are generally preferable. These include tar coatings, asphalt emulsions, and special portland cement paints. For best results, surface washes should be applied on the surface where the water enters. Because they vary so in nature, they should be applied according to the manufacturer's specifications.

HOT-WEATHER CONCRETING

Making concrete in hot weather poses special problems, among which are reduction in strength and the cracking of flat surfaces due to rapid drying. Concrete also may harden before it can be consolidated because of rapid setting of the cement and excessive absorption of mixing water. This makes it difficult to finish flat surfaces.

The most important considerations in hot-weather concreting are to keep materials and mixed concrete cooler than 90° F, prevent absorption, protect against too rapid evaporation, place the concrete without delay, and begin curing immediately. Here are a few specific suggestions:

1. During extremely hot weather, start jobs in the late afternoon.
2. Sprinkle stockpiles of coarse aggregate with water to cool the material by evaporation. Chill the mixing water by refrigeration or with ice—making sure that the ice has all melted before placing the concrete.
3. To prevent absorption of water from the mix, sprinkle the wood forms and the surface on which the concrete is to be placed with water just before the concrete is laid. Sprinkle coarse aggregates just before they are added to the batch.
4. Erect windbreaks of canvas or polyethylene sheet to prevent strong, hot winds from drying exposed surfaces while they are being finished.
5. Place concrete as soon after mixing as possible. Level it immediately. Then cover it with a temporary cover of burlap kept continuously wet. When hard enough for final finishing, uncover and finish only a small area at a time, protecting it again after finishing by replacing the wet cover.
6. Start curing as soon as the surface is hard enough to resist marring. In extremely hot weather use the "ponding" method described under "Curing" for at least the first 12 hours. After that, keep the concrete *continuously* wet to avoid alternate wetting and drying. Cure for at least 7 days.

COLD-WEATHER CONCRETING

Concrete may be placed in winter provided it is protected against freezing. A single cycle of freezing and thawing during the first few days may not lower the eventual strength of the concrete, but it will decrease its watertightness and reduce its resistance to weathering. Several such cycles at an early age, however, will permanently affect its strength, water resistance, and wearing qualities. This is the reason why walks and driveways placed late in the fall often deteriorate within a few years. Below are some of the steps to follow to avoid cold-weather problems:

1. When the air temperature is very low, you must heat the materials. The temperature of the concrete as it is placed in the forms should be between 50° and 70° F. If the air temperature is between 30° and 40° F, heat the mixing water. If the temperature is below 30° F, heat the sand also, and sometimes the coarse aggregate. Be sure no lumps of frozen aggregate are in the concrete when it is placed. To prevent flash setting of the concrete do not overheat the materials. Water temperature should be kept below 140° F. Do not place concrete on frozen ground. Thawing will produce unequal settling.

2. Accelerators to speed the setting of the concrete may be used with care. About 1 pound of calcium chloride per sack of cement will hasten hardening safely. Add it in the form of a solution, considered as part of the mixing water. Never use more than 2 pounds per sack because of the danger of flash set. Never use antifreeze compounds or other materials to lower the freezing point of concrete. The amounts required will seriously reduce the strength and wearing qualities of the concrete.

3. When using normal portland cement, keep the temperature at 70° F for the first 3 days, or 50° F for 5 days. Do not let concrete freeze for the next 4 days. Then let concrete cool gradually at the rate of 1 to 2 degrees per hour until it reaches the outside temperature.

4. In many cases a thick blanket of straw or other insulating material is sufficient protection during curing for slabs on the ground. At very low temperatures, however, housings of wood, insulation board, waterproofed paper or tarpaulins over wood frames, plus artificial heat, may be necessary. Moist, warm air should be circulated between slab and housing. If the concrete is indoors, and heating units are used, be sure to keep the concrete moist by sprinkling it or evaporating water into the air.

PREVENTING SURFACE DEFECTS

Many defects that soon develop on the surface of new concrete are caused by improper construction techniques, or by these combined with unsuitable weather. Here are some of the most common defects, with suggestions on how to prevent them:

SCALING

In this the surface of a hardened slab breaks away in scales up to about ³⁄₁₆ inch thick.

Causes	Preventive measures
Cycles of freezing and thawing right after concrete has been placed.	Keep the temperature of newly placed concrete above 50° F for at least 5 days when using normal portland cement.
Later cycles of freezing and thawing in normal portland cement concrete, also the use of deicing salts in connection with them.	Coat cured concrete with linseed oil mixture described later in this chapter, or use air-entrained concrete in place of regular concrete.
Performing any of the finishing operations—such as screeding, floating, or troweling—while free water is on the surface. By mixing this water into the top of the slab, these operations will bring to the surface a layer of cement that is not bonded to the concrete under it. This layer will scale off after the concrete sets.	Don't perform any finishing operation while free water is present. First let the water evaporate from the surface, or remove the water by dragging a rubber garden hose over it.

CRAZING

Crazing is the formation of an overall pattern of fine cracks on newly hardened concrete due to surface shrinkage.

Causes	Preventive measures
Rapid drying of the slab surface generally caused by hot sun, high air temperature, drying winds, or any combination of these.	Cover with burlap or canvas immediately after screeding or leveling the surface of the newly placed concrete. Keep this cloth damp until ready for floating and troweling. Begin the moist cure of the concrete as soon as possible without marring the surface.
Second floating and troweling while there is too much moisture on the surface or while the concrete is still too plastic. Doing this will bring too much water and fine materials to the surface. If the surface water then evaporates too fast, the result may be shrinking and crazing.	Don't start second floating and troweling until excess moisture has evaporated, and the concrete has begun to set. To avoid excess moisture, increase the amount of fine and coarse aggregate in the mix or use air-entrained concrete.

(Continued)

PREVENTING SURFACE DEFECTS (*continued*)

Many defects that soon develop on the surface of new concrete are caused by improper construction techniques, or by these combined with unsuitable weather. Here are some of the most common defects, with suggestions on how to prevent them:

DUSTING

This is the appearance of a powdery coating on the surface of newly hardened concrete.

Causes	Preventive measures
Too much clay or silt in the concrete. These harmful materials degrade the cement at the surface, causing it to dust off later.	Use only clean and well-graded coarse and fine aggregate.
Second floating and troweling while there is still excess surface water on the concrete slab.	Delay these operations until all free water has disappeared from the surface and the concrete has started its initial set.
Dry heat from winter-protection heaters may lower the relative humidity around the concrete excessively, causing the concrete to dry out too fast. This will produce weak concrete as well as dusting by preventing proper hydration of the cement.	Place water jackets on the heaters to increase the relative humidity, and employ any of the previously described methods for moist curing. Move the heaters periodically so that no area will become overheated.
No curing or insufficient curing.	Proper curing for sufficient time is necessary. Uncured concrete will be weak and its surface easily worn off by foot traffic.

COLD-WEATHER TREATMENT FOR CONCRETE

Winter damage to driveways, sidewalks, steps, patios, and other structures of exposed concrete is caused by repeated cycles of freezing and thawing of water entrapped in the pores of the concrete. It takes the form of scaling and pitting known to the cement trade as "spalling." The process is aggravated by the use of salt and other deicing chemicals.

You can prevent spalling by the application of an inexpensive compound you can make from linseed oil and mineral spirits. This compound has been endorsed by the Bureau of Public Roads of the U.S. Department of Commerce and has been used successfully for some years on highways, bridge decks, parking lots, and other outdoor concrete installations throughout the country.

To make it, simply mix together equal quantities of mineral spirits (obtainable in paint and hardware stores under this name or as "turpentine substitute" or "paint thinner") and boiled linseed oil. The linseed oil reacts with oxygen in the air to form a tough film through which moisture and destructive salt solutions cannot penetrate. The mineral spirits makes the oil easier to spread and enables it to penetrate deeper into the concrete.

The compound is most effective if applied to new concrete at the end of the curing period, which is about 28 days. It has been successfully applied, however, after 7 to 10 days' curing. It will also inhibit damage to old concrete where spalling has already begun.

The compound dries and cures best if the atmospheric temperature is 70° F or above, although it has been successfully applied at temperatures as low as 35° F. The surface to be treated should be dry and free from dirt and debris.

On highways and other large areas the compound is generally applied by spraying. The best means of application for the small user is a cheap short-nap paint roller that can be thrown away after use. A long handle will make the work easier. A brush is not recommended, except to touch up edges, because with a brush the rate of application is hard to control and too much compound is left on the surface.

Two coats should be applied—the first at the rate of about 40 square yards per gallon; the second at about 67 square yards per gallon. The first coat should be completely dry before applying the second. At 70° F or above, drying should be complete within a few hours.

Under moderate weather conditions and ordinary usage, the first application may last up to 3 years. Under severe conditions, reapplication may be required each year for the first 3 or 4 years. After that, every third or fourth year should suffice.

The treatment leaves no greasy residue after drying. At first the concrete may be slightly darkened, but this tends to bleach out and become unnoticeable with time.

HOW TO COLOR CONCRETE

By adding color to concrete you may be able to create many pleasing decorative effects around your home and garden. Stepping stones, patios, swimming pool decks, floors, walks, and driveways, and so on, may all be livened by this means.

To color concrete you have four methods to choose from: (1) mix dry color through the whole material; (2) place a foundation layer in the usual way, and then top this with a layer of colored concrete; (3)

sprinkle the concrete before it hardens with a special "dry-shake" mixture of pigment, cement, and sand; (4) color a finished slab with stain, dye, or paint. The first three methods are outlined below, the fourth is described in Chapter 2.

Pigments for Concrete

Only commercially pure mineral pigments should be used, as other pigments are apt to fade or to reduce the strength and wearing qualities of the stucco, mortar, or concrete in which they are used. You may buy them as "cement colors" or "limeproof colors" under brand names, or you may get them under their chemical names as listed here:

Blues	Cobalt oxide
Browns	Brown iron oxide
Buffs	Synthetic yellow iron oxide
Greens	Chromium oxide green
Reds	Red iron oxide
Grays or Slate effects	Black iron oxide or carbon black; common lampblack should not be used

These pigments may be blended to get intermediate colors or tones. Red, yellow, and brown dry pigments are the least expensive; blues and greens may cost up to three times as much. Use the smallest amount of pigment necessary to get the tint or shade required. Always weigh the amount you use, so you can duplicate or alter a future mix. Never, however, add more than 10 percent of the weight of the cement.

CONCRETE COLORED ALL THE WAY THROUGH. This costs the most for pigment but is the easiest to make. Full-strength pigments will usually produce a deep color when 7 pounds are mixed with 1 bag of cement. Extra deep shades may take 10 pounds, while 5 pounds will do for medium shades, 3 pounds for light shades, and 1½ pounds for a pleasing pastel tint. For cleaner, brighter colors use white portland cement instead of the normal gray type and also white sand. Regular cement will do for black or dark grays. To prevent streaking, blend the dry cement thoroughly with the pigment before adding to the mix. Mix longer than usual to further distribute the color, then place, finish, and cure as you would ordinary concrete.

COLORED TOP-LAYER CONCRETE.   Begin by placing a base layer of uncolored concrete in the usual manner. As soon as this layer has stiffened and the surface water has disappeared, place on top of it ½ to 1 inch of colored concrete, made as described above. This method requires a little more labor, but there may be a considerable saving in the cost of materials.

THE DRY-SHAKE METHOD.   This is the least expensive, but it is the most difficult to carry out satisfactorily. If you want to risk it, you'd better buy a ready-made dry-shake mix of mineral oxide, white portland cement, and special fine aggregate. The manufacturer will specify the area a given amount should cover.

After the concrete has been placed and screeded, and the surface water has evaporated, work over the surface with a magnesium or aluminum float. This will remove any ridges or depressions that might cause variations in color intensity, and also bring to the surface sufficient moisture to combine with the dry coloring material. Then immediately shake about two-thirds of the mixture as evenly as you can over the surface.

In a few minutes the powder will appear moist. It should then be worked into the surface with the float. As soon as this floating is finished, distribute the remainder of the dry-shake material evenly over the surface. Work this also in with the float. If you want the surface to be smoother, now go over it with a trowel.

CURING COLORED CONCRETE.   This must be cured as thoroughly as ordinary concrete. During drying and curing, take care to avoid any staining by dirt or foot traffic. After curing, give interior surfaces at least two coats of concrete floor wax containing the same mineral-oxide pigment used in or on the concrete.

HOW TO CLEAN CONCRETE

If concrete floors, walls, or walks become discolored beyond the capabilities of ordinary methods to clean them, here are several more drastic ones that should do the job:

Cleaning with Mortar

Repair all defects in the surface, and let the repair material set. Then make a cleaning mortar of 1 part portland cement and 1¼ parts fine sand, mixed with enough water to make a thick paste. If a light-colored surface is desired, use white portland cement. Apply the mortar to the surface with a brush, and immediately after scour the surface with a wood float such as is used in making concrete. After an hour or two, remove excess mortar from the surface with a trowel, leaving that which sticks in the pores. After the surface has dried, rub it with dry burlap to remove all visible remaining mortar. Complete each section without stopping. Mortar left on the surface overnight is very difficult to remove.

Rubbing with Burlap

Another mortar-cleaning method consists in rubbing the mortar over the surface with clean burlap. The mortar in this case should have the consistency of thick cream, and the surface should appear almost dry. Wait long enough to prevent smearing, but not long enough for the mortar to harden, and then wipe off the excess with clean burlap. Let the remainder set for 2 hours, after which keep it damp to cure it for the next 2 days. Then let it dry and sand it vigorously with No. 2 sandpaper. This removes all excess mortar not removed by the sand rubbing and leaves a surface of uniform appearance. For best results, mortar cleaning should be done in the shade on a cool, damp day.

Acid Cleaning

You can wash a concrete surface with acid if the staining is not too severe. First wet the surface and, while it is still damp, scrub it thoroughly with a 10-percent solution of hydrochloric acid. (The "muriatic" acid sold in paint and hardware stores is generally a 20-percent solution of hydrochloric acid. If you use this, just dilute it with an equal amount of water.) Then rinse off the acid with plain water. (*Caution:* Wear rubber gloves, a rubber or plastic apron or jacket, and protective goggles when scrubbing with hydrochloric acid. It is harmful to skin and clothing.)

PREPARING CONCRETE FLOORS FOR PAINTING

Because most concrete floors are below ground level, moisture may creep to the surface from the underside in sufficient quantity to cause the paint film to peel. Unless they have aged at least 6 months, there also may be free alkali on the surface that will attack the paint.

To neutralize the alkalinity and also to provide a slightly rougher surface for better adhesion, all concrete floors should be acid etched before painting.

To do this, scrub the surface with a solution of 1 part concentrated muriatic acid in 3 parts water, using a stiff fiber brush. (*Caution:* Muriatic acid is corrosive. Mix in a glass or polyethylene container, wear rubber gloves when applying it, and don't spatter on clothes or furniture.)

Allow about 1 gallon of solution to each 100 square feet of surface. Let it remain until all bubbling stops and then flush it off thoroughly with plain water. If the surface has not dried uniformly within a few hours, some of the acid still remains, so flush it again.

Depending upon the porosity of the surface, the floor will dry in several hours or it may take a day or more. As soon as it is completely dry, it may be painted.

If the finish on an old floor is poor, it should be removed before etching. Rubber-base paints require special solvents, but most other paints may be removed with a solution of 1 pound of lye in 5 pints of water (or 1 13-ounce can to 2 quarts). (*Caution:* Handle lye with care, as it is poisonous and caustic. Never mix it in hot water or in an aluminum container. Wear rubber gloves while handling it.)

After the paint has softened, remove it with steel wool or a scraper. Flush the surface with plain water to remove remaining paint and lye. Then etch with the muriatic solution mentioned above, applied at a rate of about 75 square feet to the gallon.

HARDENERS FOR CONCRETE FLOORS

Concrete floors that are not to be painted can be hardened, and so given longer life and freedom from "dusting," by treating with a diluted solution of sodium silicate prepared as follows:

Sodium silicate solution (commercial grade, 40° Baumé)	1 gallon
Water	3 gallons

Mix thoroughly and apply three coats, letting each dry a day or more before putting on the next. Succeeding coats will penetrate better if you scrub preceding coat with a stiff fiber brush and water.

Another hardener for concrete floors is a solution of zinc sulfate. This darkens the concrete somewhat, but produces a hard, uniform surface.

Here is a formula recommended by the Portland Cement Association:

Sulfuric acid, concentrated	¼ ounce
Water	2 gallons
Zinc sulfate	3 pounds

Stir the sulfuric acid into the water and then stir in the zinc sulfate until thoroughly dissolved. (*Careful:* The acid is extremely corrosive; if you spatter any on yourself or surroundings, flush off immediately with plenty of plain cold water.) Apply two coats—the second, 4 hours after the first. Before applying the second coat, scrub the surface with hot water and mop it dry.

REINFORCING CONCRETE

Here is a trick that makes reinforcing rods or mesh do the best possible job of internal bracing. Remember that concrete has great compressive strength, but much weaker tensile strength. Therefore place the rods where the concrete has the most tendency to pull apart under the load. In other words, if a slab is to be supported under its middle, with its ends unsupported, place the reinforcing rods near the top of the slab. On the other hand, if the slab is to be supported at its ends, embed the rods near the bottom. In either case, however, be sure that the rods are far enough from any surface so they are strongly keyed in the concrete.

REPAIRING CRACKS IN CONCRETE

For this purpose, use regular cement mortar, made by mixing 1 part portland cement with 3 parts fine sand and adding enough water to make a puttylike consistency. Before packing in the mortar, widen the crack, dust it out, and wet it with water.

PATCHING A CONCRETE FLOOR OR SIDEWALK

A sidewalk that has settled, a crack in the basement floor, or other damaged concrete can often be restored by timely patching. Here are the steps that ensure a good job:

1. Thoroughly clean the areas to be patched and roughen them with a chisel. Then go over the surface with a wire brush and wash away all dust and loose particles with clean water.

2. Dampen the surface that is to be patched, but leave no excess water on the surface.
3. Make a thick, creamy mixture of portland cement and water and brush it on the prepared surface. The patch should be applied before this creamy mixture dries.
4. Make a stiff mix of 1 part portland cement, 2 parts sand, and 2 parts pea gravel. Tamp this mixture firmly into the cavity and smooth off lightly with a wood float. After the concrete begins to stiffen, finish with a steel trowel or wood float. For narrow cracks where pea gravel cannot be used, use mortar made of 1 part portland cement and 3 parts sand.
5. Keep the freshly patched place damp for a minimum of 5 days.

WORKING WITH MORTAR

Mortar for Concrete Masonry

Good mortar for bonding together concrete blocks must have sufficient strength, good workability, and a property called *water retentivity,* which resists rapid loss of water to blocks that may be highly absorptive. The latter is very important, because concrete blocks, unlike some types of brick, should never be wetted to control suction before the application of mortar. The accompanying table shows formulas for mixes to be used under ordinary and under unusually severe conditions.

MORTAR MIXES FOR CONCRETE BLOCKS

(Proportions by volume)

Type of service	Portland cement	Hydrated lime	Mortar sand (in damp, loose condition)
For ordinary service	1	½ to 1¼	4½ to 6
To withstand unusually heavy loads, violent winds, or severe frost conditions	1	0 to ¼	2¼ to 3

Use clean sharp sand of a type suitable for making concrete, but with all grits and pebbles larger than ¼ inch screened out. Mix the dry ingredients first with a hoe or a shovel until no variations in color are visible. Then form in a ring, add a little water at a time to the center of this ring, and hoe the mixture into the water until the combination forms a smooth and plastic paste. If the paste is too stiff, add water sparingly.

Mortar for Brick Masonry

Unless properly mixed and applied, mortar will be the weakest part of brick masonry. Both the strength and the watertightness of brick walls depend largely on the strength of the mortar bond.

The general instructions described earlier for mixing mortar for cementing concrete blocks apply also to mixing mortar for bricks. There is one exception, however, in the application. Porous or high-suction brick, if laid dry, will absorb enough water from the mortar to prevent the cement from properly setting. Therefore, such brick must be drenched with a hose and then allowed to surface dry before they are laid. A rough way to tell if a brick should be wet before laying is to sprinkle a few drops of water on one of its sides. If these drops sink in completely in less than 1 minute, the brick should be wet before laying it.

One of the types of mortar in the table below should suit almost any kind of brick-construction job.

MORTAR MIXES FOR BRICK MASONRY

(Proportions by volume)

Type of service	Portland cement	Hydrated lime	Mortar sand, in damp, loose condition
For general use in work below ground level and in contact with earth, such as walks, foundations, and retaining walls	1	¼	3
For general use, especially where high lateral strength is needed	1	½	4½
This is the commonest and most economical mortar for general use, and is suitable for most exterior walls above ground	1	1	6
Still less expensive, this mortar will do for solid load-bearing walls where compressive forces do not exceed 100 pounds per square inch and which will not be exposed to freezing and thawing in the presence of great moisture	1	2	9

Retempering Mortar

Mortar that has become too stiff on the mortar board to work with properly because of evaporation may be restored to workability by thorough remixing and the addition of sufficient water. Mortar that has stiffened because it has started to set, however, cannot be thus retempered and should be discarded. If you can't determine the cause of stiffening, make it a rule to discard mortar that is more than 2½ hours old when the air temperature is 80° F or higher, or more than 3½ hours old at lower temperatures.

Speeding the Setting of Mortar

By adding up to 2 percent of calcium chloride to the weight of the cement, you can hasten the setting of mortar and cause it to gain full strength earlier. Dissolve the calcium chloride in a small amount of water and add this solution with the mixing water. A trial mix will give you an idea of the proper amount of the chemical to produce the desired rate of hardening.

Antifreeze Chemicals

The use of calcium chloride or other chemicals to lower the freezing point of mortars during winter construction should be avoided. The amount of such chemicals required for any appreciable effect would ruin the strength and other desirable qualities of the mortar.

Estimating the Number of Concrete Blocks Needed

If you are using the standard 8 × 8 × 16-inch blocks—they are really 7⅝ × 7⅝ × 15⅝—multiply the wall height by the length. Multiply the result by 1.2. Your answer is the number of blocks required. For example, to find out how many blocks to buy for a wall 16 feet long by 8 feet high: 16 × 8 × 1.2 gives 154 blocks, approximately.

Size	Mortar needed for 100 square feet of wall area	Per 100 blocks
4 inches high	13½ cubic feet	6 cubic feet
8 inches high	8½ cubic feet	7½ cubic feet

BRICK SIZES AND TYPES

Standard bricks made in the United States are 2¼ by 3¾ by 8 inches. English bricks are 3 by 4½ by 9 inches. Roman bricks are 1½ by 4 by 12 inches. The actual dimensions of brick may vary a little because of shrinkage during burning. Here are some common types of brick:

1. *Building brick* formerly called common brick, is made of ordinary clays or shales and is burned in kilns. It is used generally where it can't be seen, as in the backing courses in solid or cavity brick walls.
2. *Face brick* has better durability and is better looking than backup or building brick, and so is used in the exposed face of a wall. It is produced in various shades of brown, red, gray, yellow, and white.
3. *Pressed brick* is made by a dry press process and has regular smooth faces, sharp edges, and perfectly square corners. Ordinarily it is used entirely as face brick.
4. *Glazed brick* has one surface of each brick glazed in white or some color. This glasslike coating makes such brick particularly suited for walls in hospitals, dairies, laboratories, or other buildings where cleanliness and ease of cleaning are necessary.
5. *Cored brick* is made with two rows of holes extending through its beds to reduce weight. It is just about as strong and as moisture-resistant as solid brick, and may be used to replace the solid type wherever lighter weight is desired.
6. *Fire brick* is made of a special type of fire clay that will stand the heat of fireplaces, furnaces, and other locations of intense heat without cracking or otherwise deteriorating. It is usually larger than regular brick and is often molded by hand.

PLASTERING

Plastering whole walls and ceilings is not a job for the novice do-it-yourselfer. To produce finished plaster work over large surfaces requires long experience. In case you would like to experiment on a modest scale, however, here is the general procedure.

A professional plaster job usually consists of three coats—a rough or "scratch" coat is applied directly to the wood or metal lath; a "brown" coat is applied over this; and a thin, smooth finishing coat is finally skimmed over the brown coat, which has been roughened to make it hold. The first two coats are made of gypsum or hydrated lime plaster mixed with sand and with cattle or goat hair (or in cheaper jobs, jute,

QUANTITIES OF MATERIAL REQUIRED FOR BRICK WALLS*

Wall area (square feet)	WALL THICKNESS							
	4 inches		8 inches		12 inches		16 inches	
	Number of bricks	Cubic feet of mortar	Number of bricks	Cubic feet of mortar	Number of bricks	Cubic feet of mortar	Number of bricks	Cubic feet of mortar
1	6.17	0.08	12.33	0.2	18.49	0.32	24.65	0.44
10	61.7	0.8	123.3	2	184.9	3.2	246.5	4.4
100	617	8	1,233	20	1,849	32	2,465	44
200	1,234	16	2,466	40	3,698	64	4,930	88
300	1,851	24	3,699	60	5,547	96	7,395	132
400	2,468	32	4,932	80	7,396	128	9,860	176
500	3,085	40	6,165	100	9,245	160	12,325	220
600	3,712	48	7,398	120	11,094	192	14,790	264
700	4,319	56	8,631	140	12,943	224	17,253	308
800	4,936	64	9,864	160	14,792	256	19,720	352
900	5,553	72	10,970	180	16,641	288	22,185	396
1,000	6,170	80	12,330	200	18,490	320	24,650	440

* Quantities are based on ½-inch-thick mortar joint. For ⅜-inch-thick joint, use 80 percent of these quantities. For ⅝-inch-thick joint, use 120 percent.

wood fiber, or asbestos) to give the plaster greater strength. The finishing coat usually consists of plaster of Paris mixed with hydrated lime.

A typical formula for the scratch coat might be: 25 pounds of hydrated lime, 100 pounds of dry plastering sand, and ¼ pound of hair or fiber. These ingredients are mixed with water to produce a workable paste stiff enough to cling to the lath and not drop off. The plaster is applied with enough force to cause it to penetrate the openings between the lath and so anchor it firmly. The batch mentioned should cover about 2¼ square yards on wood lath to a thickness of ¼ inch.

The scratch coat is roughened with a comb before it sets hard, to give "teeth" to hold firmly the brown coat, which is applied after the scratch coat has dried. The brown coat usually has a smaller proportion of lime and hair than the scratch coat—say, 12 pounds of hydrated lime, 60 pounds of sand, and 1 ounce of hair, for a batch that would cover the same area to the same thickness. This coat should be applied as straight and as evenly as possible, and within about ⅛ inch of the final finished surface desired.

For a white smooth finish, mix 10 pounds of hydrated lime with 2½ pounds of plaster of Paris. Water is then added to this mixture to form a thick paste, which is applied to the brown coat in two or three very thin layers, one after the other. The brown coat should be thoroughly dry. To make the surface still smoother, go over it as soon as it has initially set with a brush wet with plain water, followed by a steel trowel. Dampen the surface only enough to soften it slightly, then buff it with the trowel.

REPAIRING PLASTER

Cracks, holes, and other surface imperfections on plaster walls can be repaired easily. If the ingredients are at hand, you can make up your own patching plaster or crack filler from one of the following formulas. If they are not, you can buy excellent and inexpensive ready-made preparations at your local paint or hardware store. If a hole is deep, the filling should be built up in two or three layers, letting one set before applying the next. For repairing very thin surface imperfections better use a ready-made spackling compound, which contains a glue as well as plaster for better adhesion.

Filling Cracks in Plaster Walls

Cracked plaster walls can be repaired with plaster of Paris combined with a small amount of slaked lime and mixed with thin glue size. Mix only enough for about 15 minutes' work at a time, as this crack filler hardens quickly.

If plaster walls are to be painted with oil paints, the cracks may be filled with thick white lead paste to which either whiting or plaster of Paris has been added. If the walls have already been painted, the crack filler may be colored with oil pigment to match.

Patching Plaster or Crack Filler

An inexpensive patching plaster or crack filler can be made as follows:

Plaster of Paris	1 pound
Casein glue or yellow dextrin	2 ounces
Whiting	2 ounces

Dental plaster of Paris, if available, is better than the ordinary grade because it does not shrink so much. Mix thoroughly. Stir the mixture into water to make a thick paste, mixing only as much as you can use immediately. Apply to dents or bruises with a flexible putty knife, let dry hard, and sand clean. Apply more after drying, if not puttied up to level the first time.

To prepare a crack filler or cold-water putty, the following may also be used:

Dental plaster of Paris	12 ounces
Yellow dextrin	3 ounces
French ochre or other dry color	1 ounce

Mix thoroughly, then work up only enough with water for immediate use.

Corrective for Soft Plaster

This final coat of plaster sometimes develops soft, chalky areas in dry weather due to too rapid drying. These may be hardened by moistening with this solution:

Zinc sulfate	¼ ounce
Alum	¼ ounce
Water	32 fluid ounces

Plaster Stipple Coat

A stipple coat for use on interior walls or craftwork projects to which you wish to give a stippled and glazed finish can be mixed as follows:

Soft white lead paste	5 pounds
Plaster of Paris	10 pounds

Use flatting oil to make as thin or heavy a consistency as required. For most wall work, thin to a very soft paste that can be brushed on from $\frac{1}{16}$ to $\frac{1}{8}$ inch thick. Then stipple the coating with a floor-scrubbing brush dipped in water, a wad of crumpled paper, or the cut face of a sponge, according to the texture desired. Do not coat too much wall surface before stippling, and avoid any regular pattern effects. Let dry overnight before painting or other finishing.

ROOFING

Nowadays eight of ten homes are roofed with asphalt-strip shingles. Wood shingles, cedar shakes, and asbestos cement roofs comprise the balance. Let's quickly survey these more common roofing materials.

Asphalt Shingles

Today you have a wider choice of asphalt shingles than in former years. When asphalt shingles are manufactured, a felt or fiberglass base is saturated with oily asphalt (not natural asphalt, but the residue left after the fractional distillation of crude oil), and then the top surface is coated with a filled asphalt formulated for best weather resistance. Rock or colored ceramic granules are impressed into this top coating. The heavier the shingle, generally speaking, the better the quality. Since World War II, three-tab asphalt strip shingles weighing 235 pounds per square (100 square feet), which ordinarily last some twenty years before the asphalt dries out and the shingles curl, have been used to roof nearly all moderately priced housing. These shingles are serviceable, inexpensive, and easy to lay—but they look commonplace, and for this reason other roofing materials often were used on more expensive homes.

Then in 1970 one manufacturer, Bird & Sons, Inc., introduced a much heavier two-layer asphalt shingle, a shingle having a cut-out top layer that gave the roofing a texture similar to that of random-laid wood shingles. Style-conscious architects welcomed the idea.

Now every major asphalt shingle manufacturer has a similar two-layered textured asphalt shingle on the market. One manufacturer calls his product Shake-Shingles; another calls his Shangles. Some are random-laid, and some are laid in patterns. These two-layer shingles weigh from 350 to 400 pounds per square, cost roughly twice as much as single-layer 235 pound shingles, and all last 25 years plus.

All asphalt shingles with a rock- or ceramic-granule surface are fire-retardant and most carry an Underwriters' Lab "C" rating. Asphalt shingles with a fiberglass base are even more fire-resistant and are available with an "A" rating. A-rated roofing is required by local codes on homes in some high fire-risk areas, and in many areas it is required on commercial buildings. In most parts of the country, however, using an A-rated rather than a C-rated roofing material on your house will not reduce your fire insurance premium. Nearly all better quality asphalt shingles now are self-sealing for wind resistance. Spots of heat-softening asphalt cement automatically seal down the overlaying shingle when hot summer sunshine warms the roof.

Essentially the same materials used in the manufacture of asphalt-strip shingles can also be used on the job to lay built-up roofing, which is laid by laminating layers of asphalt-saturated felt in mopped asphalt and surfaced with crushed gravel. Ordinarily a built-up roof is the most satisfactory roofing available for flat or very low-pitched roofs.

Cedar Shingles

In years past, cedar shingles were widely used because they were cheap. They're no longer cheap and, moreover, laying wood shingles is slower work requiring more skill than is needed to lay asphalt shingles. A skilled workman can lay over 100 square feet (1 square) of wood shingles per day. Because of the high cost of application, roofers always use best-quality vertical-grain No. 1 Blue Label shingles on roofs. A wood-shingled roof will last some thirty years. Some circumstances (when the attic under the roof lacks ventilation, for example) justify treating the shingles before they are laid with preservative to extend their life. Some mills supply shingles factory-stained in attractive colors.

Shingles are sawed. Shakes are split. Cedar shakes have a rough, rustic look that no other roofing really matches. They have excellent thermal characteristics, and they are not difficult to lay. Like wood shingles, shakes can be applied over either spaced or solid roof sheathing.

Asbestos Cement Shingles

These have obvious advantages: They are completely fireproof and nearly everlasting, but they also have two drawbacks—they're much more expensive than other roofing materials, and they are considerably heavier. Manufacturers' literature gives application instructions. A special cutter, which can be rented, is needed to install them. Roof valleys generally are flashed with sheet stainless steel, and the shingles are fastened with stainless steel nails. Before selecting asbestos cement shingles for your roof, be sure that the roof framing will support their weight.

There are other roofing materials that you may want to consider—roll roofing, metal shingles, slates and tiles—but these are less commonly used.

Estimating Your Needs

When you've selected a roofing material, the next problem will be to figure out how much of it you'll need. To calculate the area of your roof, first figure the ground area of your house, including eave and cornice overhang in square feet, multiplying length by width. Next determine the roof's pitch, or degree of slope, sighting over a protractor to find the angle of the roof above horizontal. Then, using this angle, make a drawing using a carpenter's square and measure the "rise" in inches per foot of "run," and add a percentage as below to ground area of the house.

3-inch rise per foot add 3 percent

4-inch rise per foot add 5½ percent

5-inch rise per foot add 8½ percent

6-inch rise per foot add 12 percent

8-inch rise per foot add 20 percent

12-inch rise per foot add 42 percent

18-inch rise per foot add 80 percent

Dividing the total by 100 will give you the number of squares of roof area. Then add one square of roofing for each 100 lineal feet of valley to determine the total number of squares of roofing needed.

From the roof's area in squares you can also figure the number of rolls of 15-pound felt underlayer you'll need. This special asphalt-saturated roofer's felt is recommended for use under all asphalt or asbestos cement shingles. It minimizes condensation problems. Do not use heavier vapor-barrier material in place of roofer's felt. The underlayer not only protects the roof deck from any wind-driven rain that might work in under the shingles, but it also protects the shingles from contact with resinous spots in the deck, which because of chemical incompatibility might damage the shingles. A standard roll of 36-inch-wide 15-pound felt underlayer covers four squares of roof deck.

Other Roofing Materials

The quantity of other materials you'll need will depend upon the roof and the roofing applied. Usually metal or vinyl drip strips should be used along the roof's eaves, and also, unless the roof has wood drip strips, along the rakes to cover the edges of the sheathing. Along the eaves, install the drip strip under the underlayer. Along the rake, nail it over the underlayer. Measure the number of lineal feet of roof edge to figure the number of lengths needed.

The material needed for valley linings will depend upon the valley treatment used. Use the valley treatment the roofing manufacturer recommends unless you're an experienced roofer. Most manufacturers of asphalt-strip shingles now recommend "closed" valleys, with the courses of shingles laid right across the valley on a 90-pound roll-roofing lining. A woven valley offers the advantage of adding extra thicknesses of roofing in the valley, which is the roof's most vulnerable point. But these extra layers of roofing form noticeable humps along the valley, which some roofers find objectionable, and those who do still prefer traditional open valleys—open-valley flashing can be either doubled 90-pound roll roofing, painted galvanized sheet metal, or sheet copper.

Most asphalt-shingle manufacturers make special shingles for capping hips and ridges that match their standard shingles. The hot-dip galvanized roofing nails used should be long enough to penetrate the deck's sheathing. You'll need about 2½ pounds of 1½-inch nails per square of roofing, together with a few pounds of 1-inch nails for the 15-pound felt underlayer.

WALL PANELING

There are various wall paneling materials on the market—plywood, fiberboard, gypsum board, and hardboard being the most popular. These drywall materials are easy to install because they are available in 4 × 8-foot panels and vary in thickness from ¼ to ⅝ inch thick depending on the material. They may be fastened to the walls with nails or contact cement. (For details on the latter, see Chapter 5.)

To estimate the number of panels required, measure the perimeter of the room. This is merely the total of the widths of each wall in the room. Then divide the perimeter by 4 to determine the number of 4 × 8-foot panels needed.

For example, if the walls of a room measure 14 feet + 14 feet + 16 feet + 16 feet, this would equal 60 feet, which divided by 4 gives 15 panels required. To allow for areas such as windows, doors, fireplaces, etc., use the following deductions:

Door	½ panel
Window	¼ panel
Fireplace	½ panel

Since this room has a fireplace, two doors, and two windows, the actual number of panels needed for the room would be 13 pieces (15 pieces minus 2 total deductions). If the perimeter of the room falls in between the figures in table, use the next highest number to determine panels required. These figures are for rooms with 8-foot ceiling heights or less. For walls over 8 feet high, select a paneling that has V grooves and that will "stack," allowing panel grooves to line up perfectly from floor to ceiling.

WALLCOVERING

Wallcoverings, including wallpapers, are still a popular form of decoration. To estimate the amount of wallcovering required for a job, keep in mind that the roll is a standard unit of measurement in the wallcovering industry. The material may come in double A or triple A roll bolts, but the roll is still the standard unit of measurement, and each roll contains approximately 36 square feet.

However, when hanging the material you will always have a certain amount of waste while trimming and cutting the strips to size, so you will actually obtain approximately 30 square feet of usable material out of each roll.

To figure how many rolls you will need for a given room, first measure the distance around the room. Then multiply this figure by the distance from the baseboard to the ceiling. This will give the number of square feet of wall area. For example:

Your room is 15 by 20 feet and 8 feet high. The distance around the room is 15 + 15 + 20 + 20 = 70 feet. Multiply this by the height of the wall: $70 \times 8 = 560$ square feet of wall area. But there are doors and windows that require no paper, and you must deduct this space. For ex-

ESTIMATING WALLCOVERING

Distance around room (feet)	Single rolls for wall areas at ceiling height of			Number of yards for borders	Single rolls for ceilings
	8 feet	9 feet	10 feet		
28	8	8	10	11	2
30	8	8	10	11	2
32	8	10	10	12	2
34	10	10	12	13	4
36	10	10	12	13	4
38	10	12	12	14	4
40	10	12	12	15	4
42	12	12	14	15	4
44	12	12	14	16	4
46	12	14	14	17	6
48	14	14	16	17	6
50	14	14	16	18	6
52	14	14	16	19	6
54	14	16	18	19	6
56	14	16	18	20	8
58	16	16	18	21	8
60	16	18	20	21	8
62	16	18	20	22	8
64	16	18	20	22	8
66	18	20	20	23	10
68	18	20	22	24	10
70	18	20	22	25	10
72	18	20	22	25	12
74	20	22	22	26	12
76	20	22	24	27	12
78	20	22	24	27	14
80	20	22	26	28	14
82	22	24	26	29	14
84	22	24	26	30	16
86	22	24	26	30	16
88	24	26	28	31	16
90	24	26	28	32	18

Note: This quick-reference chart is based on a single roll covering 30 square feet; deduct one single roll for every two ordinary size doors or windows or every 30 square feet of opening. It is wise to buy one or two extra rolls in case you ruin some of the covering in hanging. Most dealers will take back uncut rolls. You may wish to keep some covering for patching.

ample, your room contains one door, 7 feet by 4 feet, and two windows, each one 5 feet by 3 feet. Multiply height by width to get the square feet in each.

$$7 \times 4 \times 1 = 28 \text{ square feet of door space}$$

$$5 \times 3 \times 2 = 30 \text{ square feet of window space}$$

Add these to get the total amount of space you will deduct from the room size:

$$28 + 30 = 58 \text{ square feet}$$

Subtract this from the total:

$$560 \text{ square feet} - 58 \text{ square feet} =$$
$$502 \text{ square feet of wall area to be papered.}$$

Now divide this figure by 30; this room would require approximately 17 rolls of wallcovering. Estimate the number of rolls of ceiling covering needed in the same way, multiplying the length of the ceiling by the width to get the square feet.

For a quick reference aid in estimating the amount of coverage needed, use the table on page 189.

RESILIENT FLOORING

Practicality, convenience, ease of application, and long wear are a few of the reasons why resilient flooring continues to be one of the most popular choices of homeowners everywhere. With the tremendous variety of materials, designs, and colors available, it is possible to create just about any floor scheme that strikes your fancy. For example, you can install a floor of one color, or you can combine different colors into a custom-floor design that matches room requirements and individual taste. If you prefer the natural look, you will find countless resilient materials that closely resemble the appearance of slate, brick, wood, terrazzo, marble, and stone. Many of these floors feature an embossed surface texture that adds a striking note to the design.

Types of Resilient Floors

Resilient floors are manufactured in two basic types: sheet materials and tiles. The latter are cemented in place to serve as a permanent floor.

Sheet materials are also cemented in place, but in some cases can be installed loosely like rugs. Tiles generally come in 9- or 12-inch squares; sheet materials are available in continuous rolls up to 12 feet wide.

Estimating Number of Tiles Needed

The accompanying table will aid you in figuring the number of tiles to complete an installation job. For instance, if you are working with a floor area that is 280 square feet (a 14×20-foot family room), and you want to use 9×9-inch tiles, the table indicates 356 tiles for 200 square feet and 143 tiles for 80 square feet, a total number of 499 tiles.

When ordering tiles, it is most important to consider the waste factors. In our example, the allowance for waste is 7 percent of the total number of tiles, or an extra 35 tiles. This would make a grand total of 534 tiles. Since tiles are usually boxed 80 to a carton, this would mean that we need over 6¾ cartons. Even if the dealer is willing to split a carton, it would be wise to take the seven full cartons. This assures an adequate supply of tiles from the same lot and also allows for replacement if any should be needed.

ESTIMATING TILE QUANTITIES

Square feet	Number of tiles needed (inches)			Square feet	Number of tiles needed (inches)		
	9 × 9	12 × 12	9 × 18		9 × 9	12 × 12	9 × 18
1	2	1	1	60	107	60	54
2	4	2	2	70	125	70	63
3	6	3	3	80	143	80	72
4	8	4	4	90	160	90	80
5	9	5	5	100	178	100	90
6	11	6	6	200	356	200	178
7	13	7	7	300	534	300	267
8	15	8	8	400	712	400	356
9	16	9	8	500	890	500	445
10	18	10	9	600	1,068	600	534
20	36	20	18	700	1,246	700	623
30	54	30	27	800	1,424	800	712
40	72	40	36	900	1,602	900	801
50	89	50	45	1,000	1,780	1,000	890

GUIDE TO RESILIENT FLOORING

Material	Backing	How installed	Where to install	Ease of installation	Ease of maintenance	Resilience and durability	Quiet
TILE MATERIALS							
Asphalt	none	adhesive	anywhere	fair	difficult	poor	very poor
Vinyl	none	adhesive	anywhere	easy	very easy	excellent	poor
Asbestos vinyl	none	adhesive	anywhere	easy	easy	good–excellent	fair
Rubber	none	adhesive	anywhere	fair	easy	good	good
Cork	none	adhesive	on or above grade	fair	fair (with vinyl, good)	good	excellent
SHEET MATERIALS							
Inlaid vinyl	felt	adhesive	above grade	fair	easy	good	fair
	foam and felt	adhesive	above grade	difficult	easy	good	good
	asbestos	adhesive	anywhere	very difficult	easy	excellent	fair
	foam	adhesive	anywhere	very difficult	easy	excellent	good
Printed vinyl	felt	loose-lay	above grade	easy	fair	poor	poor
	felt	adhesive	above grade	fair	easy	fair	poor
	foam and felt	loose-lay	above grade	easy	easy	fair	good
	asbestos and foam	adhesive or loose-lay	anywhere	fair–easy	easy	good	good
	foam	loose-lay	anywhere	easy	easy	good	good

ALLOWANCE FOR WASTE

1–50 square feet	14 percent
50–100 square feet	10 percent
100–200 square feet	8 percent
200–300 square feet	7 percent
300–1,000 square feet	5 percent
Over 1,000 square feet	3 percent

5

Glues, Adhesives, Cements, and Sealing Compounds

Today, there is a seemingly endless variety of glues, adhesives, and cements on the market. To make a proper selection, two factors must be taken into consideration:

TYPE OF MATERIAL.   Are you trying to join porous or nonporous material? Wood, paper, and cloth are porous materials that can be bonded by a wide variety of glues. Nonporous materials such as glass, tile, metal, porcelain, and most plastics generally require a different type of glue. If you are trying to join two dissimilar materials such as vinyl and wood, you will need a glue that will do an adequate job on both.

CONDITIONS.   Will the joint be exposed to moisture, heat, or cold? Do the parts to be joined fit snugly together, or is a good filler needed? Also, what kind of stress will the joint be subjected to? Some glues are very strong when the joint is subjected to shear forces, but weak when the materials are in tension. Another consideration is the toxic effect of the glue. If you are working in an area with poor ventilation, or repairing a child's toy, a nontoxic glue is essential.

194

Types of Glues, Adhesives, and Cements

Fortunately, the glues found in retail stores are limited to the five following categories. If you remember them, selecting an adhesive for your needs ceases to be a chore.

CYANOACRYLATE. This adhesive—better known as *super glue* because of its great tensile strength—sets (hardens) as soon as chemicals in the glue combine with moisture in the air. It is the quickest setting glue being sold to consumers. Surfaces bonded together with cyanoacrylate require no clamping and take hold within 30 to 90 seconds. Full strength is attained in 12 to 24 hours.

Cyanoacrylate bonds together practically all solid, nonporous materials, either to themselves or to another nonporous surface. This includes metal, rubber, jewelry, china, glassware, most plastics, most ceramics, and some hardwoods.

The key word here is *nonporous.* Cyanoacrylate should not be used on such porous materials as softwoods. (A few cyanoacrylates will adhere to softwoods; the addition of an ingredient called orthonol is the "secret.") Cyanoacrylate resists water, extreme temperature, and most chemicals. (*Caution:* Cyanoacrylate should not be used with abandon. The glue will bond skin together almost instantaneously, and there have been cases of people having to have surgery to get fingers unglued.) You can tell if the glue is a cyanoacrylate, because the term appears on the package.

It is not economical to use cyanoacrylate if another type of glue can be used instead. Cyanoacrylate is the most expensive adhesive sold.

SOLVENT-TYPE GLUES. Solvent-type glues consist of an adhesive base (vinyl resin or acrylic resin), perhaps fillers and pigments, and a solvent that makes the mixture spreadable. As the solvent evaporates, the adhesive sets. The ingredients in solvent-type adhesive include toluene, methyl ethyl ketone, and acetone. You may see reference to this on the package.

All solvent-type adhesives—or water-type adhesives—are not the same. The degree of adhesion depends on the adhesive base. For example, glues using a *vinyl* resin adhesive base bond wood, metal, glass, concrete, and most plastics to themselves or each other.

Adhesives using an *acrylic* resin adhesive base bond wood, metal, glass, and concrete to themselves or each other, but do not accommodate plastic. However, acrylic resin adhesive does, and in addition, bonds masonry and plaster.

The so-called liquid solder, aluminum and steel mender, plastic solder, and silicone glues are also usually of the solvent-type adhesive. The latter, available in white, black, and clear, are waterproof and withstand a wide temperature range, are flexible and will join fabrics, glass, ceramics, metal, tiles, paper, and leather. Silicone glue is also used as a caulking around showers and tubs. It is a fairly strong adhesive, but do not try to paint over it—paint will not stick to most silicone glues.

Consider, too, so-called contact cements. They do several things, chief among them being that they make plastic laminates adhere to wood—which is something the others will not do—because contact cement has a neoprene rubber base. As its name implies, it bonds on contact. A coat of cement is applied to both surfaces to be joined, the glue is allowed to dry just enough to become tacky, and the surfaces are pressed together. The bond is immediate and the pieces cannot be positioned once stuck together. It is water resistant and strong in shear, but most cements are flammable and the fumes are toxic.

While most so-called panel adhesives are of solvent-base adhesive, a few are water based. Actually, one of the surest ways of determining that you are buying a solvent-type adhesive is a warning on the package that says something like this: "Danger: Extremely flammable. Vapors may cause flash fire. Harmful if swallowed. Vapors harmful, toxic."

Another type of contact cement made by the same company states, "No fire hazard. No sniffing problem." This notice appears on water-type contact cement, which is not flammable or toxic.

Solvent- and water-type adhesives do the same job as long as they have the same adhesive base—acrylic resin, vinyl resin, or neoprene rubber. Because solvent evaporates quicker than water, the only difference is in the length of time it takes for the adhesive to set.

WATER-TYPE GLUES.   The composition and action of water-type glues are the same as that of solvent-type glue, except that water is used as a vehicle. Although water-type adhesives work slower than solvent-type glue, they contain no toxic solvents. They are safe to breathe and will not ignite if exposed to flame. Another advantage of water-type glue is that your tools are easily cleaned with soapy water.

White glue is one of the most common and useful household glues because it sets relatively fast, dries almost clear, and works well on wood, leather, cork, and paper. It is strong, but not water resistant, and it softens under heat. A similar type of glue, aliphatic resin, is stronger and more tolerant of high temperatures.

There is also a water-type glue in powdered form. This is a plastic resin glue; it's used for bonding all types of woods. The powder is mixed with water, spread, and clamped. Of course, one of the oldest water-type powdered glue is casein glue. Made from milk protein and mixed with water to form a paste, it has good strength and is water resistant once dry. It works well on wood, and like vegetable glue, it is nontoxic and a good choice for children's toys.

TWO-PART GLUES.   In this category are epoxy and resorcinol. One part contains the glue, and the other contains a catalyst or hardener. When the two parts are mixed together in correct proportion, chemical action takes place and the glue sets.

Epoxy is fast-setting, with hardening taking place in from 5 minutes to 1 hour, depending on the formulation. Epoxy is formulated primarily for working with metals.

Resorcinol glue provides complete waterproofing. It is a wood glue that is used primarily for repairing boats, but it can be used also for repairing outdoor furniture and other wooden fixtures that are exposed to water.

There are two drawbacks to two-part adhesives. First, the mixture must be exact. Disproportionate amounts result in a weak repair.

Second, both epoxy and resorcinol have a short pot life. Once the two parts are mixed together, you must work rapidly to complete repairs before the glue begins to harden.

ANIMAL HIDE GLUES.   These are among the oldest types of wood glue (if not the oldest), and the source of all the old jokes about broken-down, swaybacked horses and the glue factory. Yes, the glue is made from the hides, bones, sinews, and hide fleshings of animals. Most animal glues come in dry form and are prepared for use by soaking in water and then melting, and are applied hot. Liquid animal glues, ready to use at room temperature, are also available. Animal glues come in different grades, the higher grades being preferable for joint work, and the lower grades for veneering. Hot animal glues develop strength first by cooling and gelling and later by drying, and are often preferred for spreading on irregularly shaped joints and for furniture. The chief disadvantages of these glues are their relatively high cost, the importance of temperature control in their use, and the low moisture resistance of the joints.

MAKING YOUR OWN ADHESIVES AND SEALERS

Hide Glue

Although the ready convenience of liquid, casein, and synthetic resin glues has caused these newer products to largely replace hot hide glue in the home workshop, this versatile and time-tested adhesive is still widely used in commercial wood fabrication and by the meticulous cabinetmaker. It combines qualities obtainable in no other type of adhesive at comparable cost.

Hide or animal glue can be bought by the pound in flake or ground form. If protected from moisture, this dry glue will keep indefinitely. The proper proportion of glue to water must be determined by experiment, if it is not stated on the glue you buy, as this may vary somewhat with a particular glue and job.

As a test, try 1 part glue to 2 parts water, measured by weight. Add the glue to the cold water and stir until the glue is thoroughly wet. Let soak for an hour, or until the glue is thoroughly swollen. Melt the glue by heating the combination to 145° F, either in a regular glue pot or in a Pyrex or stainless steel container heated by hot water. (It will lose strength if overheated.) After stirring into a smooth solution, it is ready to use at 140° to 145° F.

Don't make the glue too thin under the common misconception that it must thoroughly penetrate the wood in order to produce tendrils or hooks that will mechanically attach the glue to the pores of the wood. This can only result in weak and glue-starved joists. Hide glue does not work by hooking on. It apparently bonds a substance to itself because of a true electrochemical attraction between its own molecules and those of the substance. (For example, hide glue will grip smooth, nonporous glass with a bond stronger than the glass.) For maximum strength of adhesion, make the glue just thick enough so it will form a thin but continuous film between the wood surfaces.

Here are the basic rules for making a perfect bond:

1. Apply the glue with a brush in a thin continuous film to one surface only of the matching parts to be joined.
2. Permit the glue film to thicken slightly to a tacky condition before applying pressure.
3. Apply enough pressure to squeeze out the excess glue and to bring perfect contact over the entire assembled area.
4. Maintain this pressure until the initial set of the glue is strong enough to keep the parts from separating.

When held at the recommended temperature of 140° to 145° F, and covered to prevent evaporation, hot animal glue will keep in usable condition for at least 8 hours.

If further mechanical operations are to be done on a glued piece, it is best to wait at least overnight to allow the glue to develop its maximum strength.

If you use this type of glue in small quantities, it may be more convenient to buy it in combined powder form, ready to mix with water. For large-scale gluing, you may want to mix your own at the place where it is to be used. In this case, do not mix more than you need, or mix it too soon, for it will remain usable in wet form for only 6 or 7 hours.

	Parts by weight
Casein	100
Water	150
Sodium hydroxide	11
Water	50
Hydrated lime	20
Water	50

Mix in glass, enameled, or stainless steel vessels. Soak the casein in the proportion of water indicated for 15 to 30 minutes. Add the solution of sodium hydroxide in water (*Caution:* Be careful with sodium hydroxide; it is caustic to skin and surroundings) and stir thoroughly until the casein is completely dissolved. Then add the lime suspended in its proportion of water and stir until smooth.

A casein glue with better water resistance can be made by omitting the sodium hydroxide and adding sodium silicate and a salt of copper. Here is a formula of this type developed by the Forest Products Laboratory:

	Parts by weight
Casein	100
Water	200
Hydrated lime	25
Water	100
Sodium silicate solution	
40° Baumé	70
Cupric chloride or	
cupric sulfate	2 to 3
Water	30 to 50

Stir the casein in the water, and let soak as in the previous formula. Stir into it the dissolved copper salt. Mix the hydrated lime and water in another container and, while stirring constantly, add it to the casein-water-copper mixture. In about 1 minute after the lime and casein have been united, the glue will thicken a little. Immediately pour in the sodium silicate and continue stirring until the glue is free from lumps.

OTHER ADHESIVES

Adhesive	Characteristics	Typical uses	What materials
Hot melt	Chalksize polyethylene-base cartridges used in electric glue gun; fast-setting, waterproof	Spot gluing; small-job repairs like broken or loose chair rungs, wood-to-metal joints	Wood, paper, cloth, leather, fiberglass, rough surfaces
Household cement	Crystal clear, waterproof	Mending china and glass	China, glass, metal, leather, canvas, wood
Liquid rubbery	For flexible repairs; caulks, bonds, insulates, rustproofs	Motor belts, weatherstrips, rubber inflatables, tents, tarps	Rubber, fabrics, plastics, glass, metal
Model cement	Colorless, fast-drying	Building and repairing models, toys	Polystyrene, balsa wood
Old-fashioned glue	Liquid hide or fish in bottles or cans	Furniture assembly and repair	Wood, leather, cloth, cardboard, glass, china
Plastic mender	Waterproof, flexible mender for most plastics	Swimming pools, rainwear, inflatables	Vinyl, acrylic, phenolic and styrene plastics; also china, glass, paper, leather, canvas
Vinyl seal	Repairs vinyl plastic without patches	Seals leaks and rips in pools, rafts, shower curtains, raincoats, beach toys, seat covers	Vinyl plastic
Fabric mender	Use instead of sewing	Repairing rips, tears, burns, reinforcing worn spots in fabric	Cotton, wool, canvas, Leatherette, felt
Marine repair	Nonrusting, flexible	Repairing water or gas tanks, anchoring screws, bolts, fittings, filing gouges and dry rot in planking	Wood, fiberglass, metal

OTHER ADHESIVES (continued)

Adhesive	Characteristics	Typical uses	What materials
Fixture	Weatherproof, waterproof, fast grab	Mounting house numbers, brackets, electric boxes	Wood, brick, concrete, glass, ceramic tile, metal
Chair fixer	Use with flexible needle for repairing furniture without disassembling	Loose chair rungs, table legs, drawers, etc.	Wood
Rubber cement	Fast drying, noncurling	Graphic art, paper	Paper, cloth, wood, leather, rubber
Mastics	Synthetic latex or rubber-based adhesives that are used in caulking guns or troweled or for floors and walls	Used for ceiling tiles, floor tiles, wall paneling	Wood, ceramic tile, panel boards, ceiling tiles, floor tile of various material

How to Make Your Own Paste

The word "paste" come from the late Latin word "pasta," which means roughly a thick mixture of flour and water. Down through the ages this useful adhesive, used largely for sticking paper, has been made either from this combination, from water and a derivative of flour such as starch or gluten, or from some admixture of ingredients that looks and acts like its ancestor. Here are a few sample formulas:

FLOUR PASTE.   This simple and inexpensive paste is excellent for children's paper work and as a general household paste for emergencies.

Wheat flour	4 tablespoons
Cold water	6 tablespoons
Boiling water	1½ cups

Blend the flour into the cold water to make a smooth paste. Stir this into the boiling water in a saucepan. Boil over very low heat for about 5 minutes, stirring and smoothing constantly to remove lumps. Use when cold.

STARCH PASTE.   Here is a thinner paste that is just as easy to make:

Cornstarch	3	tablespoons
Cold water	4	tablespoons
Boiling water	2	cups

Blend the starch into the cold water to make a smooth paste. Stir this into the boiling water. Stir until the opaque white liquid becomes translucent. Use when cold.

HOUSEHOLD PASTE.   This paste may be used for making scrapbooks, mounting photographs, preparing paper decorations, and so on:

White dextrin	9	ounces
Water	15	fluid ounces
Sugar	½ ounce	
Glycerin	½ fluid ounce	
Alum	¼ fluid ounce	

Stir the dextrin (which should be the white and not the yellow variety) in 13 ounces of the water and heat to 140° F, with continued stirring, until completely dissolved. Dissolve the sugar, glycerin, and alum in the rest of the water. Add this solution to the first one and heat to 176° F until the combined solution becomes clear.

LIBRARY PASTE.   For mounting valuable pictures and clippings on paper, here is the formula for a paste used by a number of important museums and libraries:

Wheat flour	18 ounces
Water	4¾ pints
Alum	¼ ounce
Formaldehyde	¼ fluid ounce

Blend the flour with part of the water to form a thin paste. Heat the rest of the water to a boil and dissolve the alum in it. Then stir the flour paste into the boiling water. Continue to heat, with constant stirring, for another 5 minutes over a very low flame or in the top of a double boiler. Then add formaldehyde to the mixture. The formaldehyde will help to preserve the paste for some time.

WALLPAPER PASTES.   Here is a good paste for hanging wall-coverings:

Wheat flour	8 ounces
Water	1 quart
Powdered rosin	⅓ ounce

Blend the flour into 8 ounces of the water to make a smooth paste. Bring the rest of the water to a boil in a saucepan or the top part of a double boiler. Then stir in the flour paste, bring nearly to a boil again, and sprinkle in the rosin. Hold at this temperature for about 5 minutes while stirring and smoothing constantly to remove lumps. If the paste is too thick when cool, stir in a little more hot water.

● Here is another wheat flour paste that uses alum in place of rosin:

Wheat flour	1 pound
Cold water	1 pint
Boiling water	3 pints
Alum	½ ounce
Hot water	2 ounces

Blend the flour into the cold water to make a smooth paste. Stir this into the boiling water, and continue stirring and boiling very gently until the liquid thickens. Dissolve the alum in the small amount of hot water and then stir this into the paste.

● Some paperhangers prefer a paste made from rye flour, which depends more on gluten than on starch for its adhesiveness. Here is a typical formula for rye flour paste:

Rye flour	1 pound
Cold water	1 pint
Boiling water	1½ quarts
Powdered rosin	½ ounce

Blend the rye flour with the cold water to make a smooth paste. Stir this into the boiling water and sprinkle in the rosin. Reheat nearly to boiling and stir for several minutes until the paste is smooth. If the paste is too thick when cool, it may be thinned with a little hot water.

FLEXIBLE PASTE.   The glycerin in this paste helps keep it pliant. It is useful for cloth or paper where the joints must be flexed.

Cornstarch	2 ounces
White dextrin	1 ounce
Cold water	4 fluid ounces
Borax	½ ounce
Boiling water	1 quart
Glycerin	2 fluid ounces

Mix the cornstarch and dextrin in the cold water to make a smooth paste. Dissolve the borax in the boiling water, add the glycerin, and then stir the dextrin-starch mixture into this solution. Reheat nearly to the boiling point, and stir for several minutes longer until the paste is smooth.

HOBBY AND CRAFT PASTE.   Made from household ingredients, this paste is good for fastening together paper toys and decorations, mounting photos, and so on:

Cornstarch	¼ cup
Water	¾ cup

Corn syrup (Karo), light	2	tablespoons
White vinegar	1	teaspoon

Combine these ingredients in a medium-size saucepan. Cook, stirring constantly, over medium heat until mixture is thick. Remove from heat. In another vessel, stir together the following until smooth:

Cornstarch	¼ cup
Water	¾ cup

Immediately stir, a little at a time, into the thickened mixture. Stir smooth after each addition. Finally, to act as a preservative, stir in:

Oil of wintergreen	¼ teaspoon

The resulting paste may be used immediately, but will set up to thicker consistency in 24 hours. Stored in a covered container, it will keep about 2 months.

Mucilage

Gum acacia	2	ounces
Cornstarch	2	ounces
Sugar	8	ounces
Benzoic acid	50	grains
Water	20	fluid ounces

Use powdered gum acacia. Soak it in part of the water until it becomes jellylike. Mix the cornstarch and sugar with enough water to make a smooth paste. Combine these mixtures, add the rest of the water in which you have dissolved the benzoic acid, and boil gently until the solution becomes clear.

Another mucilage substitutes glycerin for the starch and sugar:

Gum acacia	2	ounces
Glycerin	2	fluid ounces
Benzoic acid	50	grains
Water	30	fluid ounces

Prepare the gum acacia as in the previous formula. Stir the resulting jelly into the water in which has been dissolved the glycerin and benzoic acid. Boil gently, with stirring, until smooth and clear.

Cement for Porcelain and Earthenware

Porcelain and earthenware articles that are not heated in use can be repaired or cemented together securely with ordinary sealing wax or stick shellac. The trick is to first heat the parts sufficiently so they will melt the shellac or wax. A little of either of these materials is smeared on the edges to be joined and the parts are then held or clamped tightly together until cool. If melted wax or shellac is applied to cold edges, the joint will break apart at the slightest strain.

China Cement

Stir plaster of Paris into a thick solution of gum arabic until it becomes a viscous paste. Apply to broken edges of china and clamp the parts tightly together until the cement has hardened.

Marble Cement

This is a good cement for mending marble or any other kind of stone:

Litharge	20 parts
Quicklime	1 part
Boiled linseed oil	enough to make thick paste

Mix the litharge and lime thoroughly. Then work the linseed oil into this mixture to form a thick paste. It sets in a few hours, having the appearance of light stone.

Another marble cement can be made of the following:

Portland cement	12 parts
Hydrated lime	6 parts
Fine sand	6 parts
Kiselguhr	1 part
Sodium silicate solution	enough to make thick paste

Mix the dry ingredients thoroughly and then mix into a thick paste with the sodium silicate solution. The object to be cemented need not be warmed. The cement will set within 24 hours and be as hard as the original stone.

Aquarium Cement

This term is applied to various waterproof cements used in making tanks constructed of glass panels fitted in metal frames. One of the most reliable aquarium cements is litharge–glycerin cement, described in a separate item below. Here is another:

Litharge	3 parts
Plaster of Paris	3 parts
Fine white sand	3 parts
Powdered rosin	1 part
Boiled linseed oil	enough to make thick putty

Mix the dry ingredients well, and then work in enough of the boiled linseed oil to make a thick putty. Let it stand 4 or 5 hours before using it, kneading it occasionally during this time. Apply it by working it well into all the joints of the tank, then let it set for several days. Finally test for leaks by filling the tank with water. Before putting fish in the tank, wash the tank out several times.

Cement for Roof Flashings

Where sheet metal meets chimneys, or where it is desired to repair open seams in a metal roof without soldering, use white lead and washed and dried sand mixed into a thick paste with boiled linseed oil and a few drops of a drier. If white lead paste is used, only a small amount of linseed oil will be needed. The sand acts as a filler that keeps the joint from opening up.

Skylight Cement

Red lead, powder	8 ounces
Litharge	16 ounces
White lead, dry	24 ounces
Linseed oil	8 fluid ounces
Varnish	8 fluid ounces

If white lead paste is used instead of the dry form, decrease the amount of linseed oil, adding just enough oil to give the desired consistency.

Oil-Proof Cements

A stopper for small leaks in water- and oil-containing vessels, which can be easily removed when a permanent repair is to be made, can be made of the following:

Water	7 parts
Gelatin powder	2 parts
Glycerin	1 part

Put the water in the top part of a double boiler, add the gelatin and let it soak for about an hour. Then heat the water to about 140° F. As soon as the gelatin melts, stir until it is uniformly distributed throughout the water. Finally stir in the glycerin. Apply it warm to the leaks. It will stiffen rapidly.

An emergency stopper for small leaks in oil-containing pipe lines and containers can be made by mixing up a stiff paste of flour and molasses. Work it well into holes or cracks.

Where you can temporarily shut.off pressure, a tight seal can be made with a stiff paste of sodium silicate or water glass with whiting or precipitated chalk.

For a permanent seal against oil leaks, as well as water and acid, try litharge–glycerin cement, described below.

The following cement will produce a leakproof barrier between joints on gasoline, water, or oil lines:

Powdered iron	1 part
Portland cement	1 part
Litharge	1 part
Sodium silicate solution	enough to make paste

Mix these powders thoroughly and then stir in enough sodium silicate solution to make a paste of the desired consistency. The cement will harden in about 20 minutes.

Litharge–Glycerin Acid-Resisting Cement

Here is a cement useful for a number of applications for which ordinary cements would be neither practical nor desirable. It will withstand an unusual degree of combined heat and moisture. Its most conspicuous feature, however, is its resistance to practically all acids, provided they are not of full strength. It may be used for making watertight connections between iron pipes and porcelain fittings. It also makes an excellent aquarium cement.

Make it by mixing thoroughly—preferably by grinding in a mortar—enough litharge with 95-percent glycerin to form a paste of the desired consistency.

This combination remains soft for only 10 minutes, then sets in the form of a chemical compound of incredible hardness. The addition of about 10 percent of inert matter such as silex, Fuller's earth, or asbestos flock will delay the setting time considerably and also help prevent cracking.

Other Acid-Resisting Cements

Mix asbestos powder in sodium silicate solution to the consistency of thin paste. If allowed to dry for 24 hours, the resulting cement will resist the strongest acids.

Kaolin or china clay mixed to a thick paste with boiled linseed oil also makes an acid-resisting cement.

Quicklime mixed to a thick paste with boiled linseed oil is a time-tested formula for a cement that will resist both heat and acids.

Iron Cement

Here is a cement that can be used to fill holes and cracks in cast-iron parts, make steam-tight joints, or cement iron parts into stone or cement:

Fine iron filings	40 parts
Flowers of sulfur	10 parts
Sal ammoniac	1 part
Portland cement	20 parts
Water	enough to make thick paste

First mix the dry ingredients thoroughly together. Then blend in the water, after adding a few drops of a wetting agent or a household liquid detergent to help the water wet the sulfur. Mix just before using, as this cement sets quickly.

It works by chemical reaction. Mixed with sulfur in the presence of an electrically conducting solution of sal ammoniac, the iron first rusts and then reverts to iron sulfide. In doing so, the iron expands, cementing the mass solidly together.

Sodium Silicate Cements

When mixed into a thick paste with certain white or colored dry pigments, sodium silicate solution or water glass will harden overnight into a strong and waterproof cement that can be used for mending and filling cracks in ceramics and other materials. Here are some of the colors you can make and the pigments to use to make them:

WHITE: Whiting or precipitated chalk.

GRAY: Zinc dust. This combination will make an exceedingly hard cement, which, on buffing, will exhibit the white and brilliant appearance of metallic zinc. It may be used to mend and fill ornaments and objects of zinc. It will also stick well to metals, stone, and wood.

BRIGHT GREEN: Powdered copper carbonate.

DARK GREEN: Chromium oxide green pigment.

BLUE: Cobalt blue.

ORANGE-RED: Dry red lead.

BRIGHT RED: Vermilion.

Common or Glazier's Putty

This is an inexpensive and good putty for general use:

Whiting	16 ounces
Boiled linseed oil	9 fluid ounces

Mix the whiting into the oil until it becomes of the usual putty consistency. Because of the differences in the fineness of the whiting, the proportions may vary somewhat. If you have time, let the putty stand in a tightly closed glass or plastic container for a week; if it has then become too soft, work some more whiting into it.

White Lead Putty

Professional painters often consider white-lead putty to be the best for all-round use. You can make this by mixing white-lead paste (white lead ground in linseed oil) with whiting. Work in enough of the whiting to make the putty stiff, but still tacky.

Colored Putty

Colored putty to match paint or to lend a touch of contrast can be made by mixing oil paint with the regular putty. Use colors-in-oil or the thick pigment from the bottom of the paint can. To prevent a streaky appearance, work it well into the putty.

For Removing Hardened Putty

Washing soda	10 ounces
Water	16 ounces
Soap flakes	4 ounces
Hydrated lime	12 ounces

Dissolve the washing soda in the water and then stir in the soap flakes and the lime. Apply this solution to the putty. After several hours the putty should be soft enough to be easily removed.

House-Joint Caulking Compounds

Whiting	10 ounces
Boiled linseed oil	10 ounces
Asbestos fiber	4 ounces

Mix about three-quarters of the whiting thoroughly into the oil and then stir the asbestos into this mixture. If the compound is not thick enough, blend in more of the whiting.

A more up-to-date, but more complex, caulking compound can be made as follows:

Drier	2 ounces
Boiled linseed oil	18 fluid ounces
Asbestos fiber	10 ounces
Asbestine	10 ounces
Powdered talc	5 ounces
Kerosene	4 ounces

Because they become finally so thick, mixing this and the preceding compound is quite strenuous work and is best done by a heavy mixing machine.

Mix the drier with the linseed oil. Mix thoroughly together the dry ingredients. Then combine the latter into the oil by rigorous stirring. A heavy mixing machine would help here, but the job can be done by a little strenuous effort and a strong wooden paddle. After the dry materials are blended with the oil, work in the kerosene.

Pipe Joint Sealers

White-lead or red-lead paste, just as it comes from the can, is excellent for making threaded pipe joints gastight, watertight, and airtight. Apply it to the threads before screwing the parts together.

Commercial pipe-joint compounds may consist of the following:

White lead ground in oil	8 ounces
Red lead ground in oil	8 ounces
Linseed oil	4 fluid ounces

Mix the ingredients thoroughly and keep any that is not to be used immediately in an airtight container.

FOR AIR AND GAS PIPE CONNECTIONS.   Several coats of shellac make an easy and effective seal for joints in gas and air lines. Just paint it on with a brush. Because a shellac film is brittle, the pipes can be easily taken apart at any time.

FOR STEAM-PIPE JOINTS.   To permanently stop leaks in steam pipes where plugging or caulking is not practicable, mix enough powdered manganese dioxide with raw linseed oil to make a thick paste. Apply this to the joint or leak. Take off steam pressure, but keep the pipe warm enough to cause absorption of the oil. This cement should be very hard within 24 hours.

FOR RESISTANCE TO HEAT, ACIDS, AND OIL.   Use the litharge–glycerin cement described above, mixing the litharge with about 10 percent of asbestos flock.

Gasket Compounds

Many cements may be used with rings of asbestos and other materials to form gaskets. Asphalt, tar, and pitch are simple ones. Mixtures that will stand heat, steam, and acids can be made by mixing sodium silicate solution with asbestos, with asbestos and slaked lime, with fine sand, or with fireclay, to form a thick liquid. Paint this liquid on the rings, or let them soak in it until they are thoroughly impregnated.

6

First Aid
and
Safety

PRINCIPLES OF FIRST AID

First aid is the immediate care given to anyone injured or taken suddenly ill. It may be the only care needed, as in the case of minor injuries. Or it may be temporary care given until medical help can be obtained.

The best preparation is a formal course in first aid, such as those offered by the Red Cross. A course, or guidebooks such as those offered by the Red Cross, will teach you what to do as well as *what not to do* (which in many cases is more important). As a basis, though, this chapter offers useful guidelines that can help you save a life, prevent further injury, and even limit the chances for injury-producing accidents.

WHEN IMMEDIATE ACTION IS CRITICAL

You must react promptly if you encounter any or all of the following at the scene of an accident:

1. Danger of further injury (thus the need for emergency evacuation).
2. A victim not breathing or lacking a pulse.

3. Severe bleeding.
4. A case of poisoning.

While you are administering first aid in these instances, direct someone to call for emergency medical help and arrange to transport the victim to a medical facility.

Emergency Evacuation

If the victim's life is endangered from an explosion, poisonous gas, electrical contact, or other immediate peril, he should be moved to a safer place. But first consider whether you can move the victim without being killed, injured, or overcome yourself. When moving an injured person, take care not to cause further injuries. Always move the victim lengthwise rather than sidewise. Avoid doubling the victim up. Once the victim is in a safe place, tend to his breathing, bleeding, poisoning, and shock.

Breathing

If the victim *appears to be unconscious,* do this:

1. Check for consciousness by tapping his shoulders and shouting for his attention.
2. If there is no response, check for breathing.
   a. If he is not breathing, open his airway by rotating his head back with one of your hands on his forehead and the other hand placed under the back of his head and neck. This will open his airway.
   b. Place your ear next to the victim's mouth and nose—listen, feel, and look for breathing. If the victim is now breathing, keep his airway open.

If he is still *not* breathing:

1. Pinch his nose with your fingers.
2. Place your mouth over his mouth, forming a tight seal.
3. Blow four quick breaths into his mouth. (If an obstruction prevents passage of air, remove the obstruction as described in the section "Choking," pages 219–221.)
4. Check with your fingers for a carotid pulse located on either side of the victim's Adam's apple. Use your middle and index finger to check pulse for at least five seconds.
   a. If the victim *has a pulse* and is *still not breathing, begin doing mouth-to-mouth resuscitation.*

b. *If the victim has a pulse and is breathing, monitor both pulse and breathing and get emergency medical help.*

c. *If the victim has no pulse and is not breathing* begin CPR (Cardio-Pulmonary Resuscitation), if you have been trained to do so. This basically involves applying rhythmic pressure to the breastbone with the heel of the hand while alternately administering mouth-to-mouth resuscitation. But to do this effectively, you must be trained by an instructor and have practiced on a manikin. Instruction is available from local chapters of the Red Cross and the Heart Association.

MOUTH-TO-MOUTH RESUSCITATION.   Breathe into an adult victim's mouth at a rate of 12 times per minute. To monitor effectiveness of your efforts, watch the victim's chest rise with your breaths and fall as you remove your mouth. With a child, make your breaths shallower, at a rate of 20 per minute.

Continue mouth-to-mouth efforts until the victim begins breathing on his own or until qualified help arrives, or until you can no longer continue. Remember, many victims are revived only after prolonged resuscitation effort.

Bleeding

There are two major categories of wounds: (1) open wounds, with broken skin, and (2) closed wounds, with injury to underlying tissues and no break in the skin.

Open wounds. These can cause heavy loss of blood and, if they do, you need to act quickly to control blood loss and to prevent contamination of the wound.

1. Control the bleeding:
   a. Apply direct pressure with a clean cloth or, if necessary, with your bare hand over the wound.
   b. Elevate the injury while maintaining direct pressure. (But *do not* elevate a limb if you suspect a bone fracture.)
   c. If direct pressure and elevation fail to control bleeding of a limb, then also apply pressure to the appropriate artery to slow blood flow.
      (1) For the arm, apply pressure to the brachial artery between the two muscles along the inside of bone of the upper arm. (Use the flat of your fingers.)
      (2) For the leg, use the femoral artery, located at the leg-hip joint, on top of the pelvis bone. (Use the heel of your hand to slow blood flow.)

BRACHIAL ARTERY   FEMORAL ARTERY

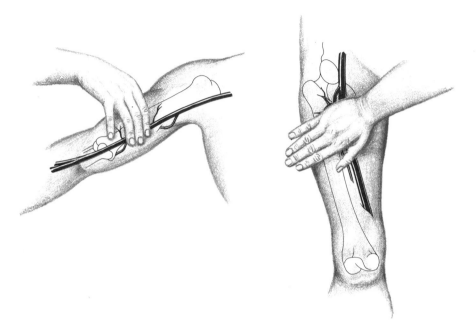

d. If pressure to the artery (combined with direct pressure to the wound and elevation of the limb) fails to stop *heavy flow* of blood, a tourniquet may be needed to prevent death due to blood loss. (*Caution:* A tourniquet is a dangerous device; once applied it should not be loosened or removed except on the advice of a physician. A tourniquet may save a life but it also risks the victim's limb.)

CLOSED WOUNDS.   There is little you can do for severe internal wounds, except to make the victim comfortable and obtain emergency medical help fast. *Never* offer fluids to a person if you suspect severe internal injuries. For small closed wounds (bruises that will turn black and blue), apply a cold pack to prevent swelling.

Poisoning

INGESTED POISONS.   When poison has been taken through the mouth, do this:

For a *conscious* victim:

1. Dilute the poison with milk or water.

2. Call a poison control center or other medical center for advice. (Be prepared to give this information: amount of poison, victim's age and weight.)
3. Save the poison container label for identification of the poison by medical people.
4. If the victim vomits, save the vomit for laboratory analysis.
5. If the victim loses consciousness, keep his airway open.

For an *unconscious* victim:

1. Keep his airway open.
2. Call for emergency medical help.
3. If the victim is not breathing, give mouth-to-mouth resuscitation. If the victim also has no pulse, a *trained* person should begin cardio-pulmonary resuscitation (CPR).
4. *Do not* give fluids. *Do not* induce vomiting.
5. Save the poison container label for medical people.

INHALED POISONS.   If a victim has been overcome by gases, such as carbon monoxide:

1. Remove him to fresh air. Be careful not to be overcome by the gases yourself.
2. If the victim is *not breathing but has a pulse,* give mouth-to-mouth resuscitation.
3. If the victim is *not breathing and has no pulse,* have a *trained* person begin cardio-pulmonary resuscitation (CPR).
4. Obtain emergency medical help.

POISONING FROM STINGS AND BITES (INSECTS, MARINE LIFE).   Prevention is vital, especially if you are allergic to specific stings and bites.
What to do:

1. Check for emergency medical identification (bracelet, necklace, and/or card in wallet), indicating an allergic reaction.
2. For minor reactions to bites and stings:
   a. Apply cold packs.
   b. Use soothing lotions such as calamine.
   c. Remove the stinger, if possible.
3. For severe reactions:
   a. If the victim stops breathing, give mouth-to-mouth resuscitation. If the victim also has no pulse, a trained person should begin cardio-pulmonary resuscitation (CPR).

    b. Apply a constricting band between the site of the sting and the heart. (*Caution:* Do not apply tightly; tighten only until you can still slip a finger under the band.)

    c. Keep the sting or bite area below the level of the victim's heart.

    d. Transport the victim to a medical facility as soon as possible.

SNAKE BITES.   Prevention of snake bites is the key. In snake season, move with a wary eye and wear protective clothing. Do not step or reach where a snake might be hidden from view.

Of the many kinds of snakes, few are poisonous. And often, bites from poisonous varieties introduce little or no poison into the victim. Still, all bites can lead to infection and should receive prompt medical attention.

What to do:

1. Immobilize the bitten limb and keep it below the level of the heart.
2. Try to identify the type of snake without endangering yourself.
3. Transport the victim to a hospital immediately, while keeping him calm and inactive.
4. If you notice swelling, discoloration, moderate pain, rapid pulse, weakness, nausea, or shortness of breath, apply a constricting band 2 to 4 inches above the area. (Tighten only until you can still slip a finger underneath.)
5. If there are serious reactions such as rapid swelling and numbness, severe pain, slurred speech, shock, or convulsions:

    a. Apply a constricting band 2 to 4 inches above the swelling, if you haven't already done so in response to milder symptoms (again, just tight enough so you can slip a finger underneath).

    b. Make a ½-inch long cut just through the skin over the suspected venom deposit. (*Caution:* Cuts should be made along the long axis of the limb to avoid cutting blood vessels. *Do not* make "X" cuts.)

    c. Apply a snake-bite suction cup or use your mouth to draw venom for at least 30 minutes.

6. If you *cannot* reach a hospital within 4 to 5 hours and *any* symptoms develop, follow procedures described in Item 5, above.

CONTACT WITH POISONOUS PLANTS.   Contact with many plants can cause allergic reactions characterized by some or all of the following: itching, redness, rash, headache, and fever. More serious reactions include intense burning, blisters, fever, and severe illness. For relief, do this:

1. Remove contaminated clothing. Wash the affected area thoroughly with soap and water. Apply rubbing alcohol.
2. Apply a soothing skin lotion (such as calamine) if the rash is mild.
3. If the victim has a severe reaction, get medical assistance.

Preventing Plant Poisoning. If it is necessary to work among poisonous plants, you should wear protective clothing. Some protection also may be obtained by first applying a protective lotion. After exposure to plants, wash off the lotion thoroughly with soap and water. Contaminated clothing and tools should also be washed with soap and water to prevent later spread of the poison.

Shock

Shock is a depressed state of all body functions. This is a serious condition and should be watched for in all accidents or injuries. Shock can kill even though the injury may not seem to be life-threatening or even severe. A victim in shock will be weak, and will have a weak rapid pulse and a high breathing rate. The skin may be pale, moist, clammy.

1. Give all necessary first aid for breathing failure, bleeding, or other injury.
2. Keep the victim lying down.
3. Maintain a normal body temperature.
4. Get medical help.

In general, keeping the victim flat will improve his blood circulation. If the victim does not have a neck or back injury, or head or chest injury, raise his feet 8 to 12 inches. Or if the victim has slight difficulty in breathing you can raise the head and shoulders. If medical help is going to be delayed, fluids by mouth will help. (*Caution:* Never give fluids if the victim is unconscious, or if he is vomiting or likely to vomit.) Give a warm solution of salt, soda, and water (1 level teaspoon of salt and ½ level teaspoon of baking soda to each quart of water). Give an adult about ¼ pint (4 ounces) every 15 minutes—less for children.

Choking

Often referred to as a "cafe coronary" because it is frequently mistaken for a heart attack in dining establishments, choking is the sixth leading cause of accidental deaths. And it is the leading cause of accidental death among small children.

COMMON SYMPTOMS. The victim may grasp at his throat. He may be unable to speak, breathe, or cough. He may look terrified and display frantic motions. He may soon turn blue in the face and lose consciousness. By contrast, heart-attack victims may be able to talk or breathe at first. Also, consider that most choking incidents occur when the victim has been eating. If the victim is conscious, you may be able to confirm that he is choking simply by asking him to nod if he is choking.

What to do:

Conscious victim with a complete airway obstruction:

1. Bend him at the waist (seated or standing) and apply four sharp back blows to his spine between the shoulder blades with the heel of your hand.
2. Reach in front of victim, placing your fist thumbside against the victim's abdomen, slightly above the navel and below the tip of the breastbone. Then with your other hand clasped over your fist, administer four quick upward thrusts. These thrusts should be firm enough to force out air from the lungs without being so violent that they injure ribs or other organs.
3. Repeat the back blows and abdominal thrusts until the obstruction is dislodged.

Unconscious victim:

1. With the victim on his back, open his airway by rotating his head back.
2. Attempt to give him four quick breaths, as in mouth-to-mouth resuscitation.
3. If unable to force your breaths into the victim's lungs, *again rotate his head.*
4. Attempt to give four more quick breaths.
5. If unable to get breaths into the victim's lungs this second time, do the following:
   a. As you kneel, quickly roll the front of the victim against your thighs and give four back blows in rapid succession.
   b. Roll the victim onto his back and apply four abdominal thrusts. (To do this, kneel at the victim's side. Use the heel of one hand, fingers pointing toward victim's head, and place the other hand on top, midway between the navel and tip of the breastbone.)
   c. Lift the victim's chin and tongue with one hand and sweep the index finger of your other hand deep into the victim's throat, attempting to hook and dislodge the object.

d. If you do not succeed in clearing the object, repeat the steps you have performed: Attempt four quick breaths; deliver four back blows; administer four manual thrusts; perform finger probes until you can remove the obstruction and/or get air into the lungs.

For infants and small children, follow the above steps (for conscious or unconscious victims as appropriate). However, use less force so as not to cause injury.

BURNS

Chemical Burns

Flush the burned area well with water to dilute and remove the chemical. Do not try to neutralize acid with alkali or alkali with acid. This may do more harm than good. Check with a poison control center for further guidance.

If the chemical has gotten into a person's eye, flush the eye gently but thoroughly with water for at least 20 minutes. Do not use an eyecup. Cover the eye with a sterile compress and get medical attention. If an eye is badly burned, cover both eyes.

Heat Burns

Heat burns are given three classifications: first-degree burns, in which the skin is reddened; second-degree burns, in which skin is reddened and blistered; and third-degree burns, in which the skin and sometimes the underlying tissue is cooked or charred.

The danger to the body does not depend so much on the degree as on the extensiveness of a burn. The severity of a burn is related to the degree and area involved. So a mild burn over a large area can be more dangerous than a second-degree burn of small size. Shock is usually severe in burns over a large area. As a general rule, first-aid for burns involves relief of pain, reduction of the chance of contamination and consequent infection, and the treatment of shock.

If the burn is small, apply cold water to it until the pain is relieved, cover the burn with several sterile gauze pads, piled one on the other, and held in place by a lightly applied bandage. If the skin has broken blisters, do not use cold water but apply the gauze pads without any medication and without causing additional damage.

If the burn is large, and especially if the skin is charred, take extra care. Keep the person quiet and lying down to reduce chances of shock. Cut away clothing from burned area. To prevent contamination, wash your hands thoroughly with soap and water. Do not apply oil, ointment, antiseptic, or any other medication. Cover the burned area with half a dozen or more layers of sterile dry gauze. Treat for shock. Get the victim to a burn-care center as soon as possible.

Sunburn

Ointments and other suntan preparations should be used *only for prevention* of sunburns. If there is redness only, soak the burned area in cold water and cover it with dry sterile dressings. Give as much liquid as possible. Aspirin will help relieve the pain. For a severe sunburn, treat with cold water and get medical attention.

OTHER COMMON PROBLEMS

Cuts, Scratches

These are probably the most frequent home injury. No matter how superficial they may appear, they are potentially dangerous—germs may easily enter the body through the broken skin. They should be treated right away.

Before treating a cut or a scratch, wash your hands thoroughly. Using sterile gauze or a freshly laundered handkerchief or towel, wash the area around the cut or scratch with soap and water. Wash outward from the cut, then wash the cut itself, using soap, water, and sterile gauze. Try to get as much dirt out of the wound as you can. Cover the wound with a sterile compress and fasten in place with a bandage. On very small cuts and scratches, a combined compress and adhesive band will do.

If a cut or scratch has been properly treated, it should not become infected. Infection, however, may possibly show up several days later. Any of these signs is evidence: a reddened, painful area around the wound; pus and red streaks; swelling in the wounded area, chills and fever in the victim.

See a doctor right away if any of these signs appear.

Electric Shock

Symptoms of electric shock are unconsciousness, no breathing, face and lips blue, flushed, or pale, pulse weak or absent. There may also be burns in the area of contact.

If the person is still in contact with the current, the thing to do immediately is to break that contact without endangering yourself. If a switch or plug is near at hand, open the switch or pull the plug. If you cannot do this quickly enough, remove the wire or move the person with a dry wooden pole, rope, or other nonconducting object.

Begin artificial respiration immediately if breathing has stopped. After breathing has been restored, keep the person warm and quiet until professional help arrives. Treat for burns, if necessary, looking for where electricity entered the victim and exited. And treat for shock.

Eye Irritation

Don't try to remove anything more than a windblown object such as dust, dirt, or a small insect. If a particle does not come out readily, let a doctor remove it.

First, try to flush out the particle with warm water (have the person lie on his back and pour plenty of water into the eye; *don't use an eyecup!*). Blinking during this bath may help. If this doesn't work, pull the eyelid away from the eyeball. With moist sterile gauze or cotton, lift out the particle.

Fainting

Hunger, shock, fatigue, poor ventilation—even seeing or hearing something pleasant or unpleasant—can cause fainting.

To revive a person who has fainted, place him on his back with his head lower than the rest of his body. Loosen all tight clothing and apply cold compresses to his face and forehead. If someone feels faint, have him sit down and put his head between his knees.

Heat Exhaustion

Early symptoms of heat exhaustion, which can be produced by exposure to heat either indoors or outdoors, are weariness, fatigue, and a feeling of faintness. Later the person may break out in profuse, but cold, perspiration; he may turn almost white; his temperature will be normal.

Remove the person to a cool place, have him lie down, and loosen his clothing. Cover him with a light blanket. If he is conscious, give him a saltwater solution (1 teaspoon of salt in ½ glass of water) every 15 minutes. Call a doctor immediately.

Heatstroke

Heatstroke is more serious than heat exhaustion. It demands immediate medical treatment.

The victim of heatstroke will have a fever up to 105° F or even higher. His pulse will be rapid and strong. His face will be flushed and his skin hot and dry. He may even lose consciousness.

Get the person out of the heat source and into a cooler area immediately. Have him lie on his back and remove as much clothing as possible. Apply cold compresses to his head. Cool his body by wrapping him in a sheet and pouring cold water on small portions at a time, or use cold cloths and cold packs. If a tub is available, place him in a tub of cold water. Get medical assistance as quickly as possible.

Nosebleeds

These may occur spontaneously as well as following injury to the nose. Children often have nosebleeds as the result of strenuous exercise, a cold, or high altitudes. In most cases, the bleeding is more annoying than serious.

Often, sitting quietly and leaning forward will stop the bleeding. If this doesn't do it, apply pressure directly at the site of bleeding. If bleeding persists insert into the bleeding nostril a clean pad of gauze (not absorbent cotton) and press firmly on the outside of the nostril. If the bleeding stops, leave the packing in place for a while. If bleeding continues seek medical attention.

Removing Foreign Objects

In small open wounds, wood splinters and glass fragments often remain in the surface tissues or in tissues just beneath the surface. As a rule, such objects irritate only the victim; they do not usually incapacitate a person or cause systemic body infection. They can cause infection, however, if they are not removed. Use tweezers sterilized over a flame or in boiling water to pull out any foreign matter from the surface tissues. Objects embedded just beneath the skin can be lifted out with the tip of a needle that has been sterilized in rubbing alcohol or in the heat of a flame. Foreign objects, regardless of size, that are embedded deeper in the tissues should be left for removal by a physician.

The fishhook is probably one of the more common types of foreign objects that may penetrate the skin. Often, only the point of the hook enters, not penetrating deeply enough to allow the barb to become effective; in this case, the hook can be removed easily by backing it out. If the fishhook goes deeper and the barb becomes embedded, the wisest course is to have a physician remove it. If medical aid is not available, remove the hook by pushing it through until the barb protrudes. Using a cutting tool, cut the hook either at the barb or at the shank and remove it. Cleanse the wound thoroughly and cover it with an adhesive compress. A physician should be consulted as soon as possible because of the possibility of infection, especially tetanus.

Some penetrating foreign objects, such as sticks and pieces of metal, may protrude loosely from the body or even be fixed, such as a stake in the ground or a wooden spike or metal rod of a fence on which the victim has become impaled. Under no circumstances should the victim be pulled loose from such an object. Obtain help at once, preferably from ambulance or rescue personnel who are equipped to handle the problem. Support the victim and the object to prevent movements that could cause further damage. If the object is fixed or protrudes more than a few inches from the body, it should be held carefully to avoid further damage, cut off at a distance from the skin, and left in place. To prevent further injury during transport of the victim, immobilize the protruding end with massive dressings. The victim should then be taken to the hospital without delay.

SAFETY IN THE SHOP

Safety is an important consideration in any shop, and certain safety rules should be stressed. The first one is to be sure that anyone working with hand or power tools is shop oriented, that he knows his way around the shop. Invite the entire family to join you in the planning and building of projects, but be sure you supervise their activity, especially when youngsters are involved.

Safety Rules

1. KNOW YOUR POWER TOOL. Read the owner's manual carefully. Learn each tool's application and limitations as well as the specific potential hazards peculiar to it.

2. GROUND ALL TOOLS. Most power tools are equipped with an approved three-conductor cord and a three-prong grounding-type plug to fit the proper grounding-type receptacle. The green conductor in the cord is the grounding wire. Never connect the green wire to a live terminal.

3. KEEP GUARDS IN PLACE.   Use all the safety devices the tool provides. For example, a radial arm saw may have a "splitter" and "antikickback dogs." If you rip a board without them, you may get away with it—but you may not. The tool may hurl the ripping like a deadly spear. Too bad if anyone is standing in its path. A table saw can hurl things too, unless they are properly secured. A drill press has other tricks: it can grab work and become a battering windmill.

4. REMOVE ADJUSTING KEYS AND WRENCHES.   Form a habit of checking to see that keys and adjusting wrenches are removed from a tool before turning it on.

5. KEEP WORK AREA CLEAN.   Cluttered areas and benches invite accidents. Floor must not be slippery due to wax or sawdust.

6. AVOID DANGEROUS ENVIRONMENTS.   Don't use power tools in damp or wet locations. Keep work area well lit. Provide adequate surrounding work space.

7. KEEP CHILDREN AWAY.   All visitors should be kept a safe distance from the work area. Also make the workshop kidproof with padlocks, master switches, or by removing starter keys.

8. NEVER FIGHT A TOOL.   Don't force it beyond its capability. Don't use it in ways or for purposes for which it is not intended. Don't attempt freehand cuts, or cuts without proper support. If an operation seems to hold special hazards, don't attempt it without thinking for a moment what the price may be.

9. WEAR PROPER APPAREL.   Avoid wearing loose clothing, gloves, neckties, or jewelry that could get caught in moving parts. Rubber-soled footwear is recommended for best footing.

10. SECURE WORK.   Use clamps or a vise to hold work when practical. It is safer than using your hand and frees both hands to operate the tool.

11. DON'T OVERREACH.   Keep proper footing and balance at all times.

12. MAINTAIN TOOLS WITH CARE. Keep tools sharp and clean for best and safest performance. Follow instructions for lubricating and changing accessories.

13. DISCONNECT TOOLS. Before servicing or when changing accessories such as blades, bits, cutters, etc., always disconnect the power cord.

14. AVOID ACCIDENTAL STARTING. Make sure switch is in OFF position before plugging in. Also never leave a running power tool unattended.

15. USE RECOMMENDED ACCESSORIES. Consult the owner's manual for recommended accessories. Follow the instructions that accompany the accessories. The use of improper accessories may cause hazards.

16. DON'T DAYDREAM. If you find yourself daydreaming as you work, snap out of it or postpone your efforts to a time when you feel more alert. When you daydream, you are not thinking of what you're doing. You are also more likely to be startled. Even when you are alert, when you are using a power tool, you are not apt to hear the approach of a visitor. Instruct your family to wait until anyone using a power tool has finished what he is doing and cannot be imperiled in case he is startled.

17. NEVER STAND ON TOOL. Serious injury could occur if the tool is tipped or if the cutting tool is accidentally contacted. Do not store materials above or near the tool so that it is necessary to stand on the tool to reach them.

18. CHECK DAMAGED PARTS. Before further use of the tool, a guard or other part that is damaged should be carefully checked to ensure that it will operate properly and perform its intended function—check for alignment of moving parts, binding of moving parts, breakage of parts, mounting, and any other conditions that may affect its operation. A guard or other part that is damaged should be properly repaired or replaced.

19. DIRECTION OF FEED. Feed work into a blade or cutter against the direction of rotation of the blade or cutter only. Keep out of line of the saw blade, front and rear, and see that no one else ever moves in line with it. This is the area where those

deadly spears are seeking a target. Let only enough blade project on a table saw or portable saw to cut the work. The saw cuts better that way, binding is minimized, and the chances of throwing wood spears are reduced.

20. DON'T FORGET TO THINK.   This eliminates most accidents before they happen.

Electricity Cautions

A large sign in a well-known research laboratory carries this warning: "Touch electrical equipment with one hand only."

This is the old one-hand-in-the-pocket trick. It works this way—if you touch a hot line with one hand, the jolt will travel down your arm and through your body to the ground. You'll feel it, but it will not kill you. But if you touch with both hands, the jolt passes up one arm, across your body, and down the other, completing the circuit. The path goes right through your heart.

An insidious thing about electricity is that it can paralyze your muscles. You may not be able to open the hand that clutches a hot wire and let go. You may be conscious but helpless to do anything to save yourself. So avoid getting into such a predicament. Switch off power at the service entry box before you work on a line. Turning power off at the room toggle switch is not enough; sometimes fixtures are incorrectly wired and may be hot even when switched off. The switch may be on the ground line instead of on the hot line.

Ladder Safety

If a ladder has bad rungs, poor footing, or is rickety or improperly slanted, don't climb it until these hazards are corrected. If a ladder slips or moves as you climb, it is not placed properly. If you are using a straight ladder, its base should be away from the supporting wall a distance equal to one quarter of its height.

Before getting on a step ladder, see that it is fully opened and its braces locked. When you get on, don't climb higher than the second step from the top. Never, never stand on the top platform.

In climbing a ladder, carry tools in your pocket, scabbard, or other tote device, but not in your hand. When working on a ladder, try at all times to keep one hand free. You may want to grasp the ladder. If your ladder is set in a doorway, see that the door is open or that it is locked—then no one will bump the ladder and knock you off. Before you move a stepladder, be sure you have not left your hammer on its top. It may come sailing off.

The light weight of magnesium or aluminum ladders is an asset, but the lightness and the metal can also be hazards. A strong wind can blow them down and leave you stranded on a roof. And since magnesium and aluminum conduct electricity, they are risky to use around electric lines and during electrical storms.

Lifting

A back injury may not kill you, but it can give you uncomfortable moments the rest of your life if you slip a disc, tear a ligament, or pull a tendon. The rule for avoiding back injuries when lifting is to bend the knees and keep the back straight. You have to bend your back a little, of course, but minimize it. When you have a lifting job that is just too awkward or heavy, get help—a block and tackle and/or a neighbor.

Menaces Miscellaneous

When you saw, do not use your knee to brace work. When you hammer, hold the nail you are driving only long enough to start it, and make the starting hammer strokes slow and measured so you can't miss. When you drill, keep your hand away from the bit. It may jump. The same goes for a screwdriver, especially one of the wrong size, or one whose tip has become rounded.

Use gloves to protect your hands when handling broken glass or rough masonry.

If your shop is in a basement or attic, and there is a low overhead en route, identify the hazard plainly, so no one could possibly be unaware of it. Avoid having a door that opens onto a downflight of steps. It should open away from the steps. Repair loose or broken steps and handrails as soon as you discover them.

Store inflammables outdoors. Keep oily rags in a sealed can; they sometimes catch fire by spontaneous combustion.

Eye and Face Protectors

You have only two eyes, of course, and replacements are hard to come by. That should be reason enough to protect your eyes whenever you use hand or power tools. And if there is any possibility of facial injuries, you should also use a face protector. Wearing these devices gives you an added benefit—you will work better because you will not be flinching and squinting.

A pair of safety glasses is probably the best choice when you do hand-tool work, power woodworking and metalworking, chipping, light grinding, and similar jobs and *not* "street" glasses with tempered glass lenses, which are shatter-resistant but are not safety spectacles.

The safety glasses you wear should be personally fitted, approved safety spectacles with glass lenses. Rims should fully surround the lenses. If you already wear glasses, the safety lenses can be ground to your prescription. (Of course, if you wear contact lenses, safety specs are a necessity.)

KINDS OF PROTECTION NEEDED

Job	Hazards	Eye/Face protective equipment*
Gas welding, cutting, soldering, brazing	Sparks, molten metal, harmful rays	G with shade #2 lenses for soldering, welding, brazing; for light cutting, shade #3 or #4
Arc or carbon-arc welding of steel	Same	H with shade #10 lens up to and including $\frac{5}{32}$-inch electrodes; shade #14 for carbon-arc welding; D under helmet desirable
Chemical and glass handling	Splash, burns, glass breakage	B with F
Chipping, paint scraping	Flying particles	A, B, C, D, or E
Power woodworking	Flying chips, dust	A, B, C, D, or E with F to protect face when necessary
Grinding, power wire-brushing	Flying particles	A, B, C, D, or E; add F for heavy grinding and wire-brushing
Power metalworking (machining)	Flying particles	A, B, C, D, or E
Hand-tool work	Flying particles	A, B, C, D, or E
Dusty operations	Dust particles	B
Visitors in work area	Flying particles	I

* Key: **A.** Flexible-fitting goggles

  B. Hooded vent flexible-fitting goggles

  C. Rigid body cushioned-fitting goggles

  D. Safety spectacles with side shields

  E. Eyecup safety goggles

  F. Face shield

  G. Welding goggles

  H. Welding helmet

  I. Plastic "visitors" spectacles

(Continued)

These safety glasses will withstand considerable impact, unless the lenses are scratched or pitted (such lenses should be replaced). When they do break, safety lenses tend to "spiderweb" and stay put within the rims.

Safety specs with built-in shields offer protection from particles that might hit you from the side. Clip-on side shields are available, but the clip should have a mechanism that cannot be easily dislodged with a blow. Should that happen, the shield itself could cause an eye injury.

Keep a pair of inexpensive plastic safety specs on hand, too, as "visitor" glasses. Everyone who wanders into your work area should also be protected.

Safety glasses are the most comfortable eye protectors for sustained wear, and the best bet for serious do-it-yourselfers. But the flexible-fitting plastic goggles are also suitable for the jobs listed above. You can get goggles with hooded vents, which are useful when you work under extremely dusty conditions or when you handle chemicals.

If there is any chance that you may get hit in the face while working, wear a face shield.

7

Calculations and Conversions

HOW TO COMPUTE CIRCUMFERENCE, AREA, AND VOLUME

All dimensions should be expressed in terms of the same unit—say in inches or centimeters. The computed areas will then be in terms of square inches or square centimeters, and the volumes in terms of cubic inches or cubic centimeters, and so on depending on the unit used.

Circumference

CIRCUMFERENCE OF A CIRCLE: Diameter times 3.1416.

Area

TRIANGLE: Multiply length of base by height and divide by 2.

SQUARE: Square the length of one side.

RECTANGLE: Multiply the length of the base by the height.

REGULAR POLYGONS

Pentagon (5 sides):   Square length of one side and multiply by 1.720.

232

Hexagon (6 sides):   Square length of one side and multiply by 2.598.

Octagon (8 sides):   Square length of one side and multiply by 4.828.

CIRCLE: Multiply the square of the radius by 3.1416.

ELLIPSE: Multiply long diameter by short diameter by 0.7854.

SPHERE: Multiply square of the diameter by 3.1416.

CYLINDER: Add area of both ends to the circumference times height.

CUBE: Square length of one side and multiply by 6.

Volume

PYRAMID: Multiply area of the base by the height and divide by 3.

CUBE: Cube the length of one edge.

RECTANGULAR SOLID: Multiply length by width by height.

CYLINDER: Multiply the square of the radius of the base by 3.1416, then multiply by the height.

SPHERE: Multiply the cube of the radius by 3.1416, then multiply by 4 and divide by 3.

CONE: Multiply the square of the radius of the base by 3.1416, then multiply by the height and divide by 3.

WATER WEIGHTS AND MEASUREMENTS

A gallon of water weighs 8.336 pounds and contains 231 cubic inches.

A cubic foot of water contains 7½ gallons, 1,728 cubic inches, and weighs 62.4 pounds.

To find the pressure in pounds per square inch at the base of a column of water, multiply the height of the column in feet by 0.433.

FRACTION EQUIVALENTS IN DECIMALS, MILLIMETERS, SQUARES, CUBES, SQUARE AND CUBE ROOTS, CIRCUMFERENCES AND AREAS OF CIRCLES, FROM 1/64 TO 1 INCH

Fraction*	Decimal	mm	Square	Square root	Cube	Cube root	Circle* circumference	Circle* area
1/64	.015625	.3969	.0002441	.125	.000003815	.25	.04909	.000192
1/32	.03125	.3969	.0009766	.176777	.000030518	.31498	.09817	.000767
3/64	.046875	1.1906	.0021973	.216506	.000102997	.36056	.14726	.001726
1/16	.0625	1.5875	.0039063	.25	.00024414	.39685	.19635	.003068
5/64	.078125	1.9844	.0061035	.279508	.00047684	.42749	.24544	.004794
3/32	.09375	2.3812	.0087891	.306186	.00082397	.45428	.29452	.006903
7/64	.109375	2.7781	.0119629	.330719	.0013084	.47823	.34361	.009396
1/8	.125	3.1750	.015625	.353553	.0019531	.5	.39270	.012272
9/64	.140625	3.5719	.0197754	.375	.0027809	.52002	.44179	.015532
5/32	.15625	3.9688	.0244141	.395285	.0038147	.53861	.49087	.019175
11/64	.171875	4.3656	.0295410	.414578	.0050774	.55600	.53996	.023201
3/16	.1875	4.7625	.0351563	.433013	.0065918	.57236	.58905	.027611
13/64	.203125	5.1594	.0412598	.450694	.0083809	.58783	.63814	.032405
7/32	.21875	5.5562	.0478516	.467707	.010468	.60254	.68722	.037583
15/64	.234375	5.9531	.0549316	.484123	.012875	.61655	.73631	.043143
1/4	.25	6.3500	.0625	.5	.015625	.62996	.78540	.049087
17/64	.265625	6.7469	.0705566	.515388	.018742	.64282	.83449	.055415
9/32	.28125	7.1438	.0791016	.530330	.022247	.65519	.88357	.062126
19/64	.296875	7.5406	.0881348	.544862	.026165	.66710	.93266	.069221
5/16	.3125	7.9375	.0976562	.559017	.030518	.67860	.98175	.076699

Fraction*								
21/64	.328125	8.3344	.107666	.572822	.035328	.68973	1.03084	.084561
11/32	.34375	8.7312	.118164	.586302	.040619	.70051	1.07992	.092806
23/64	.359375	9.1281	.129150	.599479	.046413	.71097	1.12901	.101434
3/8	.375	9.5250	.140625	.612372	.052734	.72112	1.17810	.110445
25/64	.390625	9.9219	.1525879	.625	.059605	.73100	1.22718	.119842
13/32	.40625	10.3188	.1650391	.637377	.067047	.74062	1.27627	.129621
27/64	.421875	10.7156	.1779785	.649519	.075085	.75	1.32536	.139784
7/16	.4375	11.1125	.1914063	.661438	.083740	.75915	1.37445	.150330
29/64	.453125	11.5094	.2053223	.673146	.093037	.76808	1.42353	.161260
15/32	.46875	11.9062	.2197266	.684653	.102997	.77681	1.47262	.172573
31/64	.484375	12.3031	.2346191	.695971	.113644	.78535	1.52171	.184269
1/2	.5	12.7000	.25	.707107	.125	.79370	1.57080	.196350
33/64	.515625	13.0969	.265869	.718070	.137089	.80188	1.61988	.208813
17/32	.53125	13.4938	.282227	.728869	.149933	.80990	1.66897	.221660
35/64	.546875	13.8906	.299072	.739510	.163555	.81777	1.71806	.234891
9/16	.5625	14.2875	.316406	.75	.177979	.82548	1.76715	.248505
37/64	.578125	14.6844	.334229	.760345	.193226	.83306	1.81623	.262502
19/32	.59375	15.0812	.352539	.770552	.209320	.84049	1.86532	.276884
39/64	.609375	15.4781	.371338	.780625	.226284	.84780	1.91441	.291648
5/8	.625	15.8750	.390625	.790569	.244141	.85499	1.96350	.306796
41/64	.640625	16.2719	.410400	.800391	.262913	.86205	2.01258	.322328
21/32	.65625	16.6688	.430664	.810093	.282623	.86901	2.06167	.338243
43/64	.671875	17.0656	.451416	.819680	.303295	.87585	2.11076	.354541
11/16	.6875	17.4625	.472656	.829156	.324951	.88259	2.15984	.371223

(Continued)

* Fraction represents diameter.

(Continued)

FRACTION EQUIVALENTS IN DECIMALS, MILLIMETERS, SQUARES, CUBES, SQUARE AND CUBE ROOTS, CIRCUMFERENCES AND AREAS OF CIRCLES, FROM 1/64 TO 1 INCH

Fraction*	Decimal	mm	Square	Square root	Cube	Cube root	Circle* circumference	Circle* area
45/64	.703125	17.8594	.494385	.838525	.347614	.88922	2.20893	.388289
23/32	.71875	18.2562	.516602	.847791	.371307	.89576	2.25802	.405737
47/64	.734375	18.6531	.539307	.856957	.396053	.90221	2.30711	.42370
3/4	.75	19.0500	.5625	.866025	.421875	.90856	2.35619	.441786
49/64	.765625	19.4469	.586182	.875	.448795	.91483	2.40528	.460386
25/32	.78125	19.8438	.610352	.883883	.476837	.92101	2.45437	.479369
51/64	.796875	20.2406	.635010	.892679	.506023	.92711	2.50346	.498736
13/16	.8125	20.6375	.660156	.901388	.536377	.93313	2.55254	.518486
53/64	.828125	21.0344	.685791	.910014	.567921	.93907	2.60163	.538619
27/32	.84375	21.4312	.711914	.918559	.600677	.94494	2.65072	.559136
55/64	.859375	21.8281	.738525	.927024	.634670	.95074	2.69981	.580036
7/8	.875	22.2250	.765625	.935414	.669922	.95647	2.74889	.601320
57/64	.890625	22.6219	.793213	.943729	.706455	.96213	2.79798	.622988
29/32	.90625	23.0188	.821289	.951972	.744293	.96772	2.84707	.645039
59/64	.921875	23.4156	.849854	.960143	.783459	.97325	2.89616	.667473
15/16	.9375	23.8125	.878906	.968246	.823975	.97872	2.94524	.690291
61/64	.953125	24.2094	.908447	.976281	.865864	.98412	2.99433	.713493
31/32	.96875	24.6062	.938477	.984251	.909149	.98947	3.04342	.737078
63/64	.984375	25.0031	.968994	.992157	.953854	.99476	3.09251	.761046
1	1	25.4000	1	1	1	1	3.14159	.785398

* Fraction represents diameter.

DECIMALS TO MILLIMETERS

Decimal	mm	Decimal	mm	Decimal	mm	Decimal	mm
0.001	0.0254	0.260	6.6040	0.510	12.9540	0.760	19.3040
0.002	0.0508	0.270	6.8580	0.520	13.2080	0.770	19.5580
0.003	0.0762	0.280	7.1120	0.530	13.4620	0.780	19.8120
0.004	0.1016	0.290	7.3660	0.540	13.7160	0.790	20.0660
0.005	0.1270	0.300	7.6200	0.550	13.9700	0.800	20.3200
0.006	0.1524	0.310	7.8740	0.560	14.2240	0.810	20.5740
0.007	0.1778	0.320	8.1280	0.570	14.4780	0.820	20.8280
0.008	0.2032	0.330	8.3820	0.580	14.7320	0.830	21.0820
0.009	0.2286	0.340	8.6360	0.590	14.9860	0.840	21.3360
0.010	0.2540	0.350	8.8900	0.600	15.2400	0.850	21.5900
0.020	0.5080	0.360	9.1440	0.610	15.4940	0.860	21.8440
0.030	0.7620	0.370	9.3980	0.620	15.7480	0.870	22.0980
0.040	1.0160	0.380	9.6520	0.630	16.0020	0.880	22.3520
0.050	1.2700	0.390	9.9060	0.640	16.2560	0.890	22.6060
0.060	1.5240	0.400	10.1600	0.650	16.5100	0.900	22.8600
0.070	1.7780	0.410	10.4140	0.660	16.7640	0.910	23.1140
0.080	2.0320	0.420	10.6680	0.670	17.0180	0.920	23.3680
0.090	2.2860	0.430	10.9220	0.680	17.2720	0.930	23.6220
0.100	2.5400	0.440	11.1760	0.690	17.5260	0.940	23,8760
0.110	2.7940	0.450	11.4300	0.700	17.7800	0.950	24.1300
0.120	3.0480	0.460	11.6840	0.710	18.0340	0.960	24.3840
0.130	3.3020	0.470	11.9380	0.720	18.2880	0.970	24.6380
0.140	3.5560	0.480	12.1920	0.730	18.5420	0.980	24.8920
0.150	3.8100	0.490	12.4460	0.740	18.7960	0.990	25.1460
0.160	4.0640	0.500	12.7000	0.750	19.0500	1.000	25.4000
0.170	4.3180						
0.180	4.5720						
0.190	4.8260						
0.200	5.0800						
0.210	5.3340						
0.220	5.5880						
0.230	5.8420						
0.240	6.0960						
0.250	6.3500						

Note: The first pair of columns is longer because the first ten items represent decimals to the thousandths place. Thereafter, decimals are rounded to the nearest hundredths.

TEMPERATURE CONVERSIONS

Temperature in everyday usage may be stated either in degrees Fahrenheit (°F) or in degrees Celsius or centigrade (°C). (Although the term "centigrade" is still often used in the United States, it was recommended by the International Committee on Weights and Measures and the National Bureau of Standards in 1948 that the term be officially changed to "Celsius," after Anders Celsius, the Swedish astronomer who invented the scale.)

Both scales are based on two fixed temperature points, the melting point of ice and the boiling point of water at normal atmospheric pressure.

On the Fahrenheit scale (named after Gabriel Daniel Fahrenheit, who devised it in 1714) the ice point is 32° and the steam point is 212°. The interval between these points is divided into 180 parts or degrees.

On the Celsius scale, the ice point is 0 and the steam point is 100, with the interval between divided into 100 parts or degrees.

By extending their scales beyond the ice point and the boiling point, both systems may be carried down to *absolute zero*, the temperature at which molecular motion ceases, and upward indefinitely as no upper limit to temperature is known.

On the Celsius scale, absolute zero is –273.16 degrees.

On the Fahrenheit scale, absolute zero is –459.69 degrees.

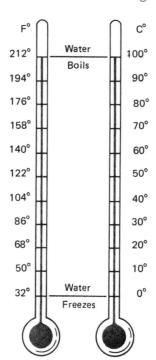

Comparison of Fahrenheit and Celsius scales, showing boiling and freezing point of water

TWO-WAY TEMPERATURE CONVERSION TABLE

°C		°F
−273.16	**−459.69**	
−184	**−300**	
−169	**−273**	−459.4
−157	**−250**	−418
−129	**−200**	−328
−101	**−150**	−238
−73.3	**−100**	−148
−45.6	**−50**	−58
−40.0	**−40**	−40
−34.4	**−30**	−22
−28.9	**−20**	−4
−23.3	**−10**	14
−17.8	**0**	32
−12.2	**10**	50
−6.67	**20**	68
−1.11	**30**	86
4.44	**40**	104
10.0	**50**	122
15.6	**60**	140
21.1	**70**	158
23.9	**75**	167
26.7	**80**	176
29.4	**85**	185
32.2	**90**	194
35.0	**95**	203
36.7	**98**	208.4
37.8	**100**	212
43	**110**	230
49	**120**	248
54	**130**	266
60	**140**	284
66	**150**	302
93	**200**	392
121	**250**	482
149	**300**	572

Find the temperature you want to convert—either Fahrenheit or Celsius (Centigrade)—among the boldface numbers in the center column. Then look to the appropriate column to the left or right to find the temperature you want to convert to.

Fahrenheit to Celsius (or Centigrade)

To convert from degrees Fahrenheit to degrees Celsius, first subtract 32 from the number of degrees F, then multiply the remainder by ⅝ (or 0.556).

Celsius to Fahrenheit

To convert from degrees Celsius to degrees Fahrenheit, multiply the number of degrees C by ⅝ (or 1.8) and add 32.

The Kelvin Scale

There is a third temperature scale that you may often read about but which you may never have occasion to use, unless you are a physicist. It is an absolute temperature scale called the Kelvin scale, after William Thomson, Lord Kelvin. This uses the Celsius unit for its degrees but places its 0 at absolute zero. The ice point then becomes 273.16° K and the boiling point 373.16° K. To convert Celsius to Kelvin, just add 273.16 degrees to the Celsius reading.

PERCENTAGE SOLUTIONS

Ordinarily percentage solutions may be made by dissolving an "X" amount of a chemical in enough water or some other solvent to make 100 parts. It becomes more complicated, however, when you have to dilute a solution of less than 100 percent to make another percent. In such a case, this simple crisscross method will help:

A   B   D   X   Y

To figure dilutions by this method:

1. Place the percentage strength of the solution to be diluted at A.
2. Place the percentage of the diluting solution at B. (Water should be entered as zero.)
3. Place the percentage desired at D.
4. Subtract D from A and place the answer at Y.
5. Subtract B from D and place at X.

Then mix X parts of A with Y parts of B to make the percent solution at D.

For example, to dilute 28-percent ammonium hydroxide to make a 5-percent solution:

$$28 \qquad 0 \qquad 5 \qquad 5 \qquad 23$$

Just add 5 parts of 28-percent ammonium hydroxide to 23 parts of water.

HOUSEHOLD WEIGHTS AND MEASURES

Weighing with Coins

Lack small weights for your balance? U.S. coins will serve quite well as substitutes. Here are their *approximate* values:

Dime	40 grains or 2½ grams
Penny	50 grains or 3⅛ grams
Nickel	80 grains or 5 grams
Quarter	100 grains or 6¼ grams
Half-dollar	200 grains or 12½ grams

An ounce equals 437.5 grains, therefore two half-dollars and a dime combined are near enough to serve as a 1-ounce weight.

Measuring with Coins

Ever caught without a ruler when you needed to know the thickness of a board? Money will help. The diameter of a U.S. cent is ¾ inch. Hold a penny against the edge of the stock and you can judge its thickness; ⅝, ¾ inch, or whatever.

Coins are also handy for determining the nominal sizes of steel water pipe. If the inside diameter of a pipe is about half the diameter of a quarter, it is nominal ⅜-inch pipe. If it is somewhat smaller than a dime, it is ½-inch pipe. If a penny fits inside loosely, you have ¾-inch pipe. In 1-inch pipe a quarter will fit loosely, but a half-dollar won't go. If the opening is twice the diameter of a dime, the pipe is 1¼ inches. Combined diameters of a nickel and a penny approximately equal the inside diameter of 1½-inch pipe. A half-dollar and a nickel add up to 2-inch pipe.

Approximate Household Measures

The following will be more accurate if you use standard measuring cups and measuring spoons.

1 teaspoon	⅙ fluid ounce
1 teaspoon	1.33 fluid drams
1 teaspoon	5 milliliters
1 teaspoon	5 medicine droppers
1 teaspoon	75 to 100 drops
1 tablespoon	½ fluid ounce
1 tablespoon	4 fluid drams
1 tablespoon	14.5 milliliters
1 tablespoon	3 teaspoons
1 cup	8 fluid ounces
1 cup	64 fluid drams
1 cup	237 milliliters
1 cup	48 teaspoons
1 cup	16 tablespoons
1 pint (liquid)	16 fluid ounces
1 pint	128 fluid drams
1 pint	473 milliliters
1 pint	96 teaspoons
1 pint	32 tablespoons
1 pint	2 cups
1 medicine dropper	about 20 drops
1 medicine dropper	1 milliliter (approx.)
1 grain	1 drop (approx.)
1 ounce	437.5 grains
1 ounce	28.35 grams
1 fluid ounce	8 fluid drams

1 fluid ounce	30 milliliters
1 fluid ounce	2 tablespoons
1 fluid ounce	6 teaspoons
1 quart (liquid)	0.946 liter
1 liter	1.056 quarts
1 gallon	8.33 pounds of water
1 gallon	231 cubic inches
1 gallon	0.1337 cubic foot
1 cubic foot of water	7.5 gallons

SHORTCUT CALCULATIONS FOR HOME AND SHOP PROBLEMS

Here are a few shortcut calculations for various home and shop problems.

TO DETERMINE PIPE SIZE FROM OUTSIDE DIMENSION. In the nominal sizes from ⅛ through 1 inch, standard, extra-strong, and double-extra-strong pipe measures approximately ⁵⁄₁₆-inch larger on the outside than its nominal size specification (or so close that the pipe cannot be confused for another size). Simply measure the outside diameter and subtract ⁵⁄₁₆ inch. Example: if the outside diameter of the pipe measures about 1⁵⁄₁₆ inches, 1⁵⁄₁₆ minus ⁵⁄₁₆ gives 1 inch nominal size.

WATER CAPACITY OF PIPES. How much flow a water pipe will deliver depends upon more than its inside diameter (pressure, pipe length, and lift are also involved). But you can quickly compare the capacities of any two pipe sizes if you remember that they vary as the squares of the diameter. That's why pipe with a 1½-inch opening will deliver more than twice as much water as one with a 1-inch opening.

NAIL SIZES. These are pretty arbitrary, but the smaller nails fall into a pattern that can take the strain off your memory. Divide the penny size of a nail by 4 and add ½ inch to get its length in inches; or subtract ½ inch from the inch length of a nail and multiply by 4 to get its size. Thus an 8-penny (8d) nail is 2½ inches long (8 divided by 4 gives

2; 2 plus ½ gives 2½). But remember this works only for nails up to 10 penny (10d) or 3 inches.

WHAT PULLEY SIZE? When stepping up or reducing speed with pulleys, you are dealing with four factors: motor speed, drive-pulley diameter, and driven-pulley diameter. You know three of these factors and you want to find the fourth—the pulley size.

This is the way to figure it: Take the pulley of known diameter and speed (this may be actual or desired speed). Multiply speed by diameter and divide the result by the known diameter or speed (again actual or desired) of the other pulley. The result is the missing figure. For instance, your joiner has a 2½-inch pulley and you want it to turn at about 4,200 rpm. What size pulley should you put on your 1,725-rpm motor to run the joiner at that speed?

Multiply 4,200 by 2½, then divide by 1,725 and you get just over 6. Using a 6-inch pulley on the motor shaft will do the trick for you.

SURFACE SPEED OF SANDER. Revolutions per minute often must be converted into surface feet per minute to give you the recommended speed for a sanding drum or sanding belt (too high a speed will scorch the material being sanded). Knowing the desired surface feet per minute, you can determine the required rpm for the drum or the driven drum on a belt sander. Divide the surface-feet-per-minute figure by the drum diameter in inches multiplied by .262. Once you have the rpm figure, use the preceding pulley formula to get the required belt-driven ratio.

SURFACE FEET OF WORK IN LATHE. Feet per minute for a given spindle speed and work (or tool) diameter can be determined by multiplying ¼ of the speed by the work or tool diameter. For example: For a lathe running 400 rpm, 3-inch work diameter, what is the sfm (surface feet per minute)? Here's how: ¼ of 400 rpm equals 100; 100 times 3 inches gives 300 sfm.

When you want to select a speed to give a desired surface speed, divide desired sfm by work or tool diameter and then multiply by 4. Example: You want 300 sfm for 3-inch work diameter. Find machine speed required this way: 300 divided by 3 inches gives 100; 100 times 4 gives 400 rpm. These mental calculations are accurate to something like 4 percent.

BEAM STIFFNESS. Stiffness refers to how much a beam will bend under a given weight. The formula for determining it is: width multiplied by the cube of the depth.

Comparing a full 2×10 with a full 4×6, you have $2 \times 10 \times 10 \times 10$ versus $4 \times 6 \times 6 \times 6$, giving a ratio of 2,000 to 846. So although the 4×6 contains more lumber and costs more, it will sag 2⅓ times as much as the 2×10 beam when it is carrying the same load.

BEAM STRENGTH.   Comparing the cross-sectional area of two beams does not necessarily give you their relative strength. For example: A full 2×10 joist will take about a 39-percent greater load than a full 4×6, although it weighs and costs one-sixth less. Use the following formula for determining the load-bearing strength: Square the dimension in the direction of the stress, and multiply that figure by the other dimension. In the case of joists, the direction of stress is, of course, through the greater dimension of the beams. With the 2×10 you therefore get $10 \times 10 \times 2$, or 200, as against $6 \times 6 \times 4$, or 144 for the 4×6. The difference in strength between dressed lumber and its nominal size is so slight that for practical purposes it can be ignored.

CYLINDRICAL TANK CAPACITY.   Remember that a circle has approximately three-fourths the area of a square drawn around it, plus 5 percent of this figure. Multiply this total by the height or length of the tank in like units of measurement to get the volume. Convert to cubic feet and multiply the resulting figure by 7½, which is the approximate number of gallons to the cubic foot.

SPHERICAL TANK CAPACITY.   A sphere has approximately half the volume of a cube drawn around it, plus 5 percent of the figure arrived at. Again, multiply the cubic footage by 7½ to get gallons.

WEIGHTS OF MATERIALS

Weights of Liquids

The old axiom "a pint's a pound the world around" is a good rule of thumb on which to estimate the weights of liquids. Actually a pint of water weighs just a fraction of an ounce over a pound. Pints of most watery fluids will tip the scale at about a pound. Alcohol, oil, gasoline, turpentine, and similar fluids weigh a little less. Other liquids, such as carbon tetrachloride and glycerin, weigh a little more.

For an approximation of the weight in pounds of a pint of the following liquids, multiply by the first number given. The second number tells you directly the number of pounds per cubic foot.

WEIGHTS OF LIQUIDS

Liquid	Specific gravity	Pounds per cubic foot
Acetone	0.792	49.4
Alcohol, ethyl	0.791	49.4
Alcohol, methyl	0.810	50.5
Benzene	0.899	56.1
Carbon tetrachloride	1.595	99.6
Ether	0.736	45.9
Gasoline	0.66–0.69	41–43
Glycerin	1.26	78.6
Kerosene	0.82	51.2
Linseed oil	0.942	58.8
Mercury	13.6	849
Milk	1.028–0.1035	64.2–64.6
Sea water	0.125	63.99
Turpentine	0.87	54.3
Water	1.0	62.4

The Meaning of Specific Gravity

The number you multiply with in the above table is labeled "specific gravity" (abbreviated sp. gr.). This is simply the ratio of the weight of a substance to that of an equal volume of water at the same temperature. It can also be considered to be the *density* of a substance in terms of grams per milliliter (or cubic centimeter), for in its densest state (at 3.98° C) 1 milliliter of pure water weighs exactly 1 gram.

Knowing the specific gravity of a substance can be useful in many ways. For instance, it can help you to figure out how much of a particular substance you can fit in a bottle, or a packing case, or the trunk of your car; or, turning things around, how much a certain volume of a given substance will weigh. Then again you can often tell one pure liquid from another just by determining its specific gravity. By the same means, you can also determine the concentration of certain acids and salt solutions, the percentage of alcohol in liquors and antifreeze, and even the charge on the battery in your car.

Determining Density with a Hydrometer

Measurement of the specific gravity of liquids is conveniently done with a hydrometer, a simple device of glass that is floated in a sample of the liquid to be tested. The calibrated stem of the hydrometer projects at a height out of the liquid depending upon the liquid's density.

Hydrometers are made with special scales for testing alcohol, milk, oils, sugar solutions, and the relative condition of battery charge. Most hydrometers, however, read either directly in specific gravity or in

SPECIFIC GRAVITY CONVERSIONS, READINGS AT 60° F (15.55° C)

Specific gravity	Light Baumé degrees	Heavy Baumé degrees	Pounds per gallon	Gallons per pound
0.6600	82		5.50	0.1818
0.6731	78		5.60	0.1786
0.6863	74		5.72	0.1748
0.700	70		5.83	0.1715
0.7071	68		5.89	0.1698
0.7216	64		6.01	0.1664
0.7368	60		6.14	0.1629
0.7527	56		6.27	0.1595
0.7692	52		6.41	0.1560
0.7685	48		6.55	0.1527
0.8046	44		6.70	0.1493
0.8235	40		6.86	0.1458
0.8434	36		7.03	0.1422
0.8642	32		7.20	0.1389
0.8861	28		7.38	0.1355
0.9091	24		7.57	0.1321
0.9333	20		7.78	0.1285
0.9589	16		7.99	0.1252
0.9722	14		8.10	0.1235
0.9859	12		8.21	0.1218
1.000	10	0	8.33	0.1200
1.007		1	8.38	0.1193
1.014		2	8.46	0.1182
1.021		3	8.50	0.1176
1.028		4	8.56	0.1168
1.043		6	8.69	0.1151
1.058		8	8.81	0.1135
1.074		10	8.94	0.1119
1.090		12	9.08	0.1101

(Continued)

(Continued)	SPECIFIC GRAVITY CONVERSIONS, READINGS AT 60° F (15.55° C)			
Specific gravity	Light Baumé degrees	Heavy Baumé degrees	Pounds per gallon	Gallons per pound
1.107		14	9.21	0.1086
1.124		16	9.36	0.1068
1.142		18	9.51	0.1052
1.160		20	9.67	0.1034
1.198		24	9.99	0.1001
1.239		28	10.32	0.0969
1.283		32	10.69	0.0935
1.330		36	11.09	0.0902
1.381		40	11.51	0.869
1.436		44	11.96	0.0836
1.495		48	12.45	0.0800
1.559		52	12.99	0.0769
1.629		56	13.57	0.0737
1.706		60	14.21	0.0704

SPECIFIC GRAVITY AND WEIGHTS OF COMMON SOLIDS

Substance	Specific gravity	Weight in pounds per cubic foot
Acrylic plastics	1.18	74
Aluminum, hard-drawn	2.7	168
Asbestos	2.0–2.8	125–175
Asphalt	1.1–1.5	69–94
Basalt	2.4–3.1	150–190
Beeswax	0.96–0.97	60–61
Brass	8.2–8.7	511–543
Brick	1.4–2.2	87–137
Bronze	8.74–8.89	545–554
Cement, portland	1.5	94
Cement, set	2.7–3.0	170–190
Chalk	1.9–2.8	118–175
Clay	1.8–2.6	112–162
Coal, anthracite	1.4–1.8	87–112
Coal, anthracite, piled		47–58

Substance	Specific gravity	Weight in pounds per cubic foot
Coal, bituminous	1.2–1.5	75–94
Coal, bituminous, piled		40–54
Concrete	2.3	145
Copper, hard-drawn	8.89	555
Cork	0.22–0.26	14–16
Earth, dry, loose		65–88
Earth, moist, compacted		95–135
Glass, common	2.4–2.8	150–175
Glass, flint	2.9–5.9	180–370
Gold, wrought	19.33	1207
Granite	2.46–2.76	165–172
Gravel, damp, loose		82–125
Gravel, dry, compacted		90–145
Gypsum	2.31–2.33	144–145
Ice	0.917	57
Iron, cast gray	7.03–7.13	439–445
Iron, wrought	7.8–7.9	487–492
Ivory	1.83–1.92	114–120
Lead	11.0	687
Lime	0.87–1.2	53–75
Magnesium	1.74	109
Marble	2.6–2.8	160–177
Nickel	8.6–8.9	537–556
Paraffin	0.87–0.91	54–57
Phenolic plastic, cast	1.27–1.31	79–82
Platinum	21.37	1334
Polyethylene	0.92	57
Sand, damp, loose		94
Sand, dry, compacted		110
Sandstone	2.14–2.35	134–147
Silver, wrought	10.6	662
Snow, fresh fallen		5–12
Snow, wet, compact		15–20
Steel	7.83	489
Styrene plastic	1.06	66
Tar	1.02	64
Tin	7.29	455
Vinyl plastic	1.4	87
Zinc	7.1	443

degrees Baumé (pronounced *boe-MAY*). The latter system of units was devised in 1768 by the French chemist Antoine Baumé in an attempt to provide a simpler scale. In fact, he devised two scales—one for liquids lighter than water, and one for those heavier. Because the Baumé hydrometer, with its uniformly spaced divisions, was easy to make and easy to read, it caught on quickly and is used for some purposes to this day. The Baumé scale is, though, purely arbitrary and so you often have to convert it into specific gravity to continue your calculations. To help you in this, see the table on pages 247 and 248.

SPECIFIC GRAVITY AND WEIGHTS OF WOODS

Wood, seasoned	Specific gravity	Weight in pounds per cubic foot
Apple	0.66–0.84	41–52
Ash	0.65–0.85	40–53
Balsa	0.11–0.14	7–9
Basswood	0.32–0.39	20–37
Beech	0.70–0.90	43–56
Birch	0.51–0.77	32–48
Blue gum	1.00	62
Box	0.95–1.16	59–72
Butternut	0.38	24
Ebony	1.11–1.33	69–83
Greenheart	1.06–1.23	66–77
Hickory	0.60–0.93	37–58
Ironwood, black	1.08	67
Lignum vitae	1.17–1.33	73–83
Mahogany, Honduras	0.66	41
Mahogany, Spanish	0.85	53
Maple	0.62–0.75	39–47
Oak	0.60–0.90	37–56
Pine, pitch	0.83–0.85	52–53
Pine, white	0.35–0.50	22–31
Pine, yellow	0.37–0.60	23–37
Redwood	0.44	27
Satinwood	0.95	59
Spruce	0.48–0.70	30–44
Teak, African	0.98	61
Teak, Indian	0.66–0.88	41–55
Walnut	0.64–0.70	40–43
Willow	0.40–0.60	24–37

SPECIFIC GRAVITY AND WEIGHT
OF GASES

The specific gravity of gases and vapors listed below is based on a system in which the specific gravity of air is 1, the atmospheric pressure normal, and the temperature 32° F or 0° C.

Gas	Weight in pounds per cubic foot	Specific gravity
Acetylene	0.0732	0.907
Air	.0807	1.000
Ammonia	.04813	0.540
Butane, iso	.1669	2.067
Carbon dioxide	.123	1.529
Carbon monoxide	.07806	0.967
Chlorine	.2006	2.486
Ether vapor	.2088	2.586
Ethylene	.07868	0.975
Helium	.01114	0.318
Hydrogen	.00561	0.070
Mercury vapor	.56013	6.940
Methane	.04475	0.554
Nitrogen	.07807	0.967
Oxygen	.08921	1.105
Propane	.1254	1.554
Sulfur dioxide	.1827	2.264
Water vapor	.05028	0.623

ENGLISH AND METRIC SYSTEMS

How Long is a Meter?

You are taught in school that the meter, the unit of length in the Metric System, is roughly 39.37 inches. Scientists who set the standards, however, have to be more precise.

As originally proposed, the meter was to be equal to one 10-millionth part of the quarter-meridian (the distance from the North Pole to the Equator) passing through Paris. To try to find out how long the quarter-meridian really was, two engineer-surveyors spent six years surveying the land between Barcelona and Dunkirk. They calculated the rest. In 1799, based on this work, a standard meter was constructed.

In 1960, the Eleventh General (International) Conference on Weights and Measures redefined the meter in terms of measurements of modern science. Today the standard meter is a unit of length equal to 1,650,763.73 wavelengths in a vacuum of the orange-red radiation of krypton 86 corresponding to the unperturbed transition between the $2p_{10}$ and $5d_5$ levels. No need now to travel to the North Pole to check your meter stick!

Multiplier Prefixes for the Metric or International System

By combining the following prefixes with such basic unit names as meter, gram, liter, volt, ampere, or ohm, you can indicate the multiples and submultiples of the Metric or International System. For example, by combining the prefix "kilo" with "volt," you can get "kilovolt," meaning "1,000 volts"; by combining "milli" with it, you get "millivolt," or "0.001 volt."

Prefix	Abbreviation	Multiplier	
tera	T	10^{12}	or 1,000,000,000,000
giga	G	10^9	or 1,000,000,000
mega	M	10^6	or 1,000,000
kilo	k	10^3	or 1,000
hecto	h	10^2	or 100
deka	da	10	or 10
deci	d	10^{-1}	or .1
centi	c	10^{-2}	or .01
milli	m	10^{-3}	or .001
micro	μ	10^{-6}	or .000001
mano	n	10^{-9}	or .000000001
pico	p	10^{-12}	or .000000000001
femto	f	10^{-15}	or .000000000000001
atto	a	10^{-18}	or .000000000000000001

MILLIMETERS TO DECIMALS

mm	Decimal	mm	Decimal	mm	Decimal	mm	Decimal
0.01	.00039	0.06	.00236	0.11	.00433	0.16	.00630
0.02	.00079	0.07	.00276	0.12	.00472	0.17	.00669
0.03	.00118	0.08	.00315	0.13	.00512	0.18	.00709
0.04	.00157	0.09	.00354	0.14	.00551	0.19	.00748
0.05	.00197	0.10	.00394	0.15	.00591	0.20	.00787

mm	Decimal	mm	Decimal	mm	Decimal	mm	Decimal
0.21	.00827	0.61	.02402	1	.03937	41	1.61417
0.22	.00866	0.62	.02441	2	.07874	42	1.65354
0.23	.00906	0.63	.02480	3	.11811	43	1.69291
0.24	.00945	0.64	.02520	4	.15748	44	1.73228
0.25	.00984	0.65	.02559	5	.19685.	45	1.77165
0.26	.01024	0.66	.02598	6	.23622	46	1.81102
0.27	.01063	0.67	.02638	7	.27559	47	1.85039
0.28	.01102	0.68	.02677	8	.31496	48	1.88976
0.29	.01142	0.69	.02717	9	.35433	49	1.92913
0.30	.01181	0.70	.02756	10	.39370	50	1.96850
0.31	.01220	0.71	.02795	11	.43307	51	2.00787
0.32	.01260	0.72	.02835	12	.47244	52	2.04724
0.33	.01299	0.73	.02874	13	.51181	53	2.08661
0.34	.01339	0.74	.02913	14	.55118	54	2.12598
0.35	.01378	0.75	.02953	15	.59055	55	2.16535
0.36	.01417	0.76	.02992	16	.62992	56	2.20472
0.37	.01457	0.77	.03032	17	.66929	57	2.24409
0.38	.01496	0.78	.03071	18	.70866	58	2.28346
0.39	.01535	0.79	.03110	19	.74803	59	2.32283
0.40	.01575	0.80	.03150	20	.78740	60	2.36220
0.41	.01614	0.81	.03189	21	.82677	61	2.40157
0.42	.01654	0.82	.03228	22	.86614	62	2.44094
0.43	.01693	0.83	.03268	23	.90551	63	2.48031
0.44	.01732	0.84	.03307	24	.94488	64	2.51969
0.45	.01772	0.85	.03346	25	.98425	65	2.55906
0.46	.01811	0.86	.03386	26	1.02362	66	2.59843
0.47	.01850	0.87	.03425	27	1.06299	67	2.63780
0.48	.01890	0.88	.03465	28	1.10236	68	2.67717
0.49	.01929	0.89	.03504	29	1.14173	69	2.71654
0.50	.01969	0.90	.03543	30	1.18110	70	2.75591
0.51	.02008	0.91	.03583	31	1.22047	71	2.79528
0.52	.02047	0.92	.03622	32	1.25984	72	2.83465
0.53	.02087	0.93	.03661	33	1.29921	73	2.87402
0.54	.02126	0.94	.03701	34	1.33858	74	2.91339
0.55	.02165	0.95	.03740	35	1.37795	75	2.95276
0.56	.02205	0.96	.03780	36	1.41732	76	2.99213
0.57	.02244	0.97	.03819	37	1.45669	77	3.03150
0.58	.02283	0.98	.03858	38	1.49606	78	3.07087
0.59	.02323	0.99	.03898	39	1.53543	79	3.11024
0.60	.02362	1.00	.03937	40	1.57480	80	3.14961

(Continued)

(*Continued*)

mm	Decimal	mm	Decimal	mm	Decimal	mm	Decimal
81	3.18898	86	3.38583	91	3.58268	96	3.77953
82	3.22835	87	3.42520	92	3.62205	97	3.81890
83	3.26772	88	3.46457	93	3.66142	98	3.85827
84	3.30709	89	3.50394	94	3.70079	99	3.89764
85	3.34646	90	3.54331	95	3.74016	100	3.93701

BOTTLE SIZES

The following is a conversion between alcohol spirit and wine bottle sizes and the new metric bottles:

Old bottle size	Fluid ounces	New bottle size	Fluid ounces
Split	6.4	187 milliliters	6.3
⅖ pint	12.8	375 milliliters	12.7
⅘ quart	25.6	750 milliliters	25.4
1 quart	32.0	1.0 liter	33.8
Magnum	51.2	1.5 liters	50.7
½ gallon	64.0	No conversion (Wineries will be using 50.7 ounces, 1.5 liter size here.)	
Jeroboam	102.4	3.0 liters	101.4
1 gallon	128.0	No conversion (Wineries will be using 101.4 ounces, 3 liter size here.)	

MISCELLANEOUS UNITS OF MEASUREMENT

AGATE.   A size of type approximately 5½ point. Also a printing measure of 1/14 inch used for column length in periodical advertising.

ANGSTROM (A or λ).   This is 0.0001 micron or 1 ten-billionth of a meter. Used in measuring the length of light waves.

ASTRONOMICAL UNIT (A.U.).   A unit used in astronomy equal to the mean distance of the earth from the sun (93 million miles).

BARREL (bbl). For liquids except petroleum, 31½ U.S. gallons; for petroleum, 42 gallons. For dry products except cranberries, 105 dry quarts or 7,056 cubic inches; for cranberries, 5,826 cubic inches. An English beer barrel holds 43.23 U.S. gallons.

BOARD FOOT (bd ft). Designates lumber 12 inches by 12 inches by 1 inch, or 144 cubic inches.

BOLT. For measuring cloth, it is 40 yards. For measuring wallpaper, the bolt equals 16 yards.

CABLE'S LENGTH. At sea, 100 to 120 fathoms, or 200 to 240 yards.

CARAT (c). 200 milligrams or 3.086 grains troy. Named from the seed of the carob plant that was once used as a weight in the Mediterranean countries. Used for weighing precious stones. When spelled karat or k or kt, the term means a twenty-fourth part in expressing the proportion of fineness of a gold alloy. For example, a gold alloy containing $^{18}\!/_{24}$ by weight of gold is 18 karats fine.

CHAIN (ch). The length of an actual chain used by surveyors. It is 66 feet, or $\frac{1}{80}$ mile long, and is divided into 100 parts called links.

CUBIT. Used thousands of years ago by the Babylonians and Egyptians, the cubit was the first unit of measurement recorded in history. It represented the distance between the elbow and the tip of the extended middle finger. A modified Egyptian cubit—the Olympic cubit—was later used by the Greeks and Romans and was equal to our 18.24 inches. In English measure, the cubit became 18 inches.

ELL. The English ell is 45 inches. In the past and in different communities, the value of the ell has ranged from 24.7 to 48 inches. At present in the Netherlands, the ell is the meter, or 39.37 inches. It is used for measuring cloth.

FATHOM (fath). Originally the distance to which a man could stretch his arms. Now standardized as 6 feet. Used chiefly for measuring cables and depth of water.

FURLONG. In Anglo-Saxon times, the furlong meant what its name said—a furrow's length, or the length of an average furrow plowed by a farmer. Today it means 40 rods or 220 yards.

HAND.   Derived from the width of the hand, this measurement is now 4 inches or 10.16 centimeters. Used for measuring the height of horses.

HOGSHEAD (hhd).   A wine and other liquid measure, once quite variable but now standardized at 63 U.S. gallons or 238.5 liters.

KNOT.   This is not a unit of distance, but a rate of speed of 1 nautical mile an hour. It is therefore not correct to say a ship travels "at 28 knots an hour"; it travels simply "at 28 knots."

LEAGUE.   A unit used in different countries and at different times to mean distances varying from about 2.4 to 4.6 miles. In English-speaking countries it now usually means 3 miles—either nautical or statute—but is generally used vaguely or poetically.

LIGHT-YEAR.   Nearly 6 trillion miles, the distance light travels in a year at the rate of more than 186,000 miles a second. Used for measuring distances in interstellar space.

LINK.   One-hundredth part of a chain, or 7.92 inches. Used by surveyors.

MAGNUM.   Wine or spirit bottle holding about ⅖ gallon or the amount such a bottle will hold.

MICRON (μ).   One thousandth of a millimeter. Used for scientific measurements.

MIL.   One thousandth of an inch. Used especially for measuring the diameter of wire. A circular mil represents the area of a circle 1 mil in diameter. The area of a cross section of wire is generally expressed in circular mils.

NAUTICAL MILE.   Theoretically equal to 1 minute or ½₁₆₀₀ part of a great circle of the earth, or roughly 1⅙ land miles. As the earth is not a perfect circle, various lengths have been assigned to it in different times and places. The British Admiralty mile, for instance, is equal to 6,080 feet or 1,853.2 meters. A U.S. unit, no longer officially used, is 6,080.2 feet or 1,853.248 meters. An international unit equal to 6,076.115 feet or 1,852 meters has been used officially by the U.S. since 1959. The nautical mile is used in both sea and air navigation.

PICA.   One-sixth inch or 12 points. Used for measurements in printing and as the name for 12-point type.

PIPE.   Wine measure equal to 2 hogsheads.

POINT.   Approximately $\frac{1}{72}$ inch or $\frac{1}{12}$ pica. Used for measuring type size.

QUIRE.   Measure for paper quantity—originally 24 sheets, but now usually 25. Twenty quires make a ream.

REAM.   Measure for paper quantity—originally 480 sheets, but now usually 500.

ROD.   Today a rod equals 5½ yards or 16½ feet. This measure was originally determined in the 16th century by lining up 16 men, left-foot-to-left-foot, as they left church on Sunday morning.

SPAN.   An English unit equal to 9 inches or 22.86 centimeters. Derived from the distance between the tip of thumb and the tip of the little finger when both are outstretched.

STONE.   A varying unit of weight that in the past has ranged from 4 to 26 pounds avoirdupois. In Great Britain it today has a legal value of 14 pounds.

TOWNSHIP.   A division of territory in surveys of U.S. public land, measuring almost 36 square miles. The south, east, and west borders are each 6 miles long. As the latter two follow the meridians of the earth, the north border is a little shorter. Often these geological townships have later become also political townships.

TUN.   The capacity of a large cask by the same name—2 pipes, 4 hogheads, or 252 old English wine gallons (which are the same as U.S. gallons).

CONVERSION OF COMMON UNITS

The following table has been compiled especially for this book in the hope that it might make conversions from one measurement unit to another faster and simpler. In it common units of weight, area, volume, power, velocity, and so on are not separated into categories as is often done, but are listed in straight alphabetical order. To use it, just find in the left column the unit you want to convert, then in the middle column the one you want to convert to. Convert merely by multiplying the number of original units by the number you find directly to the right of the second unit.

To convert from such units as spoons, cups, and other household utensils, see earlier section "Approximate Household Measures," and to convert from specialized units and others not commonly used, see "Miscellaneous Units of Measurement." Unless otherwise mentioned, all weight units are avoirdupois, and all volume units (pints, bushels, gallons, etc.) are U.S. Customary units.

CONVERSIONS OF COMMON UNITS

To convert from	To	Multiply by
Acceleration by gravity	centimeters per second	980.665
	feet per second	32.16
Acres	hectares	0.4047
	square chains	10.0
	square feet	43,560.0
	square miles	0.00156
	centiares	100.0
	square yards	119.6
Atmospheres (atm)	inches of mercury	29.921
	feet of water	33.934
	kilograms per square centimeter	1.033228
	pounds per square inch	14.6959
British thermal units (Btu)	calories	0.252
	foot-pounds	778.0
	watt-seconds	1,054.86
Bushels	bushels, imperial	0.968
	cubic feet	1.2445
	cubic inches	2,150.42
	liters	35.2393
	pecks	4.0
	pints, dry	64.0
	quarts, dry	32.0
Calories (cal)	British thermal units	3.9682
	foot-pounds	3,088.4

To convert from	To	Multiply by
Candles per square centimeter	Lamberts	3.142
Candles per square inch	Lamberts	0.4869
Carats	grains	3.086
Centares	square inches	1,549.997
	square meters	1.0
Centigrade, degrees (°C)	Fahrenheit, degrees	$\dfrac{9}{5} \times °C + 32$
Centigrams (cg)	grains	0.1543
	grams	0.01
Centiliters (cl)	liters	0.01
	ounces; fluid	0.0338
Centimeters (cm)	feet	0.0328
	inches	0.3937
	meters	0.01
Chains (surveyor's)	furlongs	0.10000
	miles, statute	0.01250
	links	100.0
Circle (angular)	degrees	360.0
Circular inch (cir in)	area of a 1-inch-diameter circle	1.0
	circular mils	1,000,000.0
	square inches	0.7854
Circular mil	area of a 0.001-inch-diameter circle	1.0
	circular inches	0.0000001
Circumference of the earth at the equator	miles, nautical	21,600.0
Circumference of the earth at the equator	miles, statute	24,874.5
Cord (cd), of wood, (4 × 4 × 8)	cubic feet	128.0
Cubic centimeters (cu cm)	cubic feet	0.00003531
	cubic inches	0.06102

(Continued)

CONVERSIONS OF COMMON UNITS (*Continued*)

To convert from	To	Multiply by
Cubic centimeters (cu cm)	liters	0.0010
	cubic meter	0.0000010
Cubic decimeters	cubic centimeters	1,000.0
	cubic inches	61.02
Cubic feet (cu ft)	bushels	0.80290
	cords, of wood	0.00781
	cubic centimeters	28,317.08
	cubic inches	1,728.0
	cubic meters	0.0283
	cubic yards	0.0370
	gallons	7.4805
	liters	28.3163
	perch, of masonry	0.04040
Cubic feet of water at 39.1° Fahrenheit (° F)	kilograms	28.3156
	pounds	62.4245
Cubic inches (cu in)	bushels, imperial	0.00045
	bushels	0.00046
	cubic centimeters	16.3872
	cubic feet	0.00058
	cubic meters	0.000016
	cubic yards	0.0000214
	gallons	0.00432
	liters	0.0164
	pecks	0.00186
	pints, dry	0.02976
	pints, liquid	0.0346
	quarts, dry	0.01488
	quarts, liquid	0.0173
Cubic meters (cu m or m³)	cubic centimeters	1,000,000.0
	cubic feet	35.3133
	cubic inches	61,023.3753
	cubic yards	1.3079
	gallons	264.170

To convert from	To	Multiply by
Cubic millimeters (cu mm or mm³)	cubic centimeters	0.001
	cubic inches	0.00006
Cubic yards (cu yd)	cubic feet	27.0
	cubic inches	46,656.0
	cubic meters	0.7646
Decagrams	grams	10.0
	ounces, avoirdupois	0.3527
Deciliters	bushels	0.284
	gallons	2.64
	liters	10.0
Decameters	inches	393.7
	meters	10.0
Decigrams	grains	1.5432
	grams	0.1
Deciliter	ounces, fluid	0.338
Deciliters	liters	0.1
Decimeters	inches	3.937
	meters	0.01
Degrees (arc)	radians	0.0175
Degrees (at the equator)	miles, nautical	60.0
	miles, statute	69.168
Degrees (deg or °)	minutes	60.0
Dozens (doz)	units	12.0
Drams (dr), apothecaries	grains	60.0
	grams	3.543
	scruples	3.0
Drams, avoirdupois	grains	27.344
	grams	1.772
	ounces, avoirdupois	0.0625
Drams, fluid	cubic inches	0.2256
	milliliters	3.6966

(Continued)

CONVERSIONS OF COMMON UNITS (*Continued*)

To convert from	To	Multiply by
Drams, fluid	minims	60.0
	ounces, fluid	0.125
Dynes	grams	0.00102
Fahrenheit	centigrade, degrees	$\dfrac{5\,(°F - 32)}{9}$
Fathoms	feet	6.0
	meters	1.8288
	yards	2.0
Feet (ft)	centimeters	30.4801
	fathom	0.16667
	inches	12.0
	links	0.66000
	meters	0.3048
	miles	0.000189
	miles, nautical	0.0001645
	rods	0.06061
	yards	0.3333
Feet of water at 62° Fahrenheit	killigrams per square meter	304.442
	pounds per square foot	62.355
	pounds per square inch	0.4334
Feet per second (fps)	knots	0.5921
	miles per hour	0.6816
Foot-pounds (ft-lb)	British thermal units	0.00129
	calories	0.00032
	meter-kilograms	0.13835
Foot-pounds per minute	horsepower	0.000003
Foot-pounds per second	horsepower	0.000018
Furlongs	chains	10.0
	feet	660.0
	meters	201.17
	miles, statute	0.12500
	yards	220.0

To convert from	To	Multiply by
Gallons (gal)	ounces, U.S. fluid	128.0
Gallons, imperial	gallons, U.S.	1.2009
Gallons (gal), imperial	liters	4.54607
Gallons, U.S.	cubic feet	0.1337
	cubic inches	231.0
	cubic meters	0.0038
	gallons, imperial	0.8327
	liters	3.7878
Gallons, U.S., water	pounds	8.5
Gills	pints, liquid	0.25
Grains	drams, avoirdupois	0.0366
	grams	0.0648
	milligrams	64.7989
	ounces, avoirdupois	0.00229
	ounces, troy and apothecaries'	0.00208
	pounds, avoirdupois	0.00014
	pounds, troy and apothecaries'	0.00017
Grams (g)	dynes	981
	grains	15.4475
	kilograms	0.0010
	milligrams	1,000.0
	ounces, avoirdupois	0.0353
	pounds, avoirdupois	0.0022
Grams per cubic centimeter	kilograms per cubic meter	1,000.0
	pounds per cubic foot	62.4
	pounds per cubic inch	0.03613
Gross	dozen	12.0
Gross, great	gross	12.0
Hands	inches	4.0
Hectares	square meters	10,000
	acres	2.471

(Continued)

CONVERSIONS OF COMMON UNITS (Continued)

To convert from	To	Multiply by
Hectograms	grams	100.0
	ounces, avoirdupois	3.5274
Hectoliters	gallons	26.417
	liters	100.0
Hectometers	feet	328.083
	meters	100.0
Horsepower (hp)	kilogram-meters per second	76.042
	foot-pounds per second	550.0
	foot-pounds per minute	33,000.0
	metric horsepower	1.0139
	watts per minute	746.0
Horsepower, metric	horsepower	0.9862
	foot pounds per minute	32,550.0
	foot pounds per second	542.5
	kilogram meters per second	75.0
Inches (in)	centimeters	2.5400
	feet	0.08333
	hands	0.25000
	links	0.12626
	meters	0.0254
	mils	1,000.0
	spans	0.11111
	yards	0.02778
Inches of mercury	feet of water	1.1341
	grams per square centimeter	34.542
	inches of water	13.6092
	pounds per square inch	0.49115
Inches of water	grams per square centimeter	2.537
	inches of mercury	0.07347
	pounds per square foot	5.1052
Kilocycles	cycles per second	1,000.0
Kilogram-meters (kg-m)	pound-feet	7.2330

To convert from	To	Multiply by
Kilogram-meters per second	horsepower	0.01305
	horsepower, metric	0.01333
Kilograms (kg)	grains	15,432.36
	grams	1,000.0
	ounces, avoirdupois	35.2740
	pounds, avoirdupois	2.2046
	tons	0.00110
	tons, long	0.00098
	tons, metric	0.001
Kilograms per cubic meter (kg per cu m or kg/m³)	pounds per cubic foot	0.06243
Kilograms per meter	pounds per foot	0.6721
Kilograms per square centimeter	pounds per square inch	14.22
Kilograms per square meter	pounds per square inch	0.2048
	pounds per square inch	0.00142
Kiloliters (kl)	liters	1,000.0
Kilometers (km)	feet	3,280.8330
	meters	1,000.0
	miles, nautical	0.5396
	miles, statute	0.6214
Kilometers per hour	knots	0.5396
	miles per hour	0.62138
Kilowatt-hours (kwhr)	British thermal units per hour	3,412.75
	horsepower hours	1.3414
Kilowatts (kw)	foot-pounds per minute	0.04426
Knots	feet per second	1.6889
	kilometers per hour	1.8532
	meters per second	0.5148
	miles per hour	1.1516
	nautical miles per hour	1.0

(Continued)

CONVERSIONS OF COMMON UNITS (Continued)

To convert from	To	Multiply by
Lamberts	candles per square centimeter	0.3183
	candles per square inch	2.054
Leagues, land	kilometers	4.83
	miles, nautical	2.6050
	miles, statute	3.0
Leagues, marine	kilometers	5.56
	miles, nautical	3.0
	miles, statute	3.45
Links	chains	0.01
	feet	0.66
	inches	7.92
	rods	0.04
	yards	0.22
Liters (l)	bushels	0.0284
	cubic centimeters	1,000.0
	cubic feet	0.035313
	cubic inches	61.02398
	gallons, imperial	0.2199
	gallons, U.S.	0.2641
	pecks	0.1135
	quarts, dry	0.9081
	quarts, liquid	1.0567
Long tons	pounds, avoirdupois	2,240.0
Lumens per square foot	foot-candles	1.0
Lux	foot-candles	0.0929
Megacycles	cycles per second	1,000,000.0
Megameters	meters	100,000.0
Meter-kilograms (m-kg)	foot-pounds	7.2330
Meters (m)	fathoms	0.5468
	feet	3.2808
	inches	39.370
	miles, nautical	0.000541

To convert from	To	Multiply by
Meters (m)	miles	0.000622
	yards	1.0936
Meters per second	knots	1.9425
	miles per hour	2.2369
Microns	inches	0.000039
	meters	0.000001
	mils	0.03937
Miles, nautical	feet	6,080.20
	kilometers	1.85325
	leagues, marine	0.33333
	meters	1,853.2486
	miles, statute	1.1516
Miles per hour (mph)	feet per second	1.4667
	kilometers per hour	1.6093
	knots	0.8684
	meters per second	0.4470
Miles, statute	chains	80.0
	feet	5,280.0
	furlongs	8.0
	kilometers	1.6093
	leagues, land	0.33333
	meters	1,609.35
	miles, nautical	0.86836
	yards	1,760.0
Milligrams (mg)	grains	0.01543
	grams	0.001
Milliliters (ml)	drams, fluid	0.2705
	liters	0.001
	ounces, fluid	0.0338
Millimeters (mm)	inches	0.03937
	meters	0.001
	microns	1,000.0
	mils	39.37
Mils	inches	0.001
	microns	25.4001
	millimeters	0.0254

(Continued)

CONVERSIONS OF COMMON UNITS (*Continued*)

To convert from	To	Multiply by
Minims	drams, fluid	0.01667
Minutes (min)	seconds	60.0
Myriagrams	grams	10,000.0
Myriameters	meters	10,000.0
Ounces (oz), apothecaries'	drams, apothecaries'	8.0
Ounces, avoirdupois	drams, avoirdupois	16.0
	grains	437.5
	grams	28.3495
	ounces, troy and apothecaries'	1.0971
	pounds, avoirdupois	0.0625
Ounces, British fluid	cubic centimeters	28.382
	cubic inches	1.732
Ounces, fluid	millimeters	29.57
Ounces, troy	pennyweights	20.0
Ounces, troy and apothecaries'	grains	480.0
	grams	31.10348
	ounces, avoirdupois	0.91149
Ounces, U.S. fluid	cubic inches	1.805
	drams, fluid	8.0
	gallons	0.00781
	liters	0.0296
Pecks (pk)	bushel	0.25
	cubic inches	537.61
	liters	8.8096
	quarts, dry	8.0
Pennyweights (dwt)	grains	24.0
Perch (of masonry)	cubic feet	24.75
Pints (pt), dry	bushels	0.015625
	cubic inches	33.60
	liters	0.5506

To convert from	To	Multiply by
Pints (pt), dry	pecks	0.0625
	quarts, dry	0.5
Pints, liquid	cubic inches	28,875
	gills	4.0
	liters	0.4732
Poundals	pounds, avoirdupois	0.03113
Pound-feet (lb-ft)	kilogram-meters	0.1383
Pounds (lb), avoirdupois	cubic feet of water	0.0160
	grains	7,000.0
	grams	453.5924
	ounces, avoirdupois	16.0
	poundals	32.1740
	slugs	0.0311
	tons, long	0.00045
	tons, short	0.0005
Pounds per cubic foot (lb per cu ft)	grams per cubic centimeter	0.01602
	kilograms per cubic meter	16.0184
	pounds per cubic inch	0.00058
Pounds per foot	kilograms per meter	1.4882
Pounds per square foot (psf)	inches of water	0.1922
	kilograms per square meter	4.8824
	pounds per square inch	0.00694
Pounds per square inch (psi)	atmospheres	0.0680
	feet of water	2.3066
	grams per square centimeter	70.3067
	inches of water	27.7
	inches of mercury	2.0360
	kilograms per square meter	703.0669
	pounds per square foot	144.0
Pounds, troy and apothecaries'	grains	5,760.0
	kilograms	0.37324

(Continued)

CONVERSIONS OF COMMON UNITS *(Continued)*

To convert from	To	Multiply by
Pounds, troy and apothecaries'	ounces, troy and apothecaries'	12.0
	pounds, avoirdupois	0.8229
Quadrants	degrees	90.0
Quarts, dry	liters	1.1012
	pecks	0.125
	pints, dry	2.0
	quarts, dry, imperial	0.968
	bushel, U.S.	0.03125
	cubic inches	67.2
Quarts, liquid	cubic inches	57.75
	liters	0.94636
Quintals	grams	100,000.0
	pounds, avoirdupois	220.46
Radians	degrees, arc	57.2958
	minutes, arc	3,437.7468
	revolutions	0.1591
Radians per second	revolutions per minute	9.4460
Ream	sheets	480.0
Ream, printing paper	sheets	500.0
Revolutions	radians	6.2832
Revolutions per minute (rpm)	radians per second	0.1059
Rods	chains	0.25
	feet	16.5
	furlongs	40.0
	links	25.0
	meters	5.029
	yards	5.5
Score	units	20.0
Scruples	grains	20.0
Seconds	minutes	0.01667

To convert from	To	Multiply by
Slugs	pounds	32.1740
Spans	inches	9.0
Square centimeters (sq cm or cm²)	square feet	0.001076
	square inches	0.1550
	square millimeters	100.0
Square chains	acres	0.1
	square feet	4,356.0
	square meters	404.7
	square miles	0.00016
	square rods	16.0
	square yards	484.0
Square decameters	square meters	100.0
Square decimeters	square meters	0.01
Square feet (sq ft)	acres	0.000022988
	square centimeters	929.0341
	square chains	0.00023
	square inches	144.0
	square meters	0.0929
	square rods	0.00368
	square yards	0.11111
Square hectometers	square meters	10,000.0
Square inches (sq in)	circular inches	1.27324
	square centimeters	6.4516
	square feet	0.00694
	square millimeters	645.1625
	square yards	0.00077
Square kilometers (sq km or km²)	hectares	100.0
	square meters	1,000,000.0
	square miles	0.3861
Square links	square feet	0.4356
	square meters	0.0405
	square rods	0.00160
	square yards	0.04840

(Continued)

CONVERSIONS OF COMMON UNITS (*continued*)

To convert from	To	Multiply by
Square meters (sq m or m²)	centiares	1.0
	square feet	10.7639
	square yards	1.1960
Square miles	square kilometers	2.590
	acres	640.0
	square chains	6,400.0
Square millimeters (sq mm or mm²)	square inches	0.00155
	square meters	0.000001
Square rods	square chains	0.06250
	square feet	272.25
	square links	625.0
	square meters	25.29
	square yards	30.25
Square yards	square chains	0.00207
	square feet	9.0
	square inches	1,296.0
	square links	20.66116
	square meters	0.83613
	square rods	0.03306
Tons, long	kilograms	1,016.0470
	pounds, avoirdupois	2,240.0
Tons, metric	kilograms	1,000.0
	pounds, avoirdupois	2,204.62
	quintals	10.0
Tons of refrigeration	BTU per hour	12,000.0
Tons, register	cubic feet	100.0
Tons, shipping	bushels	32.143
	cubic feet	40.0
Tons, short	kilograms	907.18
	pounds, avoirdupois	2,000.0
Watt-hours	Btu	3.413

To convert from	To	Multiply by
Watts	Btu per hour	3.415
	horsepower	0.00134
Yards (yd)	chains	0.04545
	fathoms	0.50000
	feet	3.0
	furlongs	0.004545
	inches	36.0
	links	0.22000
	meters	0.9144
	miles, statute	0.000569
	rods	0.18182

Other Information

RECOMMENDED NAILING PRACTICES

Proper fastening of frame members and covering materials provides the rigidity and strength to resist severe windstorms and other hazards. Good nailing is also important from the standpoint of normal performance of wood parts. For example, proper fastening of intersecting walls usually reduces wall cracking at the inside corners. The schedule below outlines good nailing practices for the framing and sheathing of a well-constructed wood-frame house.

JOINING	NAILING METHOD	NAILS		
		Number	Size	Placement
Header to joist	end-nail	3	16d	
Joist to sill or girder	toenail	2 3	10d or 8d	
Header and stringer joist to sill	toenail		10d	16 inches o.c.
Bridging to joist	toenail each end	2	8d	
Ledger strip to beam, 2 inches thick		3	16d	at each joist
Subfloor, boards 1 × 6 inches and smaller 1 × 8 inches		2 3	8d 8d	to each joist to each joist

Subfloor, plywood
   At edges
   At intermediate joists
			8d
			8d
				6 inches o.c.
				8 inches o.c.

Subfloor (2 × 6 inches T&G) to joist or girder	blind-nail (casing and face-nail)	2	16d	

JOINING	NAILING METHOD	NAILS		
		Number	Size	Placement
Soleplate to stud, horizontal assembly	end-nail	2	16d	at each stud
Top plate to stud	end-nail	2	16d	
Stud to soleplate	toenail	4	8d	
Soleplate to joist or blocking	face-nail		16d	16 inches o.c.
Doubled studs	face-nail, stagger		10d	16 inches o.c.
End stud of intersecting wall to exterior wall stud	face-nail		16d	16 inches o.c.
Upper top plate to lower top plate	face-nail		16d	16 inches o.c.
Upper top plate laps and intersections	face-nail	2	16d	
Continuous header, two pieces, each edge			12d	12 inches o.c.
Ceiling joist to top wall plates	toenail	3	8d	
Ceiling joist laps at partition	face-nail	4	16d	
Rafter to top plate	toenail	2	8d	
Rafter to ceiling joist	face-nail	5	10d	
Rafter to valley or hip rafter	toenail	3	10d	
Ridge board to rafter	end-nail	3	10d	
Rafter to rafter through ridge board	toenail	4	8d	
	edge-nail	1	10d	
Collar beam to rafter				
2-inch member	face-nail	2	12d	
1-inch member	face-nail	3	8d	

(Continued)

RECOMMENDED NAILING PRACTICES (continued)

Proper fastening of frame members and covering materials provides the rigidity and strength to resist severe windstorms and other hazards. Good nailing is also important from the standpoint of normal performance of wood parts. For example, proper fastening of intersecting walls usually reduces wall cracking at the inside corners. The schedule below outlines good nailing practices for the framing and sheathing of a well-constructed wood-frame house.

JOINING	NAILING METHOD	NAILS		
		Number	Size	Placement
1-inch diagonal let-in brace to each stud and plate (four nails at top)		2	8d	
Built-up corner studs Studs to blocking	face-nail	2	10d	each side
Intersecting stud to corner studs	face-nail		16d	12 inches o.c.
Built-up girders and beams, three or more members	face-nail		20d	32 inches o.c.
Wall sheathing 1 × 8 inches or less horizontal	face-nail	2	8d	at each stud
1 × 6 inches or greater, diagonal	face-nail	3	8d	at each stud
Wall sheathing, vertically applied plywood ⅜ inch and less thick	face-nail		6d	6-inch edge
½ inch and overthick	face-nail		8d	12 inches intermediate
Wall sheathing vertically applied fiberboard ½ inch thick	face-nail			1½-inch roofing nail
²⁵⁄₃₂ inch thick	face-nail			1¾-inch roofing nail (3 inches edge and 6 inches intermediate)
Roof sheathing boards, 4-, 6-, 8-inch width	face-nail	2	8d	at each rafter
Roof sheathing, plywood ⅜ inch and less thick	face-nail		6d	
½ inch and overthick	face-nail		8d	6 inches edge and 12 inches intermediate

COMMON NAILS REFERENCE TABLE

The "d" in nail sizes means "penny" and is the abbreviation for the Latin denarius, an ancient Roman coin. Originally, 2d, 10d, etc., referred to the cost in pennies for 100 nails. Now it refers to a definite size.

Size	Length (inches)	Diameter guage number	Diameter of head (inches)	Approximate number per pound
2d	1	15	$1\frac{1}{64}$	830
3d	$1\frac{1}{4}$	14	$1\frac{3}{64}$	528
4d	$1\frac{1}{2}$	$12\frac{1}{2}$	$\frac{1}{4}$	316
5d	$1\frac{3}{4}$	$12\frac{1}{2}$	$\frac{1}{4}$	271
6d	2	$11\frac{1}{2}$	$1\frac{7}{64}$	168
7d	$2\frac{1}{4}$	$11\frac{1}{2}$	$1\frac{1}{64}$	150
8d	$2\frac{1}{2}$	$10\frac{1}{4}$	$\frac{9}{32}$	106
9d	$2\frac{3}{4}$	$10\frac{1}{4}$	$\frac{9}{32}$	96
10d	3	9	$\frac{5}{16}$	69
12d	$3\frac{1}{4}$	9	$\frac{5}{16}$	63
16d	$3\frac{1}{2}$	8	$1\frac{1}{32}$	49
20d	4	6	$1\frac{3}{32}$	31
30d	$4\frac{1}{2}$	5	$\frac{7}{16}$	24
40d	5	4	$1\frac{3}{32}$	18
50d	$5\frac{1}{2}$	3	$\frac{1}{2}$	14
60d	6	2	$1\frac{7}{32}$	11

FINISHING NAILS REFERENCE TABLE

Size	Length (inches)	Diameter gauge number	Diameter of head gauge number	Approximate number per pound
2d	1	$16\frac{1}{2}$	$13\frac{1}{2}$	1,351
3d	$1\frac{1}{4}$	$15\frac{1}{2}$	$12\frac{1}{2}$	807
4d	$1\frac{1}{2}$	15	12	584
5d	$1\frac{3}{4}$	15	12	500
6d	2	13	10	309
8d	$2\frac{1}{2}$	$12\frac{1}{2}$	$9\frac{1}{2}$	189
10d	3	$11\frac{1}{2}$	$8\frac{1}{2}$	121
16d	$3\frac{1}{2}$	11	8	90
20d	4	10	7	62

CASING NAILS REFERENCE TABLE

Size	Length (inches)	Diameter gauge number	Diameter of head gauge number	Approximate number per pound
4d	1½	14	11	490
6d	2	12½	9½	245
8d	2½	11½	8½	145
10d	3	10½	7½	95
16d	3½	10	7	72

STANDARD WOOD SCREW DIAMETERS

Number	DIAMETER		
	Basic	Maximum	Minimum
0	.006	.064	.053
1	.073	.077	.066
2	.086	.090	.079
3	.099	.103	.092
4	.112	.116	.105
5	.125	.129	.118
6	.138	.142	.131
7	.151	.155	.144
8	.164	.168	.157
9	.177	.181	.170
10	.190	.194	.183
11	.203	.207	.196
12	.216	.220	.209
14	.242	.246	.235
16	.268	.272	.261
18	.294	.298	.287
20	.320	.324	.313
24	.372	.376	.365

DRILL AND BIT SIZES FOR SCREWS

Size of screw	SHANK OR FIRST HOLES			PILOT OR SECOND HOLES					Auger bit for counter-sink*	Countersink drill number
				Hardwood		Softwood				
	Drill number or letter	Drill size nearest fraction (in inches)	Auger bit size*	Drill number or letter	Drill size nearest fraction (in inches)	Drill number or letter	Drill size nearest fraction (in inches)	Auger bit size*		
0	52	$1/16$		70	$1/32$	75	$1/64$		—	32
1	47	$5/64$		66	$1/32$	71	$1/32$		—	20
2	42	$3/32$		56	$3/64$	65	$1/32$		3	16
3	37	$7/64$		54	$1/16$	58	$3/64$		4	4
4	32	$7/64$		52	$1/16$	55	$3/64$		4	B
5	30	$1/8$		49	$5/64$	53	$1/16$		4	F
6	27	$9/64$		47	$5/64$	52	$1/16$		5	L
7	22	$5/32$		44	$3/32$	51	$1/16$		5	O
8	18	$11/64$	3	40	$3/32$	48	$5/64$		6	S
9	14	$3/16$	3	37	$7/64$	45	$5/64$		6	T
10	10	$3/16$	3	33	$7/64$	43	$3/32$		6	X
11	4	$13/64$	3	31	$1/8$	40	$3/32$		7	$7/16$
12	2	$7/32$	3	30	$1/8$	38	$7/64$		7	$29/64$
14	D	$1/4$	4	25	$9/64$	32	$7/64$	3	8	$33/64$
16	I	$17/64$	5	18	$5/32$	29	$9/64$	3	9	$37/64$
18	N	$19/64$	5	13	$3/16$	26	$9/64$	4	10	$41/64$
20	P	$21/64$	5	4	$13/64$	19	$11/64$	4	11	$45/64$
24	V	$3/8$	6	1	$7/32$	15	$3/16$	4	12	$49/64$

* Standard auger bits are sized by sixteenths of an inch. The number stamped on the square tang represents the diameter of the bit in these units. For example, a Number 3 bit will cut a hole $3/16$ inch in diameter, while a Number 4 will cut a $1/4$-inch hole.

"POP" RIVET SELECT CHART

Rivet diameter (in inches)	Rivet material	To fit work thickness (in inches)	Rivet diameter (in inches)	Rivet material	To fit work thickness (in inches)
$\frac{1}{8}$	Aluminum	$\frac{1}{8}$ short	$\frac{5}{32}$	Aluminum	$\frac{3}{8}$ long
$\frac{1}{8}$	Aluminum (white) rivets	$\frac{1}{8}$ short	$\frac{3}{16}$	Aluminum	$\frac{1}{8}$ short
$\frac{1}{8}$	Aluminum	$\frac{1}{4}$ medium	$\frac{3}{16}$	Aluminum	$\frac{1}{4}$ medium
$\frac{1}{8}$	Aluminum	$\frac{3}{8}$ long	$\frac{3}{16}$	Aluminum	$\frac{3}{8}$ long
$\frac{5}{32}$	Aluminum	$\frac{1}{8}$ medium	$\frac{1}{8}$	Steel	$\frac{1}{8}$ short
$\frac{5}{32}$	Aluminum	$\frac{1}{4}$ medium	$\frac{1}{8}$	Steel	$\frac{1}{4}$ medium
			$\frac{1}{8}$	Steel	$\frac{3}{8}$ long

COMMON STAPLE SIZE AND THEIR USES

$\frac{1}{4}$-inch leg	$\frac{5}{16}$-inch leg	$\frac{3}{8}$-inch leg	$\frac{1}{2}$-inch leg	$\frac{9}{16}$-inch leg
Light upholstering, screens, window shades, decorations, valances	Thin insulation, storm windows, draperies, upholstery, heavy fabrics	Weather stripping, roofing papers, light insulation, electrical wires, wire mesh	Canvas, felt stripping, underlayments of carpets, fiberglass	Ceiling tile,* fencing, insulation board, metal lathing, roofing

* Special $\frac{9}{16}$-inch staples are also available for ceiling tile.

PIPE DATA AT A GLANCE

Ease of working	Water flow efficiency factor	Type of fittings needed	Manner usually stocked	Life expectancy	Principal uses
THREADED BRASS [1]					
No threading required; cuts easily, but can't be bent; measuring a job is rather difficult	Highly efficient because of low friction	Screw-on connections	12-foot rigid lengths; cuts to size wanted	Lasts life of building	Generally for commercial construction
HARD COPPER					
Easier to work with than brass	Same as brass	Screw-on or solder connections	12-foot rigid lengths; cut to size wanted	Same as brass	Same as brass
SOFT COPPER					
Easier to work with than brass or hard copper because it bends readily by using a bending tool; measuring a job isn't too difficult	Same as brass	Solder connections	Coils are usually soft	Same as brass	Widely used in residential installations

1. Threaded brass is required in some cities where water is extremely corrosive; often smaller diameter will suffice because of low friction coefficient.
2. Flexible copper tubing is probably the most popular; often a smaller diameter will suffice because of its low friction coefficient.
3. Wrought or galvanized iron is recommended if lines are subject to impact.
4. Plastic pipe is the lightest weight of all (weighing roughly one-eighth as much as metal); does not burst in freezing temperatures.

(Continued)

PIPE DATA AT A GLANCE (continued)

Ease of working	Water flow efficiency factor	Type of fittings needed	Manner usually stocked	Life expectancy	Principal uses
FLEXIBLE COPPER TUBING[2]					
Easier than soft copper because it can be bent without a tool; measuring jobs is easy	Highest of all metals since there are no nipples, unions, or elbows	Solder or compression connections	3-wall thicknesses: 'K'—thickest; 'L'—medium; 'M'—thinnest; 20-foot lengths or 15-, 30-, or 60-foot coils (except 'M')	Same as brass	'K' is used in municipal and commercial construction; 'L' is used for residential water lines; 'M' is for light domestic lines only (check code before using)
WROUGHT IRON (OR GALVANIZED)[3]					
Has to be threaded; more difficult to cut; measurements for jobs must be exact	Lower than copper because nipple unions reduce water flow	Screw-on connections	Rigid lengths, up to 22 feet; usually cut to size wanted	Corrodes in alkaline water more than others; produces rust stains	Generally found in older homes
PLASTIC PIPE[4]					
Can be cut with saw or knife	Same as copper tubing	Insert couplings, clamps, also by cement; threaded and compression fittings can be used (thread same as for metal pipe)	Rigid, semirigid, and flexible; coils of 100 to 400 feet	Long life; it is rust and corrosion proof	For cold-water installations; used for well casings, septic tank lines, sprinkler systems; check code before installing

1. Threaded brass is required in some cities where water is extremely corrosive; often smaller diameter will suffice because of low friction coefficient.
2. Flexible copper tubing is probably the most popular; often a smaller diameter will suffice because of its low friction coefficient.
3. Wrought or galvanized iron is recommended if lines are subject to impact.
4. Plastic pipe is the lightest weight of all (weighing roughly one-eighth as much as metal); does not burst in freezing temperatures.

Sizes of Wrought Iron, Galvanized Steel, and Copper Pipe

Pipe sizes are generally determined by the inside diameter of the pipe. Does it confuse you, then, to find that to get a pipe about ¼ inch in diameter on the inside and ⅜ inch on the outside you must ask for ⅛-inch pipe? The story behind this anomaly goes back to the days when materials were weaker and pipe of ⅜-inch outside diameter did have an inside diameter of only ⅛ inch. When materials became stronger and walls could be thinner, it was decided to keep the same *outside* diameter so that standard threading tools and fittings could still be used. The inside diameter of threaded iron, steel, and brass pipe therefore became somewhat larger than its nominal size. In the larger sizes the difference is small; in the smaller ones, though, it can confound you.

SIZES OF TYPES K, L, AND M COPPER TUBING

Nominal Size (Inches)	Outside Diameter	Inside Diameter		
	Types K, L, and M	Type K	Type L	Type M
⅜	0.500	0.402	0.430	0.450
½	0.625	0.527	0.545	0.569
¾	0.875	0.745	0.785	0.811
1	1.125	0.995	1.025	1.055
1¼	1.375	1.245	1.265	1.291
1½	1.625	1.481	1.505	1.527

IRON- TO COPPER-TUBE CONVERSION

Since copper tubing has a smooth bore, water flows through it with less resistance than through wrought iron. This feature permits replacement of a heavy iron pipe with a copper tube of smaller diameter. To determine possible replacement sizes involving this factor, check the table below:

Iron pipe size (inches)	Copper tube size	Iron pipe size (inches)	Copper tube size
½	⅜	1¼	1
¾	½	1½	1¼
1	¾	2	1½

DATA ON THREADED METAL

Here are the nominal and approximate actual dimensions of commonly used sizes of standard threaded wrought iron, galvanized steel, and bronze pipe:

Nominal size (inches)	Approximate inside diameter (inches)	Approximate outside diameter (inches)	Threads per inch	Tap drill (inches)
⅛	¼	⅜	27	¹¹⁄₃₂
¼	⅜	¹⁷⁄₃₂	18	⁷⁄₁₆
⅜	½	¹¹⁄₁₆	18	³⁷⁄₆₄
½	⅝	¹³⁄₁₆	14	²³⁄₃₂
¾	¹³⁄₁₆	1	14	⁵⁹⁄₆₄
1	1¹⁄₁₆	1⁵⁄₁₆	11½	1⁵⁄₃₂
1¼	1⅜	1⅝	11½	1½
1½	1⅝	1⅞	11½	1⁴⁷⁄₆₄
2	2¹⁄₁₆	2⅜	11½	2⁷⁄₃₂
2½	2⁹⁄₁₆	2⅞	8	2⅝

PIPE SIZES FOR HOME-DRAINAGE SYSTEMS (IN INCHES)

Type of fixture	Lavatory	Tub or shower	Toilet	Sink	Garbage disposal	Dishwasher	Clothes washer
Branch drains	1½	1½	3 to 4	1½ to	1½ to	1½ to	1½
Revent lines				2	2	2	
Fixture supply lines	⅜	½	⅜	½	—	½	½

Note: Main soil stack: 3 to 4 inches. Secondary soil stack: Size of largest branch drain connected to it, in most cases. Basement floor drain: 2 to 4 inches. Building drain: At least the size of main soil stack. Branch building drain: At least the size of largest secondary soil stack emptying into it. Cold-water main line serving both the cold-water system and the hot-water heater: ¾ inch to 1 inch. Cold- and hot-water main lines serving two or more fixtures: Size of largest branch line served or, if fixtures will be used simultaneously, the next pipe size larger than that used for the largest branch line.

Electricity Consumed by Common Appliances

The accompanying table may help you determine the number and capacity of electrical outlets needed in your home or shop, and to estimate the operating cost of various appliances.

Electric power is charged for by the kilowatt-hour. To find out how long it takes an appliance to use this much electricity, just divide 1,000 by the wattage of the appliance. Using this method, you find you can run a 2-watt clock for 500 hours or a 100-watt lamp for 10 hours on 1 kilowatt-hour. At the other extreme, you discover that a 5,000-watt range oven will consume the same amount of power in 1/5 hour, or 12 minutes.

ELECTRICITY CONSUMPTION: APPLIANCES

	Watts
Air conditioner, room	800 to 1500
Blanket	150 to 200
Blender	250 to 300
Broiler	1200 to 1600
Can opener	80 to 120
Clock	2 to 3
Coffeemaker	600 to 1000
Deep fryer	1200 to 1650
Dishwasher	600 to 1300
Dryer, clothes	4000 to 8700
Fan, portable	50 to 200
Food mixer	120 to 250
Freezer, home	300 to 500
Frying pan	1000 to 1300
Furnace blower	800
Garbage disposal unit	200 to 800
Grill	1000 to 1200
Heat lamp	250
Heater, portable, home	600 to 1650
Heater, portable, home, 230-volt	2800 to 5600
Heating pad	50 to 75
Hot plate, each burner	550 to 1200
Intercom radio	800 to 120
Iron, hand	660 to 1500
Ironer	1200 to 1650
Lamps, fluorescent	15 to 60
Lamps, incandescent	2 up
Microwave oven	800 to 1500
Motors: ¼ horsepower	300 to 400
½ horsepower	450 to 600
1 horsepower	950 to 1000

(continued)

ELECTRICITY CONSUMPTION: APPLIANCES (continued)

	Watts
Projector, movie or slide	150 to 550
Radio, transistor	6 to 12
Radio, tube	35 to 150
Range, oven and all burners	8000 to 16000
Refrigerator	150 to 300
Roaster	1200 to 1650
Rotisserie-broiler	1200 to 1650
Sewing machine	60 to 90
Shaver	8 to 12
Stereo	100 to 400
Television	200 to 400
Toaster	550 to 1200
Trash compactor	300 to 500
Vacuum cleaner	200 to 800
Vent hood	125 to 175
Waffle iron	600 to 1100
Washing machine	400 to 800
Water heater	2000 to 5000
Water pump	300 to 700

COPPER WIRE TABLE
(Brown & Sharpe or American Wire Gauge)

AWG B&S	Diameter in mills	Turns per linear inch		Foot per pound		Ohms per 1000 feet at 68° F
		Enamel	Double cotton covered	Bare	Double cotton covered	
1	289.3	—	—	3.947	—	.1264
2	257.6	—	—	4.977	—	.1593
3	229.4	—	—	6.276	—	.2009
4	204.3	—	—	7.914	—	.2533
5	181.9	—	—	9.980	—	.3195
6	162.0	—	—	12.58	—	.4028
7	144.3	—	—	15.87	—	.5080
8	128.5	7.6	7.1	20.01	19.6	.6405

AWG B&S	Diameter in mills	Turns per linear inch		Foot per pound		Ohms per 1000 feet at 68° F
		Enamel	Double cotton covered	Bare	Double cotton covered	
9	114.4	8.6	7.8	25.23	24.6	.8077
10	101.9	9.6	8.9	31.82	30.9	1.018
11	90.74	10.7	9.8	40.12	38.8	1.284
12	80.81	12.0	10.9	50.59	48.9	1.619
13	71.96	13.5	12.0	63.80	61.5	2.042
14	64.08	15.0	13.8	80.44	77.3	2.575
15	57.07	16.8	14.7	101.4	97.3	3.247
16	50.82	18.9	16.4	127.9	119	4.094
17	45.26	21.2	18.1	161.3	150	5.163
18	40.30	23.6	19.8	203.4	188	6.510
19	35.89	26.4	21.8	256.5	237	8.210
20	31.96	29.4	23.8	323.4	298	10.35
21	28.46	33.1	26.0	407.8	370	13.05
22	25.35	37.0	30.0	514.2	461	16.46
23	22.57	41.3	31.6	648.4	584	20.76
24	20.10	46.3	35.6	817.7	745	26.17
25	17.90	51.7	38.6	1031	903	33.00
26	15.94	58.0	41.8	1300	1118	41.62
27	14.20	64.9	45.0	1639	1422	52.48
28	12.64	72.7	48.5	2067	1759	66.17
29	11.26	81.6	51.8	2607	2207	83.44
30	10.03	90.5	55.5	3287	2534	105.2
31	8.928	101	59.2	4145	2768	132.7
32	7.950	113	62.6	5227	3137	167.3
33	7.080	127	66.3	6591	4697	211.0
34	6.305	143	70.0	8310	6168	266.0
35	5.615	158	73.5	10480	6737	335.0
36	5.000	175	77.0	13210	7877	423.0
37	4.453	198	80.3	16660	9309	533.4
38	3.965	224	83.6	21010	10666	672.6
39	3.531	248	86.6	26500	11907	848.1
40	3.145	282	89.7	33410	14222	1069

A mil is $\frac{1}{1000}$ (one-thousandth) of an inch.

Measurements of covered wires may vary slightly with different manufacturers.

Wire of size 6 and larger is always stranded. The diameters shown here, however, are those of solid wires of equivalent cross section.

What Size Wire for the Circuit?

The minimum size wire to be used in electrical circuits is determined by both safety and efficiency. In all cases, wiring installations should conform to the rules of the National Electrical Code, which is based on the recommendations of the National Fire Protection Association. This code is concerned only with preventing electrical or thermal hazards that might electrocute somebody or start a fire. Beyond the bare requirements of safety, however, circuits should be designed to not waste too much electricity in the form of useless heat so that they deliver current at the end of the line at a sufficiently high voltage to properly do the job.

WIRE GAUGES FOR FEEDER AND BRANCH CIRCUITS*

Amperes	Continuous operation		Noncontinuous operation	
	Wire size (copper)	Wire size (aluminum)	Wire size (copper)	Wire size (aluminum)
15	14	12	14	12
20	12	10	12	10
25/30	10	8	10	8
35/40	8	6	8	6
45/50	6	4	6	4
60	4	4	4	4
70	4	3	4	3
80	3	2	3	3
90	2	1	3	2
100	1	0	2	1
110	0	00	1	0
125	0	000	1	00
150	00	0000	0	000
175	000		00	0000
200	0000		000	
225			0000	

* American Wire Gauge (AWG) sizes. Continuous loads are those expected to continue for 3 or more hours; noncontinuous loads are those where 67 percent or less of the load is expected to be continuous.

RESISTANCE OF COPPER WIRE

In estimating the resistance of copper wire, it may help to remember several approximate relationships:

Size wire AWG, B&S	Ohms per 1,000 feet	Feet per ohm
10	1	1,000
20	10	100
30	100	10
40	1,000	1

An increase of 1 in AWG or B&S wire size increases resistance 25 percent.

An increase of 2 increases resistance 60 percent.

An increase of 3 increases resistance 100 percent.

ELECTRICAL CONDUCTIVITY OF METALS

With the conductivity of copper rated at 100, here are the relative conductivities of other common metals. All are measured at 68° F or 20° C.

	Relative conductivity
Aluminum	59
Brass	28
Cadmium	19
Chromium	55
Climax	1.83
Cobalt	16.3
Constantin	3.24
Copper, annealed	100
Copper, hard drawn	89.5
Everdur	6
German silver, 18 percent	5.3
Gold	65
Iron, pure	17.7
Iron, wrought	11.4
Lead	7
Manganin	3.7
Mercury	1.66

(Continued)

ELECTRICAL CONDUCTIVITY OF METALS (*continued*)

With the conductivity of copper rated at 100, here are the relative conductivities of other common metals. All are measured at 68° F or 20° C.

	Relative conductivity
Molybdenum	33.2
Monel	4
Nichrome	1.45
Nickel	12–16
Phosphor bronze	36
Platinum	15
Silver	106
Steel	3–15
Tin	13
Tungsten	28.9
Zinc	28.2

WIRING-SIZE DATA (ENCLOSED WIRES)

	Maximum ampere rating	
Wire size	Types R, RW, RU, T, and TW	Types RH and RHW
14	15	15
12	20	20
10	30	30
8	40	45
6	55	65
4	70	85
3	80	100
2	95	115
1	110	130
0	125	150
00	145	175
000	165	200

CONDUIT SIZE AND AMPERE CAPACITY OF WIRES IN CONDUIT

Number of wires (1 to 9) to be installed in conduit (exact number will vary according to local code)

Wire size	Ampere capacity	½-inch conduit	¾-inch conduit	1-inch conduit	1¼-inch conduit
14	15	4	6	9	9
12	20	3	5	8	9
10	25	1	4	7	9
8	35	1	3	4	7
6	45	1	1	3	4
4	60	1	1	1	3
5	95	1	1	1	3

Extension Cords

The 125-volt all-purpose extension cords for indoor or outdoor use are generally marked type "SJT." Two conductor cords are okay for double-insulated tools with a two-prong plug, but tools with three-prong grounded plugs must be used only with three-wire grounded extension cords connected to properly grounded three-wire receptacles. Current National Electrical Code specs call for outdoor receptacles to be protected with ground-fault detector devices.

When you buy a new extension cord, check the table below or the maker's specs and permanently mark or tag it for capacity. For example, mark a 50-foot cord "13A" to indicate it's good for a maximum 13-ampere load.

HOW TO SELECT THE PROPER EXTENSION CORD

| Cord length | Ampere rating for 110–120 V.A.C. tools | | | | | | | | | | | | | | |
	0-5A	6A	7A	8A	9A	10A	11A	12A	13A	14A	15A	16A	17A	18A	19A	20A
25 feet	18	18	18	18	18	18	16	16	16	14	14	14	14	14	12	12
50 feet	18	18	18	18	18	18	16	16	16	14	14	14	14	14	12	12
75 feet	18	18	18	18	16	16	16	16	16	14	14	14	14	14	12	12
100 feet	18	16	16	16	16	16	16	16	14	14	14	14	14	14	12	12
125 feet	16	16	16	16	16	14	14	14	14	14	14	12	12	12	12	12
150 feet	16	16	14	14	14	14	14	14	14	12	12	12	12	12	12	12

* Wire sizes are AWG (American Wire Gauge); recommendations are minimum allowable. For nameplate ampere ratings that fall between those given here, use the extension cord recommended for the next higher ampere. If the tool has a long supply cord, this should be added when figuring total extension cord length.

REQUIRED CONDUCTOR INSULATION
FOR CURRENT-CARRYING CIRCUITS UNDER 6,000 VOLTS

Trade name	Type letter	Insulation	Outer covering	Use
Code	R	code-grade rubber	moisture-resistant, flame-retardant fibrous covering	general use
Moisture resistant	RW	moisture-resistant rubber	moisture-resistant, flame-retardant fibrous covering	general use, especially in wet locations
Heat resistant	RH	heat-resistant rubber	moisture-resistant, flame-retardant fibrous covering	general use
Latex rubber	RU	90-percent unmilled grainless rubber	moisture-resistant, flame-retardant fibrous covering	general use
Thermoplastic	T and TW	flame-retardant thermoplastic compound	none	T—general use TW—in wet locations
Thermoplastic and asbestos	TA	thermoplastic and asbestos	flame-retardant cotton braid	switchboard wiring only
Asbestos and varnished cambric	AVA	impregnated asbestos and varnished cambric	asbestos braid	dry location only

Asbestos and varnished cambric	AVB	same as type AVA	flame-retardant cotton braid	dry location only
Asbestos and varnished cambric	AVL	same as type AVA	asbestos braid and lead sheath	wet location
Slow-burning	SB	three braids of impregnated fire-retardant cotton thread	outer cover finished smooth and hard	dry locations only
Slow-burning weatherproof	SBW	two layers impregnated cotton thread	outer fire-retardant coating	open wiring only

Appliance Grounding

The one electrical problem most often overlooked is improper or inadequate grounding or none at all. It has been estimated by the Injury Control Program of the National Center for Urban and Industrial Health that there are 500,000 household injuries each year as the direct result of accidents with major and portable electrical appliances used in the home. The U.S. Bureau of Vital Statistics lists over 1,000 deaths each year due to electric shock. Proper grounding would have eliminated many of these injuries and deaths.

It has been determined that electric current (amperage), not voltage, is the dangerous ingredient of electricity. Measurements of a 60-Hz, 120-V current and the predicted body reaction are given in the accompanying table:

Current	Effect
0.05 to 2 mA (5/10,000 to 2/1,000A)	Just noticeable
2 to 10 mA (2/1,000 to 10/1,000A)	Slight to strong muscular reaction
5 to 25 mA (5/1,000 to 25/1,000A)	Strong shock, inability to let go
25 to 50 mA (25/1,000 to 50/1,000A)	Violent muscular contraction
50 to 200 mA (50/1,000 to 200/1,000A)	Irregular twitching of the heart muscles with no pumping action (ventricular fibrillation)
100 mA and over (100/1,000A)	Paralysis of breathing

A person's skin, when dry, may have from 100,000 to as high as 600,000 ohms resistance; however, when the skin is wet (such as when perspiring), resistance can drop below 1,000 ohms. Let us assume a technician is working on a 120-V motor with an insulation break leaking current to an ungrounded motor frame. Ohm's law (volts/ohms = amperes) may be used to compute the amount of current received by the technician's body. If his skin is dry, the current would be 120V/ 100,000 ohms = 0.0012A, or 1.2 mA. This current would be barely noticeable. However, if the technician is perspiring, his skin resistance may be 1,000 ohms or less (with a break in the skin it can be as low as 200 ohms). Using Ohm's law, the current would be 0.12A, or 120 mA (120 V/1,000 ohms = 0.12A). This is more than a lethal current. If the motor frame had been grounded, this leaking current would have bled to the ground, and the fuse or breaker would generally have "blown." Remember, as little as 0.025A at 120 V can kill.

WATTAGE FOR HOME LIGHTING

Room	General area lighting		Local lighting		Remarks
	Bulb	Fluorescent	Bulb	Fluorescent	
Living, dining room	150	60–80	40–150	15–40	For small living rooms
Bedroom	200		40–100		Average size
Bath	100–150	80	Two 60s	Two 20s	Task lights on both sides of mirror
Kitchen	150–200	60–80	60	10 per foot of counter	Fixture over eating area or sink—150-watt bulb, 60-watt fluorescent
Halls, service	75	32			Plus low-wattage night lights
Hall entrance	100	60			
Stairway	75	32			Shielded fixtures at top and bottom controlled by three-way switch
Outdoors, entry and access	40				Wall brackets aimed down
Hall entrance	100	60			
Outdoors, yard	100–150 projector				Controlled from garage and house
Laundry	Two 150s	Two 80s			Placed over washing and ironing areas
Workshop	150	80	60	10 per foot of bench	Task lights aimed at machines
Garage	Two 100s				On ceiling, center of each side of car

AVERAGE FURNITURE DIMENSIONS

Item	Length, Inches	Depth-width, Inches	Height Inches
Dining table	60	42	29
Kitchen table	42	30	30
Card table	36	36	30
Coffee table	36–60	18–24	14–18
Coffee table (round)	36 diam.		15–18
End table	24	15	24
Drum table	36 diam.		30
Lamp table	24 diam.		30
Desk	48	24	30
Secretary	36	24	84
Lowboy	30	18	30
Highboy	36	18	60–84
Breakfront bookcase	48–60	18	78–84
Sofa	72	30	36
Love seat	48	30	36
Occasional chair	27	30	36
Occasional chair (armless)	24	30	30
Wing chair	30	30	36
Dining, desk, folding chair	15–18	15–18	30–36 (seat height 16–18)
Twin bed	78	39	20–24
Double bed	78	54	20–24
Dresser	42–60	22	32–36

BTU IMPUT FOR GAS APPLIANCES

	Approximate Input BTU per hour*
Range, free standing	65,000
Built-in oven or broiler unit	25,000
Built-in top unit	40,000
Water heater (quick recovery), automatic storage	
30-gallon tank	30,000
40-gallon tank	38,000
50-gallon tank	50,000
Water heater, automatic instantaneous	
2 gallons per minute	142,000
4 gallons per minute	285,000
6 gallons per minute	428,400
Refrigerator	3,000
Clothes dryer	35,000
Incinerator	32,000

* A *therm* is equal to 10,000 BTUs

RUBBER STOPPER SIZES
(All measurements in millimeters)

Stopper size no.	Fits openings	Top diameter	Bottom diameter	Length
00	10 to 13	15	10	26
0	13 to 15	17	13	26
1	15 to 17	19	15	26
2	16 to 18.5	20	16	26
3	18 to 21	24	18	26
4	20 to 23	26	20	26
5	23 to 25	27	23	26
5½	25 to 26	29	25	26
6	26 to 27	32	26	26
6½	27 to 31.5	34	27	26
7	30 to 34	37	30	26
8	33 to 37	41	33	26
9	37 to 41	45	37	26
10	42 to 46	50	42	26
10½	45 to 47	53	45	26

(Continued)

(Continued)	**RUBBER STOPPER SIZES** (All measurements in millimeters)			
Stopper size no.	Fits openings	Top diameter	Bottom diameter	Length
11	48 to 51.5	56	48	26
11½	51 to 56	60	51	26
12	54 to 59	64	54	26
13	58 to 63	67	58	26
13½	61 to 70	75	61	35
14	75 to 85	90	75	39
15	83 to 95	103	83	39

Precious Metals

Precious metals are gold, platinum, and silver. Equally expensive, and sometimes used, is palladium. These precious metals may be mixed with or laid over a base metal, usually copper, zinc, tin, antimony, nickel, aluminum, lead, chromium, rhodium, or iron. A mixture of metals is an alloy. The alloy may be used to attain greater durability, hardness, tarnish-resistance, or some special effect. Or it may be used to decrease cost.

Solid (24-karat) gold contains no copper to each 24 parts of gold. This is too soft for most jewelry purposes. But 14-karat gold contains 14 parts gold and 10 parts copper; 10-karat gold contains 10 parts gold, 14 parts copper. Gold-filled metal contains a thin sheet or covering of 12-karat gold, usually (soldered, welded, or brazed on) 1/10th to 1/20th the thickness of the metal. Rolled gold may have a coating of 1/30th to 1/40th the thickness of the metal. Gold-flashed or gold-washed metals may have a gold thickness of 1/100,000th of an inch. Gold-plated metals have a thin layer of gold coated by an electroplating process. White gold, red gold, and green gold are made by adding other metals in the plating process. They may be of solid gold, plated, and so on.

Sterling silver is 92½ percent silver, 7½ percent copper. Pure silver is too soft for ordinary use. Silverplate has a coating of silver over a base metal. Antiqued silver has been oxidized (tarnished) to add to the design.

MOHS' SCALE OF HARDNESS

Minerals, metals, abrasive grits, and other materials are still compared for hardness on the "Mohs scale," a rating devised in 1820 by Friedrich Mohs, noted German mineralogist. In this scale, talc, the softest mineral, is rated as 1, while diamond, the hardest, is 10. Each mineral on the scale is hard enough to scratch the one below it. Here is the basic scale:

1 talc	6 feldspar
2 rocksalt or gypsum	7 quartz
3 calcite	8 topaz
4 fluorite	9 corundum
5 apatite	10 diamond

Compared with the scale above, here are some values for other materials:

Agate	6–7	Iron	4–5
Aluminum	2–2.9	Jade	7
Amber	2–2.5	Kaolinite	2–2.5
Amethyst	7	Lead	1.5
Anthracite	2.2	Magnesium	2
Asphalt	1–2	Marble	3–4
Brass	3–4	Opal	4–6
Cadmium	2	Osmium	7
Carborundum	9–10	Platinum	4.3
Chromium	9	Pumice	6
Copper	2.5–3	Ruby	9
Diatomaceous			
earth	1–1.5	Sapphire	9
Emerald	8	Silicon	
Emery	7–9	carbide	9–10
Flint	6.8–7	Silver	2.5–7
Garnet	7.5–8.5	Steel	5–8.5
Glass	4.5–6.5	Tin	1.5–1.8
Gold	2.5–3	Tourmaline	7.3
Graphite	0.5–1	Tungsten	
		carbide	9–10
Gypsum	1.6–2	Turquoise	6
		Wax, 32° F	0.2
		Zinc	2.5

Frequency Range of Voices and Instruments

If your stereo speakers cannot reach down to 20 Hz (formerly *cycles per second*) don't worry too much. No musical instrument except a pipe organ with a 32-foot pipe can go as low. The piano comes next, with its very lowest tone at 27.5 Hz. At the other extreme, the highest fundamental tone of any ordinary musical instrument—shared by the organ, piano, and piccolo—is about 4,186 Hz.

The fundamental frequencies of the singing voice range from about 65 Hz for the lowest tone of the bass to about 1,568 Hz for the highest of the soprano. The harmonics or overtones of both instruments and voices—the extra frequencies that characterize one source of sound from another—extend to about 10,000 Hz, while frequencies in a door squeak, chirping insects, or escaping steam may go beyond 16,000 Hz. It is because of these harmonics that you need good high-frequency response in your hi-fi to get completely natural sound.

To help get a clearer idea of the frequency range of orchestral instruments and human voices, see the accompanying table based on the American standard frequency of 440 Hz for middle A. Where two frequencies are given, the first one is for special instruments.

FREQUENCY RANGE OF VOICES AND INSTRUMENTS

	Frequency In Hz (cycles per second)	
INSTRUMENT	**Lower limit**	**Upper limit**
Organ	16, 32	4186
Piano	27	4186
Contra bassoon	30	175
Harp	32	3136
Bass violin	32, 41	262
Bass tuba	41	234
Trombone	51, 82	524
Bassoon	58	623
French horn	61	699
Cello	65	880
Bass clarinet	63, 73	467
E-flat baritone saxophone	69	416
B-flat tenor saxophone	103	623
Viola	131	1318
E-flat alto saxophone	138	831
English horn	164	934

(Continued)

INSTRUMENT	Frequency in Hz (cycles per second)	
	Lower limit	Upper limit
Trumpet	164	1047
Violin	195	2093
Oboe	233	1397
Flute	261	2043
Piccolo	587	4186
VOICE		
Bass	65	294
Baritone	98	416
Tenor	123	1174
Contralto	174	933
Soprano	261	1568

FREEZING POINT OF ANTIFREEZE MIXTURES

ETHYL ALCOHOL–WATER MIXTURES

Percent alcohol by volume	Specific gravity, 60°F	Freezing point	
		°C	°F
3.1	0.9954	− 1.0	30.2
8.5	0.9884	− 3.0	26.6
14.0	0.9822	− 5.0	23.0
20.0	0.9761	− 7.5	18.5
25.0	0.9710	−10.5	13.0
29.5	0.9660	−14.0	6.8
32.5	0.9624	−16.0	3.2
36.0	0.9577	−18.8	− 2.0
40.5	0.9511	−23.6	−10.5
46.3	0.9413	−28.7	−19.7

ETHYLENE GLYCOL (PRESTONE)–WATER MIXTURES

12.5	1.019	− 3.9	25
17.0	1.026	− 6.7	20
25.0	1.038	−12.2	10
32.5	1.048	−17.8	0

(Continued)

FREEZING POINT OF ANTIFREEZE MIXTURES (continued)

ETHYL ALCOHOL–WATER MIXTURES

Percent alcohol by volume	Specific gravity, 60°F	Freezing point	
		°C	°F
38.5	1.056	−23.3	−10
44.0	1.063	−28.9	−20
49.0	1.069	−34.4	−30
52.5	1.073	−40.0	−40

TEMPERATURES USEFUL TO KNOW

Degrees Celsius (Centigrade)	Degrees Fahrenheit	
−273	−459.4	Absolute zero
−130	−202	Alcohol freezes
−78.5	−109.3	Dry ice sublimes
−38.9	−38	Mercury freezes
0	32	Ice melts
34.5	94.1	Ether boils
37	98.6	Temperature of human body
60	140	Wood's metal melts
78.5	173.3	Alcohol boils
100	212	Water boils
160	320	Sugar melts
232	450	Tin melts
327	621	Lead melts
658	1,216	Aluminum melts
700	1,292	Dull red heat
800	1,472	Pyrex glass begins to soften
1,000	1,832	Bright red heat
1,083	1,980	Copper melts
1,400	2,552	White heat
1,500	2,732	Temperature of Bunsen flame
1,530	2,786	Iron melts
1,773	3,223	Platinum melts
4,000	7,232	Temperature of electric furnace
6,000	10,800	Temperature of sun's surface

Useful Facts About Rope

The smallest cordage that is technically called "rope" is about ½ inch in circumference and $\frac{3}{16}$ inch in diameter.

- *Manila rope* is the strongest and most durable rope made of natural fibers. It is made of abaca, a relative of the banana plant, and commonly called Manila fiber because it is grown almost entirely in the Philippines and shipped chiefly from the port of Manila.

(Continued)

ROPE SIZES AND STRENGTHS
FOR THREE-STRAND MANILA AND SISAL ROPE
WITH STANDARD LAY

(For safe loads, allow at least a 5-to-1 safety factor)

	NOMINAL SIZE			MINIMUM BREAKING STRENGTH, POUNDS	
Threads	Circumference (inches)	Diameter (inches)	Weight per 100 Feet (pounds)	Manila	Sisal
6-fine	$\frac{9}{16}$	$\frac{3}{16}$	1.47	450	360
6	$\frac{3}{4}$	$\frac{1}{4}$	1.96	600	480
9	1	$\frac{5}{16}$	2.84	1,000	800
12	$1\frac{1}{8}$	$\frac{3}{8}$	4.02	1,350	1,080
15	$1\frac{1}{4}$	$\frac{7}{16}$	5.15	1,750	1,400
18	$1\frac{3}{8}$	$\frac{15}{32}$	6.13	2,250	1,800
21	$1\frac{1}{2}$	$\frac{1}{2}$	7.35	2,650	2,120
	$1\frac{3}{4}$	$\frac{9}{16}$	10.20	3,450	2,760
	2	$\frac{5}{8}$	13.10	4,440	3,520
	$2\frac{1}{4}$	$\frac{3}{4}$	16.30	5,400	4,320
	$2\frac{1}{2}$	$\frac{13}{16}$	19.10	6,500	5,200
	$2\frac{3}{4}$	$\frac{7}{8}$	22.00	7,700	6,160
	3	1	26.50	9,000	7,200
	$3\frac{1}{4}$	$1\frac{1}{16}$	30.70	10,500	8,400
	$3\frac{1}{2}$	$1\frac{1}{8}$	35.20	12,000	9,600
	$3\frac{3}{4}$	$1\frac{1}{4}$	40.80	13,500	10,800
	4	$1\frac{5}{16}$	46.90	15,000	12,000
	$4\frac{1}{2}$	$1\frac{1}{2}$	58.80	18,500	14,800
	5	$1\frac{5}{8}$	73.00	22,500	18,000
	$5\frac{1}{2}$	$1\frac{3}{4}$	87.70	26,500	21,200
	6	2	105.00	31,000	24,800

Useful Facts About Rope (continued)

- *Sisal rope* (often made from a related fiber, henequen) is next in importance to Manila rope and is about 80 percent as strong. Its fiber comes from a plant in the century plant family, and was formerly exported from Sisal, Yucatán.

- *Nylon rope,* made from synthetic fibers, is more expensive than Manila rope but about twice as strong. It also has the unique property of being able to stretch about 8 percent and then return to its original length on release of its load. This property makes it extremely useful for long tow lines, or under other conditions where a sudden strong pull might snap an ordinary rope.

- *Dacron rope* is nearly as strong as nylon, is almost impervious to moisture, is a good electrical insulator, and does not stretch at all. It is especially useful for guy lines for antennas, for outdoor clotheslines that stay taut during dry or wet weather, and for other purposes where stretch or electrical conduction would be detrimental.

- *Polyethylene rope,* one of the newest, is about one-third stronger than Manila rope and is the only rope that will float indefinitely on water. Because of this floating ability, polyethylene rope is becoming standard for lifelines and for tow ropes in water skiing.

SHOP, BLUEPRINT, AND OTHER COMMON ABBREVIATIONS

Word	Abbreviation	Word	Abbreviation
Abbreviate	ABBR		
Absolute	ABS	Acoustic	ACST
Accelerate	ACCEL	Actual	ACT.
Acceleration due to		Adapter	ADPT
gravity	G	Addition	ADD.
Accessory	ACCESS.	Adhesive	ADH
Access panel	AP	Adjust	ADJ

Word	Abbreviation	Word	Abbreviation
Advance	ADV	Assemble	ASSEM
After	AFT.	Assembly	ASSY
Aggregate	AGGR	At	@
Air-break switch	ABS	Atomic	AT
Air-circuit breaker	ACB	Attach	ATT
Air-condition	AIR CON.	Audio-frequency	AF
Aircraft	ACFT	Automatic	AUTO
Airplane	APL	Auto-transformer	AUTO TR
Airtight	AT	Auxiliary	AUX
Alarm	ALM	Avenue	AVE.
Allowance	ALLOW	Average	AVG
Alloy	ALY	Back to back	B to B
Alteration	ALT	Baffle	BAF
Alternate	ALT	Balance	BAL
Alternating current	AC	Balcony	BALC
Alternator	ALT	Ball bearing	BB
Altitude	ALT	Baseline	BL
Aluminum	AL	Basement	BSMT
American Standard	AMER STD	Base plate	BP
American Wire Gauge	AWG	Bathroom	B
Ammeter	AM	Bath tub	BT
Amount	AMT	Battery	BAT.
Ampere	AMP	Beam	BM
Ampere hour	AMP HR	Bearing	BRG
Amplifier	AMPL	Bedroom	BR
Anneal	ANL	Bench mark	BM
Antenna	ANTS.	Bent	BT
Apartment	APT	Between	BET.
Apparatus	APP	Between centers	BC
Approved	APPD	Between perpendiculars	BP
Approximate	APPROX	Bevel	BEV
Architectural	ARCH	Bill of material	B/M
Arc weld	ARC/W	Birmingham Wire Gage	BWG
Area	A	Blank	BLK
Armature	ARM.	Blocking	BLKG
Arrange	ARR.	Blower	BLO
Arrester	ARR.	Blueprint	BP
Asbestos	ASB	Board	BD
Asphalt	ASPH	Boiler	BLR

(Continued)

(*Continued*)

SHOP, BLUEPRINT, AND OTHER COMMON ABBREVIATIONS

Word	Abbreviation	Word	Abbreviation
Both sides	BS	Catalog	CAT
Bottom	BOT	Caulking	CLKG
Bottom chord	BC	Cement	CEM
Brake	BK	Center	CTR
Brass	BRS	Center line	CL
Brazing	BRZG	Center to center	C to C
Break	BRK	Centering	CTR
Breaker	BKR	Centigrade	C
Brick	BRK	Centigram	CG
British Standard	BR STD	Centiliter	CL
British thermal units	BTU	Centimeter	CM
Broach	BRO	Centrifugal	CENT.
Bronze	BRZ	Centrifugal force	CF
Broom closet	BC	Ceramic	CER
Brown & Sharp	B&S	Chain	CH
Brush	BR	Chamfer	CHAM
Building	BLDG	Change	CHG
Building line	BL	Change notice	CN
Burnish	BNH	Change order	CO
Bushing	BUSH.	Channel	CHAN
Bypass	BYP	Check	CHK
Cabinet	CAB	Check valve	CV
Cadmium plate	CD PL	Chemical	CHEM
Calculate	CALC	Chord	CHD
Calibrate	CAL	Chrome molybdenum	CR MOLY
Capacitor	CAP	Chrome vanadium	CR VAN
Capacity	CAP	Chromium plate	CR PL
Cap screw	CAP SCR	Circle	CIR
Carburize	CARB	Circuit	CKT
Case harden	CH	Circuit breaker	CIR BKR
Casing	CSG	Circular	CIR
Cast (used with other materials)	C	Circular pitch	CP
		Circulate	CIRC
Cast concrete	C CONC	Circumference	CIRC
Cast iron	CI	Clamp	CLP
Cast iron pipe	CIP	Class	CL
Cast steel	CS	Cleanout	CO
Casting	CSTG	Clear	CLR

Word	Abbreviation	Word	Abbreviation
Clearance	CL	Control switch	CS
Clockwise	CW	Controller	CONT
Closet	CL	Convert	CONV
Closing	CL	Conveyor	CNVR
Clutch	CL	Cooled	CLD
Coated	CTD	Copper oxide	CUO
Coaxial	COAX	Copper plate	Cop PL
Coefficient	COEF	Cord	CD
Cold drawn	CD	Correct	CORR
Cold-drawn steel	CDS	Corrosion resistant	CRE
Cold rolled	CR.	Corrosion-resistant	
Cold-rolled steel	CRS	steel	CRES
Column	COL	Corrugate	CORR
Combination	COMB.	Cotter	COT
Combustion	COMB.	Counter	CTR
Common	COM	Counterbalance	CBAL
Communication	COMM	Counterbore	CBORE
Commutator	COMM	Counterclockwise	CCW
Complete	COMPL	Counterdrill	CDRILL
Composite	CX	Counterpunch	CPUNCH
Composition	COMP.	Countersink	CSK
Compressor	COMPR	Countersink other side	CSK-O
Concentric	CONC	Coupling	CPLG
Concrete	CONC	Courses	C
Condition	COND	Cover	COV
Conduct	COND	Crank	CRK
Conductor	COND	Cross connection	XCONN
Conduit	CND	Cross section	XSECT
Connect	CONN	Cubic	CU
Constant	CONST	Current	CUR
Construction	CONST	Cyanide	CYN
Contact	CONT	Cycle	CY
Container	CNTR	Cycles per minute	CPM
Continue	CONT	Cycles per second	CPS
Continuous wave	CW	Cylinder	CYL
Contract	CONT	Damper	DMPR
Contractor	CONTR	Dampproofing	DP
Control	CONT	Dead load	DL
Control relay	CR	Decibel	DB

(Continued)

(Continued)

SHOP, BLUEPRINT, AND OTHER COMMON ABBREVIATIONS

Word	Abbreviation	Word	Abbreviation
Decimal	DEC	Drawing	DWG
Deep drawn	DD	Drawing list	DL
Deflect	DEFL	Drill	DR
Degree	(°) DEG	Drill rod	DR
Density	D	Drive	DR
Describe	DESCR	Drive fit	DF
Design	DSGN	Drop	D
Designation	DESIG	Drop forge	DF
Detail	DET	Dryer	D
Detector	DET	Duplex	DX
Develop	DEV	Duplicate	DUP
Diagonal	DIAG	Dynamic	DYN
Diagram	DIAG	Dynamo	DYN
Diameter	DIA	Each	EA
Diaphragm	DIAPH	East	E
Differential	DIFF	Eccentric	ECC
Dimension	DIM	Effective	EFF
Dining room	DR	Electric	ELEC
Dioxide	DIO	Electronic air cleaner	EAC
Direct current	DC	Elevation	EL
Directional	DIR	Enamel	ENAM
Discharge	DISCH	Enclose	ENCL
Disconnect	DISC	End to end	E to E
Dishwasher	DW	Entrance	ENT
Distance	DIST	Envelope	ENV
Distribute	DISTR	Equal	EQ
Ditto	DO	Equation	EQ
Division	DIV	Equipment	EQUIP.
Door	DR	Equivalent	EQUIV
Double	DBL	Estimate	EST
Double hung	DH	Evaporate	EVAP
Dovetail	DVTL	Excavate	EXC
Dowel	DWL	Exhaust	EXH
Down	DN	Existing	EXIST
Downspout	DS	Expand	EXP
Drafting	DFTG	Exterior	EXT
Draftsman	DFTSMN	External	EXT
Drain	DR	Extra heavy	X HVY

Word	Abbreviation	Word	Abbreviation
Extra strong	X STR	Flush	FL
Extrude	EXTR	Focus	FOC
Fabricate	FAB	Foot	(') FT
Face to face	F to F	Foot candle	FC
Fahrenheit	F	Footing	FTG
Fairing	FAIR.	Force	F
Farad	F	Forging	FORG
Far side	FS	Forward	FWD
Feed	FD	Foundation	FDN
Feeder	FDR	Foundry	FDRY
Feet	(') FT	Fractional	FRAC
Feet board measure	FBM	Frame	FR
Feet per minute	FPM	Freezing point	FP
Feet per second	FPS	Frequency	FREQ
Female	FEM	Frequency, high	HF
Fiber	FBR	Frequency, low	LF
Field	FLD	Frequency, medium	MF
Figure	FIG.	Frequency modulation	FM
Filament	FIL	Frequency, super high	SHF
Fillet	FIL	Frequency, ultra high	UHF
Filling	FILL.	Frequency, very high	VHF
Fillister	FIL	Frequency, very low	VLF
Filter	FLT	Friction horsepower	FHP
Finish	FIN.	From below	FR BEL
Finish all over	FAO	Front	FR
Fireproof	FPRF	Fuel	F
Fitting	FTG	Full size	FS
Fixture	FIX	Furnish	FURN
Flange	FLG	Furred ceiling	FC
Flashing	FL	Fusible	FSBL
Flat	F	Fusion point	FNP
Flat head	FH	Gage or gauge	GA
Flexible	FLEX.	Gallon	GAL
Float	FLT	Galvanize	GALV
Floor	FL	Galvanized iron	GI
Floor drain	FD	Galvanized steel	GS
Flooring	FLG	Galvanized steel wire	
Fluid	FL	rope	GSWR
Fluorescent	FLUOR	Garage	GAR

(Continued)

(Continued)

SHOP, BLUEPRINT, AND OTHER COMMON ABBREVIATIONS

Word	Abbreviation	Word	Abbreviation
Gas	G	Henry	H
Gasket	GSKT	Hexagon	HEX
Gasoline	GASO	High	H
General	GEN	High frequency	HF
Girder	G	High point	H PT
Glass	GL	High pressure	HP
Glaze	GL	High speed	HS
Government	GOVT	High speed steel	HSS
Governor	GOV	High tension	HT
Grade	GR	High voltage	HV
Grade line	GL	Highway	HWY
Graduation	GRAD	Holder	HLR
Gram	G	Hollow	HOL
Graphic	GRAPH	Horizontal	HOR
Graphite	GPH	Horsepower	HP
Grating	GRTG	Hose bib	HB
Gravity	G	Hot rolled	HR
Grid	G	Hot-rolled steel	HRS
Grind	GRD	House	HSE
Groove	GRV	Hundred	C
Ground	GRD	Hydraulic	HYD
Gypsum	GYP	I-Beam	I
Half hard	½H	Identify	IDENT
Half round	½RD	Ignition	IGN
Hall	H	Illuminate	ILLUM
Handle	HDL	Illustrate	ILLUS
Hanger	HGR	Impact	IMP
Hard	H	Impedance	IMP.
Hard-drawn	HD	Impregnate	IMPG
Harden	HDN	Inch	('') IN.
Hardware	HDW	Inches per second	IPS
Head	HD	Include	INCL
Headless	HDLS	Increase	INCR
Heat	HT	Indicate	IND
Heater	HTR	Inductance or induction	IND
Heat treat	HT TR.	Information	INFO
Heavy	HVY	Injection	INJ
Height	HGT	Inlet	IN

Word	Abbreviation	Word	Abbreviation
Inspect	INSP	Kip (1000 lb)	K
Install	INSTL	Kitchen	KIT
Instantaneous	INST	Knots	KN
Instruct	INST	Laboratory	LAB
Instrument	INST	Lacquer	LAQ
Insulate	INS	Laminate	LAM
Interchangeable	INTCHG	Lateral	LAT
Intercommunication	INTERCOM	Laundry	LAU
Interior	INT	Lavatory	LAV
Interlock	INTLK	Lead-coated metal	LCM
Intermediate	INTER	Leading edge	LE
Intermittent	INTMT	Left	L
Internal	INT	Left hand	LH
Interrupt	INTER	Length	LG
Intersect	INT	Length over all	LOA
Inverse	INV	Letter	LTR
Invert	INV	Light	LT
Iron	I	Limit	LIM
Iron-pipe size	IPS	Line	L
Irregular	IRREG	Linear	LIN
Jack	J	Linen closet	L CL
Job order	JO	Link	LK
Joint	JT	Liquefied gas	LPG
Joist	JST	Liquid	LIQ
Junction	JCT	Liter	L
Kelvin	K	Live load	LL
Key	K	Living room	LR
Keyseat	KST	Locate	LOC
Kilo	K	Long	LG
Kilocycle	KC	Longitude	LONG.
Kilocycles per second	KC	Lower	LV
Kilogram	KG	Low explosive	LE
Kiloliter	KL	Low frequency	LF
Kilometer	KM	Low pressure	LP
Kilovolt	KV	Low speed	LS
Kilovolt-ampere	KVA	Low tension	LT
Kilovolt-ampere hour	KVAH	Low torque	LT
Kilowatt	KW	Low voltage	LV
Kilowatt-hour	KWH	Lubricate	LUB

(Continued)

(Continued)

SHOP, BLUEPRINT, AND OTHER COMMON ABBREVIATIONS

Word	Abbreviation	Word	Abbreviation
Lubricating oil	LO	Micron	u or U
Lumber	LBR	Microvolt	uV or UV
Lumen	L	Microwatt	uW or UW
Lumens per watt	LPW	Miles	MI
Machine	MACH	Miles per gallon	MPG
Magnet	MAG	Miles per hour	MPH
Main	MN	Milli	M
Male and female	M&F	Milliampere	MA.
Malleable	MALL	Milligram	MG
Manhold	MH	Millihenry	MH
Manual	MAN.	Millimeter	MM
Manufacture	MFR	Milliseconds	MS
Manufactured	MFD	Millivolt	MV
Manufacturing	MFG	Milliwatt	MW
Material	MATL	Minimum	MIN
Material list	ML	Minute	(') MIN
Maximum	MAX	Miscellaneous	MISC
Maximum working pressure	MWP	Mixture	MIX.
Mean effective pressure	MEP	Model	MOD
Mechanical	MECH	Modify	MOD
Mechanism	MECH	Modulated continuous wave	MCW
Medicine cabinet	MC	Modular	MOD
Medium	MED	Molecular weight	MOL WT
Mega	M	Monument	MON
Megacycles	MC	Morse taper	MOR T
Megawatt	MW	Motor	MOT
Megohm	MEF	Moulding	MLDG
Melting point	MP	Mounted	MTD
Membrane	MEMB	Mounting	MTG
Metal	MET.	Multiple	MULT
Meter (instrument or measure of length)	M	Multiple contact	MC
Micro	u or U	National	NATL
Microampere	uA or UA	National Electrical Code	NEC
Microfarad	uF or UF	Natural	NAT
Microhenry	uH or UH	Near face	NF
Micrometer	MIC	Near side	NS

Word	Abbreviation	Word	Abbreviation
Negative	NEG	Pack	PK
Network	NET	Packing	PKG
Neutral	NEUT	Painted	PTD
Nickel-silver	NI-SIL	Pair	PR
Nipple	NIP.	Panel	PNL
Nominal	NOM	Parallel	PAR.
Normal	NOR	Part	PT
Normally closed	NC	Partition	PTN
Normally open	NO	Pattern	PATT
North	N	Penny (nails)	d
Not to scale	NTS	Perforate	PERF
Number	NO.	Permanent	PERM
Obscure	OB	Permanent magnet	PM
Obsolete	OBS	Perpendicular	PERP
Octagon	OCT	Phase	PH
Ohm	OHM	Phosphor bronze	PH BRZ
Oil-circuit breaker	OCB	Photograph	PHOTO
Oil-insulated	OI	Physical	PHYS
Oil switch	OS	Piece	PC
On center	OC	Piece mark	PC MK
One pole	1 P	Pierce	PRC
Opening	OPNG	Pipe tap	PT
Operate	OPR	Pitch	P
Opposite	OPP	Pitch circle	PC
Optical	OPT	Pitch diameter	PD
Ordnance	ORD	Plaster	PL
Orifice	ORF	Plastic	PLSTC
Original	ORIG	Plate	PL
Oscillate	OSC	Plumbing	PLMB
Ounce	OZ	Pneumatic	PNEU
Outlet	OUT.	Point	PT
Output	OUT.	Pole	P
Outside diameter	OD	Polish	POL
Outside face	OF	Port	P
Outside radius	OR	Position	POS
Out to out	O to O	Positive	POS
Over-all	OA	Potential	POT.
Overhead	OVHD	Pound	LB
Overload	OVLD	Pounds per cubic foot	PCF
Oxidized	OXD		

(Continued)

(Continued)

SHOP, BLUEPRINT, AND OTHER COMMON ABBREVIATIONS

Word	Abbreviation	Word	Abbreviation
Pounds per square foot	PSF	Received	RECD
		Receiver	REC
Pounds per square inch	PSI	Receptacle	RECP
		Reciprocate	RECIP
Power	PWR	Recirculate	RECIRC
Power amplifier	PA	Reclosing	RECL
Power factor	PF	Record	REC
Preamplifier	PREAMP	Rectangle	RECT
Precast	PRCST	Rectifier	RECT
Prefabricated	PREFAB	Reduce	RED.
Preferred	PFD	Reference	REF
Premolded	PRMLD	Reference line	REF L
Prepare	PREP	Refrigerate	REF
Press	PRS	Refrigerator	REF
Pressure	PRESS	Regulator	REG
Primary	PRI	Reinforce	REINF
Process	PROC	Relay	REL
Production	PROD	Release	REL
Profile	PF	Relief	REL
Project	PROJ	Remove	REM
Punch	PCH	Repair	REP
Purchase	PUR	Replace	REPL
Push-pull	P-P	Reproduce	REPRO
Quadrant	QUAD	Require	REQ
Quality	QUAL	Required	REQD
Quantity	QTY	Resistance	RES
Quart	QT	Resistor	RES
Quarter	QTR	Retainer	RET.
Quarter hard	¼ H	Retard	RET.
Quarter round	¼ RD	Return	RET.
Quartz	QTZ	Reverse	REV
Radial	RAD	Revise	REV
Radiator	RAD	Revolution	REV
Radio frequency	RF	Revolutions per minute	RPM
Radius	R	Revolutions per second	RPS
Range	R	Rheostat	RHEO
Reactor	REAC		
Ream	RM	Right	R
Reassemble	REASM		

Word	Abbreviation	Word	Abbreviation
Right hand	RH	Shaft	SFT
Ring	R	Sheet	SH
Riser	R	Shield	SHLD
Rivet	RIV	Shop order	SO
Roller bearing	RB	Short wave	SW
Roof	RF	Shunt	SH
Room	RM	Side	S
Room air conditioner	RAC	Siding	SDG
Root diameter	RD	Signal	SIG
Rotary	ROT.	Similar	SIM
Rotate	ROT.	Single-pole, double-throw switch	SPDT
Rough	RGH		
Round	RD	Single-pole, normally closed	SPNC
Rubber	RUB.		
Saddle	SDL	Single-pole, normally open	SPNO
Safety	SAF		
Safe working pressure	SWP	Single-pole, single-throw switch	SPST
Sand blast	SD BL	Sink	SK
Sanitary	SAN	Sketch	SK
Saturate	SAT.	Sleeve	SLV
Schedule	SCH	Slide	SL
Schematic	SCHEM	Slotted	SLOT.
Scleroscope hardness	SH	Small	SM
Screen	SCRN	Smoke	SMK
Screw	SCR	Smokeless	SMKLS
Second	SEC	Socket	SOC
Section	SECT	Soft	S
Segment	SEG	Soil pipe	SP
Select	SEL	Solder	SLD
Semifinished	SF	Solenoid	SOL
Semifixed	SFXD	Sound	SND
Semisteel	SS	South	S
Separate	SEP	Space	SP
Sequence	SEQ	Spare	SP
Serial	SER	Speaker	SPKR
Series	SER	Special	SPL
Serrate	SERR	Specific	SP
Service	SERV	Specification	SPEC
Set screw	SS	Specific gravity	SP GR
Sewer	SEW.	Specific heat	SP HT

(Continued)

(Continued)

SHOP, BLUEPRINT, AND OTHER COMMON ABBREVIATIONS

Word	Abbreviation	Word	Abbreviation
Speed	SP	Tachometer	TACH
Spherical	SPHER	Tandem	TDM
Spindle	SPDL	Tangent	TAN.
Split phase	SP PH	Taper	TPR
Spot-faced	SF	Tar and gravel	T & G
Spring	SPG	Technical	TECH
Square	SQ	Tee	T
Stabilize	STAB	Teeth per inch	TPI
Stainless	STN	Telephone	TEL
Stairs	ST	Television	TV
Standard	STD	Temperature	TEMP
Static pressure	SP	Template	TEMP
Station	STA	Tensile strength	TS
Stationary	STA	Tension	TENS.
Steam	ST	Terminal	TERM.
Steel	STL	Terminal board	TB
Stiffener	STIFF	Terra-cotta	TC
Stock	STK	Terrazzo	TER
Storage	STG	That is	IE
Straight	STR	Theoretical	THEO
Street	ST	Thermal	THRM
Strip	STR	Thermostat	THERMO
Storage	STG	Thick	THK
Structural	STR	Thousand	M
Substitute	SUB	Thread	THD
Suction	SUCT	Throttle	THROT
Summary	SUM.	Through	THRU
Supervise	SUPV	Time	T
Supply	SUP	Time delay	TD
Surface	SUR	Time-delay closing	TDC
Survey	SURV	Time-delay opening	TDO
Switch	SW	Tinned	TD
Symbol	SYM	Toggle	TGL
Symmetrical	SYM	Toilet	T
Synchronous	SYN	Tolerance	TOL
Synthetic	SYN	Tongue and groove	T & G
System	SYS	Tool steel	TS
Tabulate	TAB	Tooth	T

Word	Abbreviation	Word	Abbreviation
Total	TOT	Volt	V
Trace	TR	Volt-ampere	VA
Tracer	TCR	Voltmeter	VM
Transfer	TRANS	Volts per mil	VPM
Transformer	TRANS	Volume	VOL
Transmission	XMSN	Washer	WASH
Transmitter	XMTR	Washing Machine	WM
Transmitting	XMTG	Water	W
Transverse	TRANSV	Water closet	WC
Tread	TR	Water heater	WH
Truss	T	Water line	WL
Tubing	TUB	Waterproof	WP
Tuned radio frequency	TRF	Watertight	WT
Turbine	TURB	Watt	W
Typical	TYP	Watt-hour	WHR
Ultimate	ULT	Watt-hour meter	WHM
Ultra-high frequency	UHF	Wattmeter	WM
Unfinished	UNFIN	Weatherproof	WP
Unit	U	Weather stripping	WS
United States Gage	USG	Weep hole	WH
United States Standard	USS	Weight	WT
Universal	UNIV	West	W
Urinal	UR	Wet bulb	WB
Vacuum	VAC	Width	W
Valve	V	Wind	WD
Vapor proof	VAP PRF	Winding	WDG
Variable	VAR	Window	WDW
Variable-frequency oscillator	VFO	Wire	W
		With	W/
Velocity	V	Without	W/O
Ventilate	VENT	Wood	WD
Vent pipe	VP	Woodruff	WDF
Versus	VS	Working point	WP
Vertical	VERT	Working pressure	WP
Very-high frequency	VHF	Wrought	WRT
Very-low frequency	VLF	Wrought iron	WI
Vibrate	VIB	Yard	YD
Video-frequency	VDF	Year	YR
Viscosity	VISC	Yield point	YP
Vitreous	VIT	Yield strength	YS
Voice frequency	VF		

ABBREVIATIONS FOR COLORS

Amber	AMB	Green	GRN
Black	BLK	Orange	ORN
Blue	BLU	White	WHT
Brown	BRN	Yellow	YEL

CHEMICAL ELEMENTS

Name	Symbol	Atomic weight	Atomic number
Actinium	AC	227	89
Aluminum	Al	26.98	13
Americium	Am	243	95
Antimony	Sb	121.76	51
Argon	Ar	39.944	18
Arsenic	As	74.92	33
Astatine	At	210	85
Barium	Ba	137.36	56
Berkelium	Bk	249	97
Beryllium	Be	9.013	4
Bismuth	Bi	208.99	83
Boron	B	10.82	5
Bromine	Br	79.916	35
Cadmium	Cd	112.41	48
Calcium	Ca	40.08	20
Californium	Cf	251	98
Carbon	C	12.011	6
Cerium	Ce	140.13	58
Cesium	Cs	132.91	55
Chlorine	Cl	35.457	17
Chromium	Cr	52.01	24
Cobalt	Co	58.94	27
Copper	Cu	63.54	29
Curium	Cm	247	96
Dysprosium	Dy	162.51	66
Einsteinium	E	254	99
Erbium	Er	167.27	68
Europium	Eu	152	63
Fermium	Fm	253	100
Fluorine	F	19	9

Name	Symbol	Atomic weight	Atomic number
Francium	Fr	223	87
Gadolinium	Gd	157.26	64
Gallium	Ga	69.72	31
Germanium	Ge	72.60	32
Gold	Au	197	79
Hafnium	Hf	178.50	72
Helium	He	4.003	2
Holmium	Ho	164.94	67
Hydrogen	H	1.008	1
Indium	In	114.82	49
Iodine	I	126.91	53
Iridium	Ir	192.2	77
Iron	Fe	55.85	26
Krypton	Kr	83.80	36
Lanthanum	La	138.92	57
Lawrencium	Lw	257	103
Lead	Pb	207.21	82
Lithium	Li	6.940	3
Lutetium	Lu	174.99	71
Magnesium	Mg	24.32	12
Manganese	Mn	54.94	25
Mendelevium	Mv	256	101
Mercury	Hg	200.61	80
Molybdenum	Mo	95.95	42
Neodymium	Nd	144.27	60
Neon	Ne	20.183	10
Neptunium	Np	237	93
Nickel	Ni	58.71	28
Niobium	Nb	92.91	41
Nitrogen	N	14.008	7
Nobelium	No	254	102
Osmium	Os	190.2	76
Oxygen	O	16	8
Palladium	Pd	106.4	46
Phosphorus	P	30.975	15
Platinum	Pt	195.09	78
Plutonium	Pu	242	94
Polonium	Po	210	84
Potassium	K	39.1	19

(Continued)

CHEMICAL ELEMENTS (continued)

Name	Symbol	Atomic weight	Atomic number
Praseodymium	Pr	140.92	59
Promethium	Pm	147	61
Protactinium	Pa	321	91
Radium	Ra	226	88
Radon	Rn	222	86
Rhenium	Re	186.22	75
Rhodium	Rh	102.91	45
Rubidium	Rb	85.48	37
Ruthenium	Ru	101.1	44
Samarium	Sm	150.35	62
Scandium	Sc	44.96	21
Selenium	Se	78.96	34
Silicon	Si	28.09	14
Silver	Ag	107.873	47
Sodium	Na	22.991	11
Strontium	Sr	87.63	38
Sulfur	S	32.066	16
Tantalum	Ta	180.95	73
Technetium	Te	99	43
Tellurium	Te	127.61	52
Terbium	Tb	158.93	65
Thallium	Tl	204.39	81
Thorium	Th	232	90
Thulium	Tm	168.94	69
Tin	Sn	118.7	50
Titanium	Ti	47.90	22
Tungsten	W	183.86	74
Uranium	U	238.07	92
Vanadium	V	50.95	23
Xenon	Xe	131.30	54
Ytterbium	Yb	173.04	70
Yttrium	Y	88.91	39
Zinc	Zn	65.38	30
Zirconium	Zr	91.22	40

NAMES AND FORMULAS FOR CHEMICALS

Popular name	Chemical name	Formula
Alcohol, grain	Ethyl alcohol	C_2H_5OH
Alcohol, wood	Methyl alcohol	CH_3OH
Alum, common	Aluminum potassium sulfate	$AlK(SO_4)_2 \cdot 12H_2O$
Alumina	Aluminum oxide	Al_2O_3
Alundum	Fused aluminum oxide	Al_2O_3
Antichlor	Sodium thiosulfate	$Na_2S_2O_3 \cdot 5H_2O$
Aqua ammonia	Ammonium hydroxide solution	$NH_4OH + H_2O$
Aqua fortis	Nitric acid	HNO_3
Aqua regia	Nitric and hydrochloric acids	$HNO_3 + HCl$
Aromatic spirits of ammonia	Ammonia gas in alcohol	
Asbestos	Magnesium silicate	$Mg_3Si_2O_7 \cdot 2H_2O$
Aspirin	Acetylsalicylic acid	$C_2H_3O_2C_6H_4CO_2H$
Baking soda	Sodium bicarbonate	$NaHCO_3$
Banana oil	Amyl acetate	$CH_3CO_2C_5H_{11}$
Baryta	Barium oxide	BaO
Bauxite	Impure aluminum oxide	Al_2O_3
Bichloride of mercury	Mercuric chloride	$HgCl_2$
Black lead	Graphite	C
Black oxide of copper	Cupric oxide	CuO
Black oxide of mercury	Mercurous oxide	Hg_2O
Bleaching powder	Calcium hypochlorite	$CaOCl_2$
Bluestone	Copper sulfate	$CuSO_4 \cdot 5H_2O$
Blue vitriol	Copper sulfate	$CuSO_4 \cdot 5H_2O$
Boracic acid	Boric acid	H_3BO_3
Borax	Sodium borate	$Na_2B_4O_7 \cdot 10H_2O$
Brimstone	Sulfur	S
Brine	Strong sodium chloride solution	$NaCl\ H_2O$
"Butter of"	Chloride or trichloride of	
Caliche	impure sodium nitrate	$NaNO_3$
Calomel	Mercurous chloride	Hg_2Cl_2
Carbolic acid	Phenol	C_6H_5OH
Carbonic acid gas	Carbon dioxide	CO_2
Caustic potash	Potassium hydroxide	KOH

(Continued)

NAMES AND FORMULAS FOR CHEMICALS (*continued*)

Popular name	Chemical name	Formula
Caustic soda	Dosium hydroxide	NaOH
Chalk	Calcium carbonate	$CaCO_3$
Chile saltpeter	Sodium nitrate	$NaNO_3$
Chloroform	Trichloromethane	$CHCl_3$
Chrome alum	Chromium potassium sulfate	$CrK(SO_4)_2 \cdot 12H_2O$
Chrome yellow	Lead chromate	$PbCrO_4$
Copperas	Ferrous sulfate	$FeSO_4 \cdot 7H_2O$
Corrosive sublimate	Mercuric chloride	$HgCl_2$
Cream of tartar	Potassium bitartrate	$KHC_4H_4O_6$
Crocus powder	Ferric oxide	Fe_2O_3
DDT	Dichlorodiphenyl-trichloroethane	$(C_6H) \cdot Cl_2 \cdot CH \cdot CCl_3$
Dry ice	Solid carbon dioxide	CO_2
Dutch liquid	Ethylene dichloride	$CH_2Cl \cdot CH_2Cl$
Emery powder	Impure aluminum oxide	Al_2O_3
Epsom salts	Magnesium sulfate	$MgSO_4 \cdot 7H_2O$
Ethanol	Ethyl alcohol	C_2H_5OH
Ether	Ethyl ether	$(C_2H_5)_2O$
Fluorspar	Natural calcium fluoride	CaF_2
Formalin	Formaldehyde	HCOH
French chalk	Natural magnesium silicate	$H_2Mg_3(SiO_3)_4$
Galena	Natural lead sulfide	PbS
Galuber's salt	Sodium sulfate	$Na_2SO_4 \cdot 10H_2O$
Green vitriol	Ferrous sulfate	$FeSO_4 \cdot 7H_2O$
Gypsum	Natural calcium sulfate	$CaSO_4 \cdot 2H_2O$
Hypo	Sodium thiosulfate	$Na_2S_2O_3 \cdot 5H_2O$
Javelle water	Originally potassium hypochlorite solution, now usually sodium hypochlorite solution	$KOCl + H_2O$ $NaOCl + H_2O$
Labarraque's solution	Sodium hypochlorite solution	$NaOCl + H_2O$
Lime, unslaked	Calcium oxide	CaO
Limewater	Calcium hydroxide solution	$Ca(OH_2) + H_2O$
Litharge	Lead oxide	PbO

Popular name	Chemical name	Formula
Lithopone	Zinc sulfide plus barium sulfate	$ZnS + BaSO_4$
Magnesia	Magnesium oxide	MgO
Magnesite	Magnesium carbonate	$MgCO_3$
Marble	Calcium carbonate	$CaCO_3$
Marsh gas	Methane	CH_4
Methanol	Methyl alcohol	CH_3OH
Methylated spirits	Methyl alcohol	CH_3OH
Milk of magnesia	Magnesium hydroxide in water	$Mg(OH)_2$
Minium	Lead tetroxide	Pb_3O_4
"Muriate of" Muriatic acid	Chloride of hydrochloric acid	HCl
Natural gas	Mostly methane	CH_4
Niter	Potassium nitrate	KNO_3
Oil of bitter almonds (artificial)	Benzaldehyde	C_6H_5CHO
Oil of mirbane	Nitrobenzene	$C_6H_5NO_3$
Oil of vitriol	Sulfuric acid	H_2SO_4
Oil of wintergreen (artificial)	Methyl salicylate	$C_6H_4OHCOOCH_3$
Oleum	Fuming sulfuric acid	$H_2SO_4SO_3$
Orpiment	Arsenic trisulfide	As_2S_3
Paris green	Copper aceto-arsenite	$3Cu(AsO_2)_2 \cdot Cu(C_2H_3O_2)_2$
Pearl ash	Potassium carbonate	K_2CO_3
Peroxide	Peroxide of hydrogen solution	$H_2O_2 + H_2O$
Phosgene	Carbonyl chloride	$COCl_2$
Plaster of Paris	Calcium sulfate	$(CaSO_4)_2 \cdot H_2O$
Plumbago	Graphite	C
Potash	Potassium carbonate	K_2CO_3
Prussic acid	Hydrocyanic acid	HCN
Pyro	Pyrogalic acid	$C_6H_3(OH)_3$
Quicklime	Calcium oxide	CaO
Quicksilver	Mercury	Hg
Red lead	Lead tetroxide	Pb_3O_4
Red oxide of copper	Cuprous oxide	Cu_2O
Red oxide of mercury	Mercuric oxide	HgO
Red prussiate of potash	Potassium ferricyanide	$K_3Fe(CN)_6$
Rochelle salt	Potassium sodium	$KNaC_4H_4O_6 \cdot 4H_2O$
Rouge	Ferric oxide	Fe_2O_3

(Continued)

NAMES AND FORMULAS FOR CHEMICALS (*continued*)

Popular name	Chemical name	Formula
Sal ammoniac	Ammonium chloride	NH_4Cl
Saleratus	Sodium bicarbonate	$NaHCO_3$
Sal soda	Crystalline sodium carbonate	$NaHCO_3$
Salt	Sodium chloride	$NaCl$
Salt cake	Impure sodium sulfate	Na_2SO_4
Salt of lemon	Potassium binoxalate	$KHC_2O_4 \cdot H_2O$
Saltpeter	Potassium nitrate	KNO_3
Saltpeter (Chile)	Impure sodium nitrate	$NaNO_3$
Salts of tartar	Potassium carbonate	K_2CO_3
Silica	Silicon dioxide	SiO_2
Slaked lime	Calcium hydroxide	$Ca(OH)_2$
Soapstone	Impure magnesium silicate	$H_2Mg_3(SiO_3)_4$
Soda ash	Dry sodium carbonate	Na_2CO_3
Spirit of hartshorn	Ammonia gas in alcohol	
Spirits of salt	Hydrochloric acid	HCl
Spirits of wine	Ethyl alcohol	C_2H_5OH
Sugar of lead	Lead acetate	$Pb(C_2H_3O_2)_2 \cdot 3H_2O$
Sulfuric ether	Ethyl ether	$(C_2H_5)_2O$
Talc	Magnesium silicate	$H_2Mg_3(SiO_3)_4$
TNT	Trinitrotoluene	$C_6H_2CH_3(NO_3)_3$
Toluol	Toluene	$C_6H_5CH_3$
Vinegar	Dilute and impure acetic acid	CH_3COOH
Washing soda	Crystalline sodium carbonate	$NaHCO_3$
Water glass	Sodium silicate	Na_2SiO_3
White arsenic	Arsenic trioxide	As_2O_3
White lead	Basic lead carbonate	$(PbCO_3)_2 \cdot Pb(OH)_2$
White vitriol	Zinc sulfate	$ZnSO_4 \cdot 7H_2O$
Whiting	Powdered calcium carbonate	$CaCO_3$
Wood alcohol	Methyl alcohol	CH_3OH
Xylol	Xylene	$C_6H_4(CH_3)_2$
Zinc white	Zinc oxide	ZnO

THE GREEK ALPHABET

Lower-case letter	Capital letter	Name of letter	English equivalent
α	A	alpha	a
β	B	betà	b
γ	Γ	gamma	g
δ	Δ	delta	d
ε	E	epsilon	e
ζ	Z	zeta	z
η	H	eta	ē
θ	Θ	theta	th
ι	I	iota	i
κ	K	kappa	k
λ	Λ	lambda	l
μ	M	mu	m
ν	N	nu	n
ξ	Ξ	xi	x
o	O	omicron	o
π	Π	pi	p
ρ	P	rho	r
σ	Σ	sigma	s
τ	T	tau	t
υ	Υ	upsilon	u
φ	Φ	phi	ph
χ	X	chi	ch
ψ	Ψ	psi	ps
ω	Ω	omega	ō

Index

A